THE ASTRONAUTS

THE ASTRONAUTS

THE FIRST 25 YEARS OF MANNED SPACE FLIGHT

BILL YENNE

Exeter Books
NEW YORK
A Bison Book

First published in USA 1986
by Exeter Books
Distributed by Bookthrift
Exeter is a trademark of Bookthrift Marketing, Inc.
Bookthrift is a registered trademark of Bookthrift Marketing
New York, New York

ISBN 0-671-08194-2

Printed in Hong Kong

CONTENTS

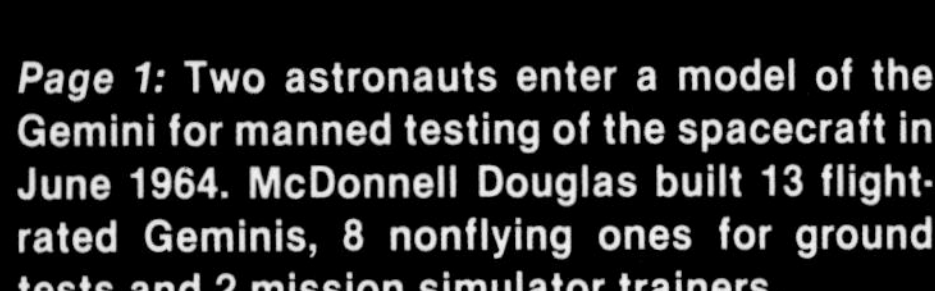

Page 1: **Two astronauts enter a model of the Gemini for manned testing of the spacecraft in June 1964. McDonnell Douglas built 13 flight-rated Geminis, 8 nonflying ones for ground tests and 2 mission simulator trainers.**

Pages 2-3: **The RMS, operated from inside the Space Shuttle Orbiter *Discovery*, was first tested during the STS-2 mission. It allows great scope in conducting extravehicular activity such as repair to the Leasat satellite during mission 51-I. William Fisher is shown here inspecting his work.**

Below: **Sherwood Spring connects pieces of the Space Station devices called EASE, 'experimental assembly of structures in extravehicular activity,' during the 61-B mission in**

EASE
NASA
EASE
MEXICO
MORELOS

INTRODUCTION

Mankind's dreams of space flight predate history. Most of earth's civilizations have had within their folklore tales of heroes who walked among the stars. Over the ages, while dreamers dreamed of reaching into and exploring the heavens, practical man was concerned with more practical matters. As late as the mid nineteenth century the conventional wisdom held that human flight, let alone human flight into space, was impossible. Yet the dream persisted, kept alive by those who dared to dream. When Jules Verne wrote *From The Earth to the Moon* in 1865, it was considered to be on the fringes of fantasy. There were, however, too many people who became intoxicated by the fantasy and ultimately too many people who asked 'why not?' It would take a mere 104 years for Verne's fantasy to become reality—the mere twinkling of an eye on the time line of history.

By the 1930s, when scientists were developing the rockets whose offspring would break the bonds of earth's atmosphere, the brave men who would eventually ride them into space were mere boys, boys enraptured by the same fantasy that had captured the imaginations of so many through the ages. In Smolensk young Yuri Gagarin was devouring Jules Verne's fiction, while half a world away in Shawnee, Oklahoma Gordon Cooper was tuning his parent's crystal set to Buck Rogers and wondering if it really would take until the

Manned operations in earth-orbit: 1950s fantasy and 1980s reality. When Frank Tinsley produced the drawing (*below*), it represented an educated guess about what it would be like to work in space. In many ways, his impression parallels what actually transpired. *Right:* Sherwood Spring assembles the prototype Space Station components in the payload bay of *Atlantis* in November 1985.

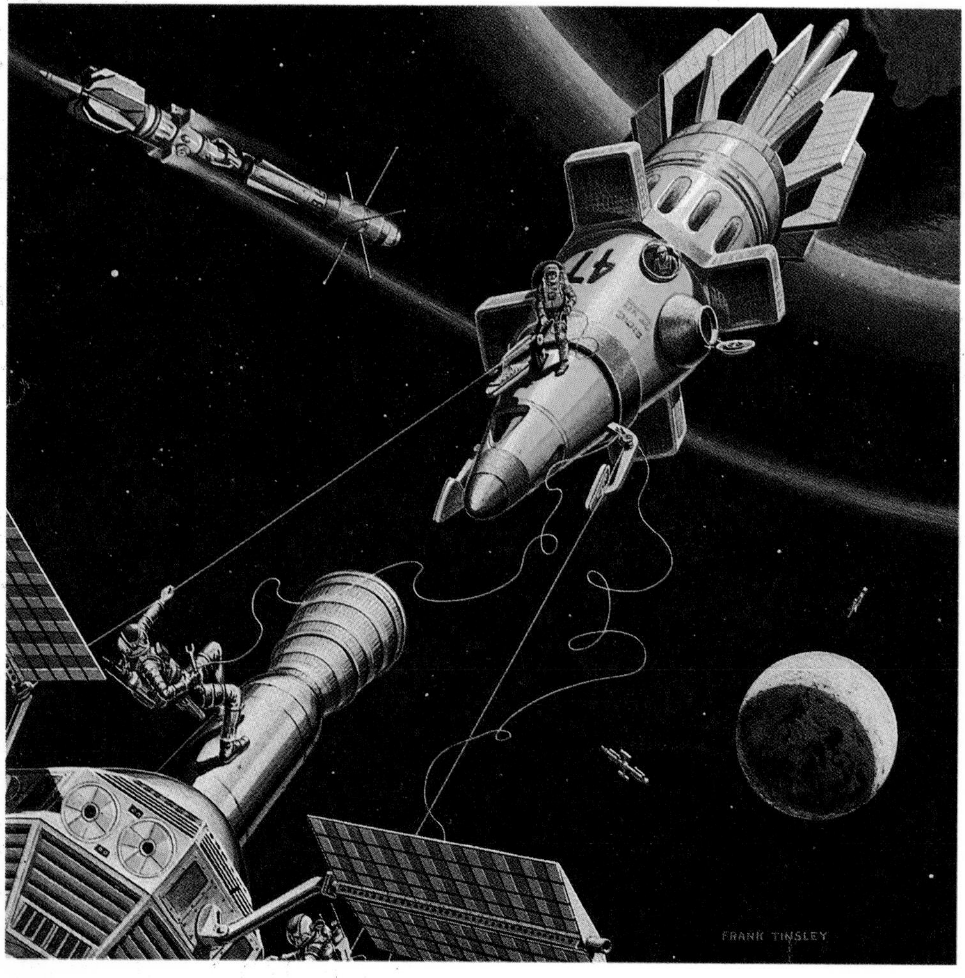

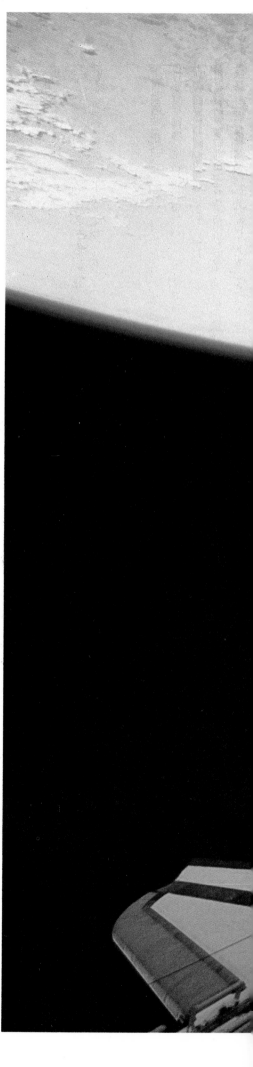

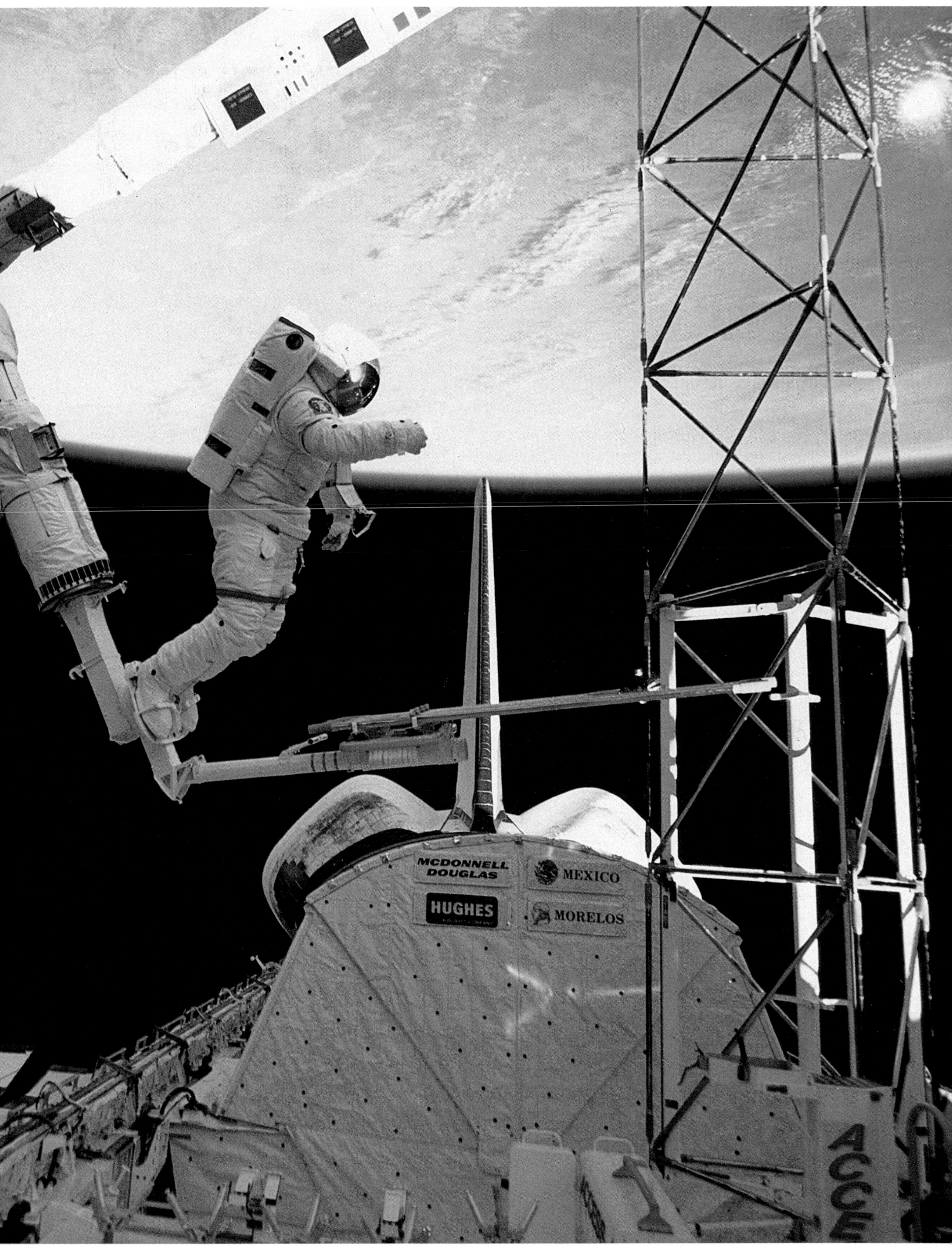
MCDONNELL DOUGLAS
MEXICO
HUGHES
MORELOS
ACCE

Above: **A German A-4 rocket is launched from Peenemünde in 1943. The rockets that took men like Gene Cernan (*right*) into space and finally to the moon were based on the A-4 and designed by many of the same men. Cernan is shown here prior to his Gemini 9 flight, which took place 24 years after the A-4 was first successfully fired. He later commanded Apollo 17, the last Apollo expedition to the moon.**

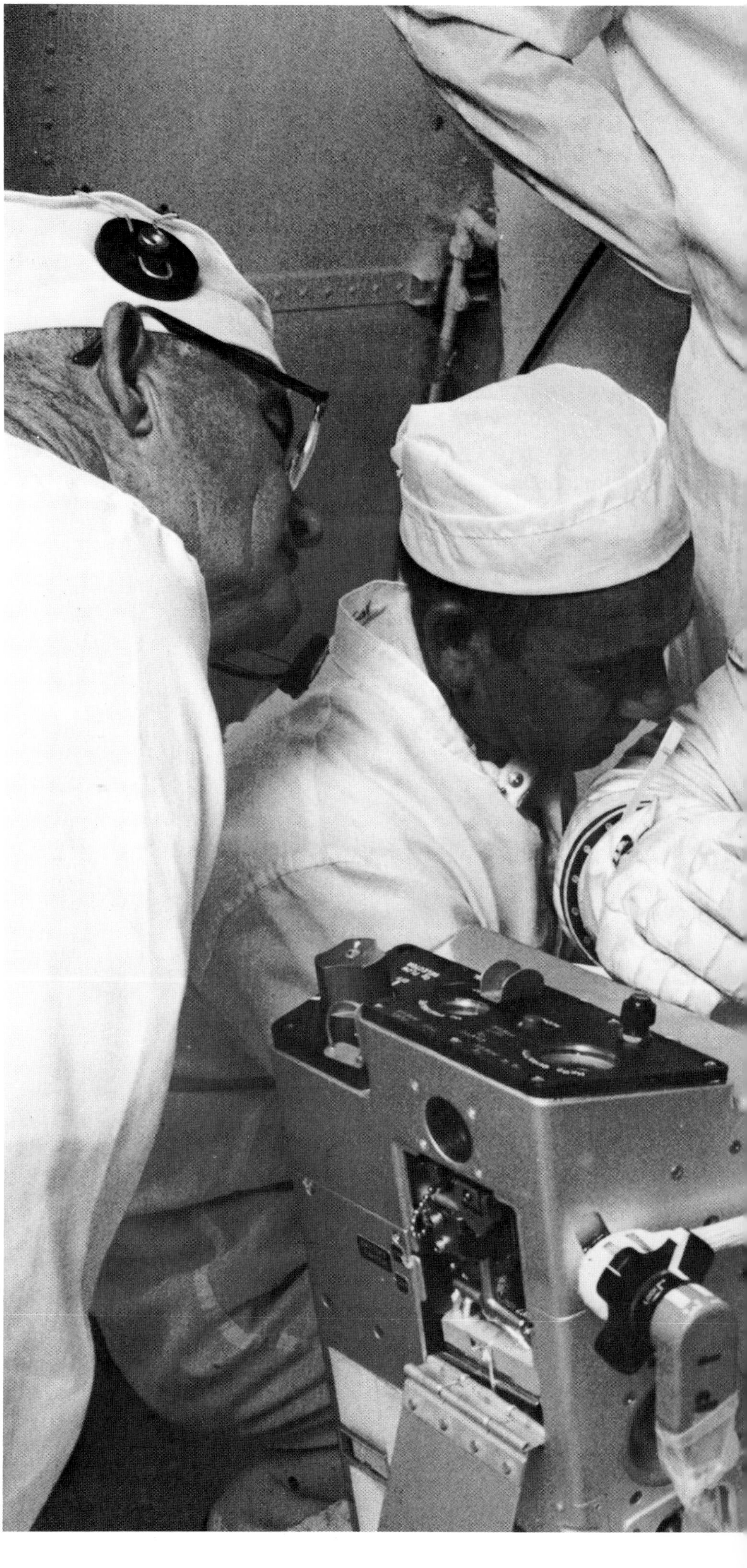

twenty-fifth century before man ventured into space.

By the 1940s in Germany, men like Wernher von Braun were building the foundations for the hardware that would make it possible to at last put a man in space. Von Braun's A-4 was a practical liquid-fuel rocket capable of supersonic flight over a range of 200 miles. Von Braun entertained the notion of a manned A-4 and a successor to the A-4 that could put a man into space, but Germany was at war and von Braun's A-4 became Hitler's V-2 (Vengeance Weapon 2), an intermediate-range ballistic missile. Had Germany turned its national attention to conquering space with the same vigor as it went about conquering the world, the results would not have been so cataclysmic. Some German test pilot would have been the first man in space and the event probably would have occurred prior to 1949.

As it was, Germany lay defeated and destroyed by 1945. Its missile program, like the nation itself, was in disarray and

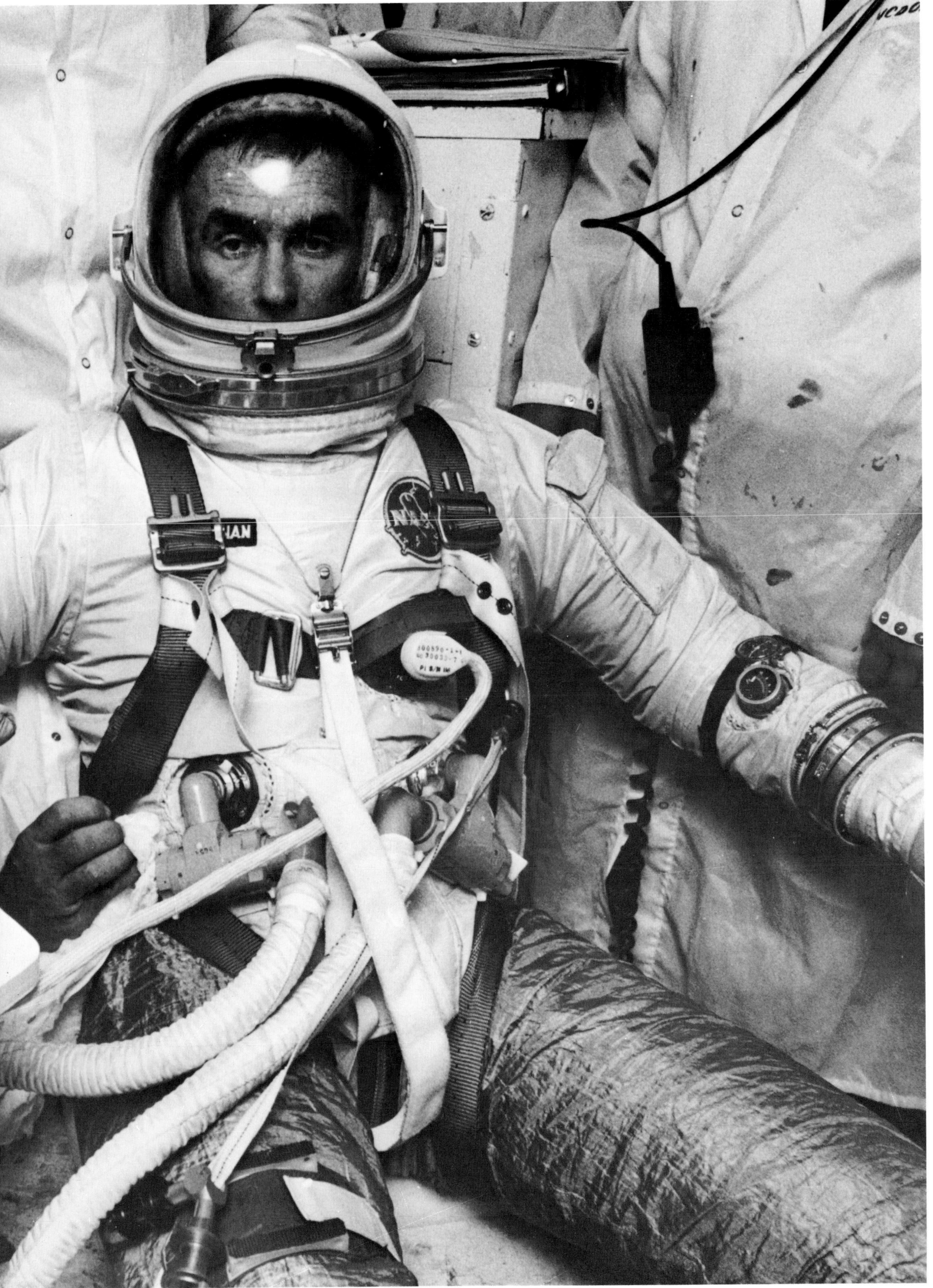

being carved into portions like a pie by the victorious allies. The best and brightest of the German rocket scientists found themselves continuing their work in either the United States or the Soviet Union. For the first time in history, two of the world's leading powers were putting both money and man hours into the notion that mankind could and would put an object, and ultimately a person, into space.

By the late 1950s it seemed to even the ardent cynics that space flight was possible, and a race was on to see which nation would do it first. Within the United States the US Navy was locked in a desperate contest with the US Army over which service would launch America's first satellite.

The interservice rivalry cost the United States the race, for on 4 October 1957 the Soviets launched Sputnik I, the first artificial satellite ever placed in orbit. By 3 November Sputnik II, carrying a dog named Laika, joined Sputnik I and was orbiting the earth every 103.7 minutes. Though Laika was dead by 12 November, the Soviet Union had triumphed. The Soviets had two satellites in orbit while the US Navy *Vanguard* had only reached an altitude of 5 feet before exploding.

On 31 January 1958 the US Army's Explorer I was carried into space atop a Jupiter C launch vehicle. The Russians had beaten the United States into space, but the US Army had beaten the US Navy. The Navy finally got its first Vanguard into space in March, but the US government was already moving to put an end to the interservice rivalry.

The National Aeronautics and Space Administration (NASA) was established in 1958 to serve as an umbrella organization for all American space activities. NASA's first launch was Pioneer 1, which reached 80,000 miles into space in an unsuccessful attempt to reach the moon. In March 1959 Pioneer 4 was successful and became the first manmade object to reach the moon. A major part of NASA's mandate was, however, to prepare to put a human into space. During 1959, in both the Soviet Union and the United States, pilots were being selected to form two elite teams to begin training for mankind's first venture beyond earth's atmosphere.

Just as they had been the first to launch satellites, the Soviets again were first to launch a human into space, but not by much. Yuri Gagarin became the first man in space on 12 April 1961, and Alan Shepard the second, three weeks later. By the end of 1962, the Americans had placed five men in space to the Soviet's four, and NASA was at last moving ahead of the Soviet Union in the space race. The United States won the biggest prize of all in July 1969 when Neil Armstrong became the first human being to set foot on the moon. Over the next three years a dozen Americans walked on the moon, an adventure that the Soviets showed no intention of emulating.

Left: The earth as seen from Apollo 17. _Above:_ Jack Lousma pauses at breakfast before STS-3 blastoff. _Below:_ November 1985 marked the first time that citizens of three nations went into space on the same craft. Aboard _Challenger_ were (_top, left to right_) Henry Hartsfield, Jr; Bonnie Dunbar; James Buchli; Reinhard Furrer and (_bottom, left to right_) Ernst Messerschmid of W Germany; Wubbo Ockels of The Netherlands; Steven Nagel and Guy Bluford.

By the 1980s countries such as France and Japan were building and launching their own spacecraft, but the achievements of the Soviets and the Americans far outdistanced them. Other countries by then had manned space programs, but their astronauts and cosmonauts flew with Americans aboard the Space Shuttle or with Soviets aboard Soyuz spacecraft. It was not until October 1985 that a third country, France, announced the contractors for its Hermes manned spacecraft. When Hermes goes into space in the 1990s and France becomes the third nation to develop an indigenous manned space program, it will have been over 30 years since those uncertain days in the spring of 1961 when the first men went into space.

With American Space Shuttle flights seeming almost routine prior to the loss of *Challenger* in January 1986, it had become easy to start taking manned space flight for granted. This disaster served to remind us that we had come so far in such a relatively short time, and that placing a human being into space is still an event of awesome complexity and of monumental importance. The fact that we have been able to do it successfully as often as we have is a tribute to all the men and women who designed and built the systems and hardware that made it possible. Far more tribute, however, must be paid to those brave men and women who followed the dream of the centuries into a reality in the dark reaches of outer space—who had become the heroes and heroines who walked among the stars.

THE UNITED STATES

FOR MANY WERE CALLED, BUT SEVEN WERE CHOSEN

When NASA was established in 1958, its immediate goal was to unify the various American space programs, but in the highlight of the new agency's agenda was the project called Mercury that would place the first American into outer space. The formal selection process began in January 1959, when NASA chose 110 military test pilots from the 508 names submitted by the Defense Department. These pilots, including 58 from the US Air Force, 47 from the US Navy and 5 from the US Marines, were evaluated for just the right mix of experience, skill and physical fitness. On 27 April 1959 NASA selected its first 7 astronauts—3 Air Force pilots, 3 Navy pilots and a Marine pilot.

Lt Malcolm Scott Carpenter (USN) was on the verge of shipping out of San Diego aboard a carrier when he got his orders to report to Langley AFB in Virginia to begin astronaut training. He was especially pleased because the two-year carrier tour would not only have kept him away from his family, but it would have been a desk job. Carpenter had flown as a test pilot out of the Naval Air Station at Pautuxent River, Maryland, but most of his experience was flying multiengined propeller-driven aircraft. Only 300 of his 2800 flying hours were in jets.

Capt Leroy Gordon Cooper (USAF) had 2300 flying hours, the fewest of the seven, but 1400 of them were in jets. The youngest of the astronauts, he came to NASA from Edwards AFB where he had been a test pilot in the F-106B supersonic interceptor program. Cooper's father had been a US Army Air Force colonel and had known some of the early pioneers of aviation such as Amelia Earhart and Wiley Post. As for Gordon Cooper himself, he made no secret of the fact that he had been an avid reader of Buck Rogers comics as a boy.

Lt Col John Herschel Glenn, Jr (USMC) was at 38 the oldest of the Mercury seven and the only Marine. He also had 5000 flying hours, the most of any of the candidates. He had been a fighter pilot during the Korean War, where he adopted the nickname 'MiG Mad Marine.'

Capt Virgil Ivan 'Gus' Grissom (USAF) also fought MiGs in Korea, where he flew 100 combat missions in F-86 Sabre jets. At the time of his selection, Grissom was a test pilot at Wright-Patterson AFB in Ohio, the Air Force's principal research and development center and a base that was to be the site of much of the astronaut training.

Lt Cdr Walter Marty 'Wally' Schirra (USN) also flew combat missions over Korea. After the war, he was a test pilot during the development of the AIM-9 Sidewinder missile, the most important and widely deployed air-to-air missile in Western military history. At one point during the testing, a Sidewinder misfired and it was only Schirra's quick thinking and quick action that saved him from being destroyed by the errant missile.

Lt Cdr Alan Bartlett Shepard (USN) had accrued 3600 hours in the cockpit, but he was flying a desk at the Navy base in Norfolk when his orders came.

Capt Donald Kent 'Deke' Slayton (USAF) was an F-105 test pilot at Edwards AFB when word came of his selection as one of the Mercury seven. He and Grissom had logged more hours (2000 each) flying jets than any of the others.

The seven astronaut candidates, along with their wives, became instant media stars. *Life* magazine bought the rights to their life accounts and began a series of cover stories about them. The rigors of public attention matched the rigors of the unusual flight training. The training included everything they had endured in pilot training and more. The seven men were subjected to high G spins at the Wright-Patterson AFB centrifuge. They

Left: **John Glenn, Jr — the 'MiG Mad Marine' of the Korean War with his FJ-2 Fury after downing a third Chinese MiG — became the first American to orbit the earth.** ***Right:*** **The original Mercury 7 astronauts were (*front row, left to right*) Walter Schirra, Jr; Donald Slayton; John Glenn, Jr; Scott Carpenter and (*back row, left to right*) Alan Shepard, Jr; Gus Grissom and Gordon Cooper, Jr.**

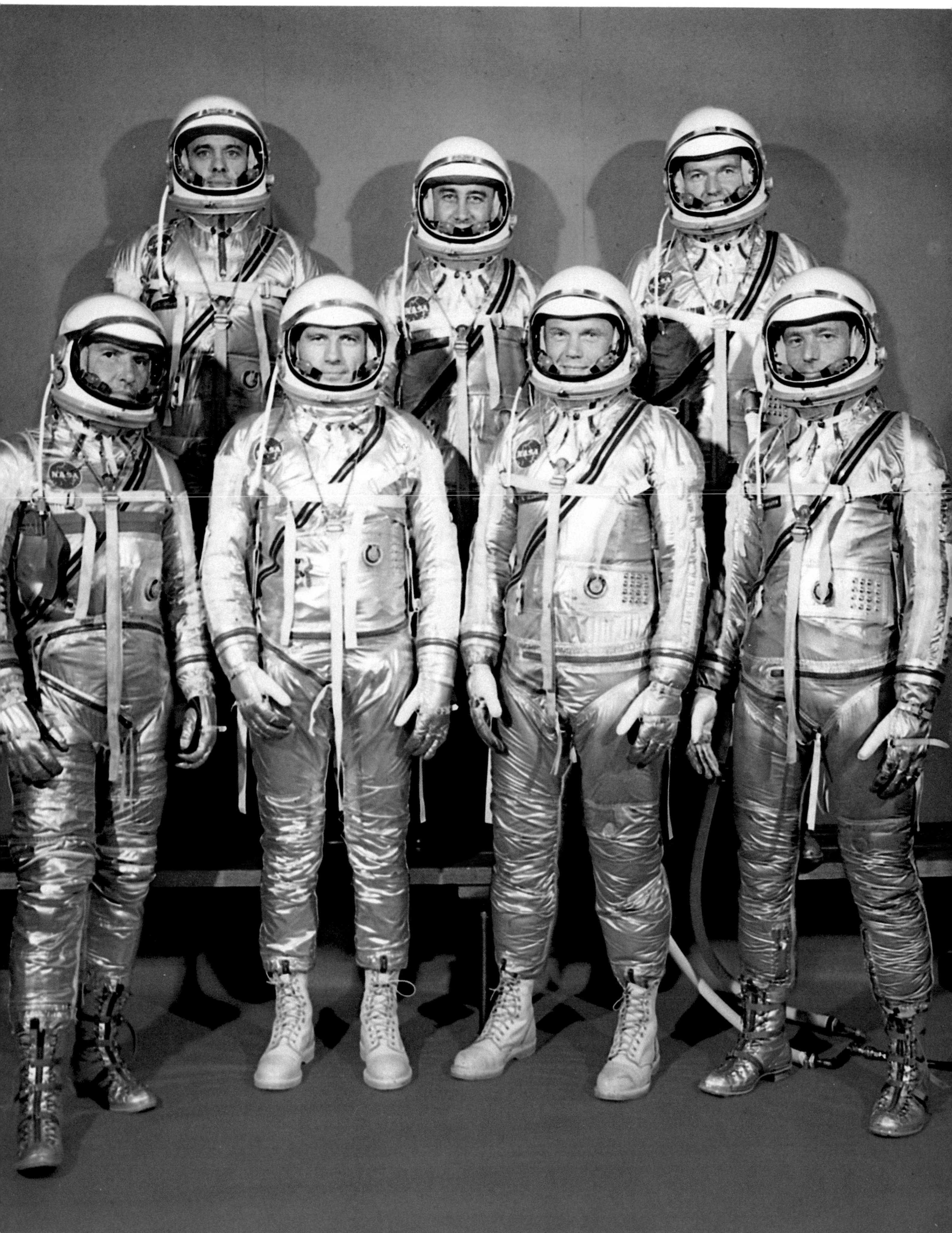

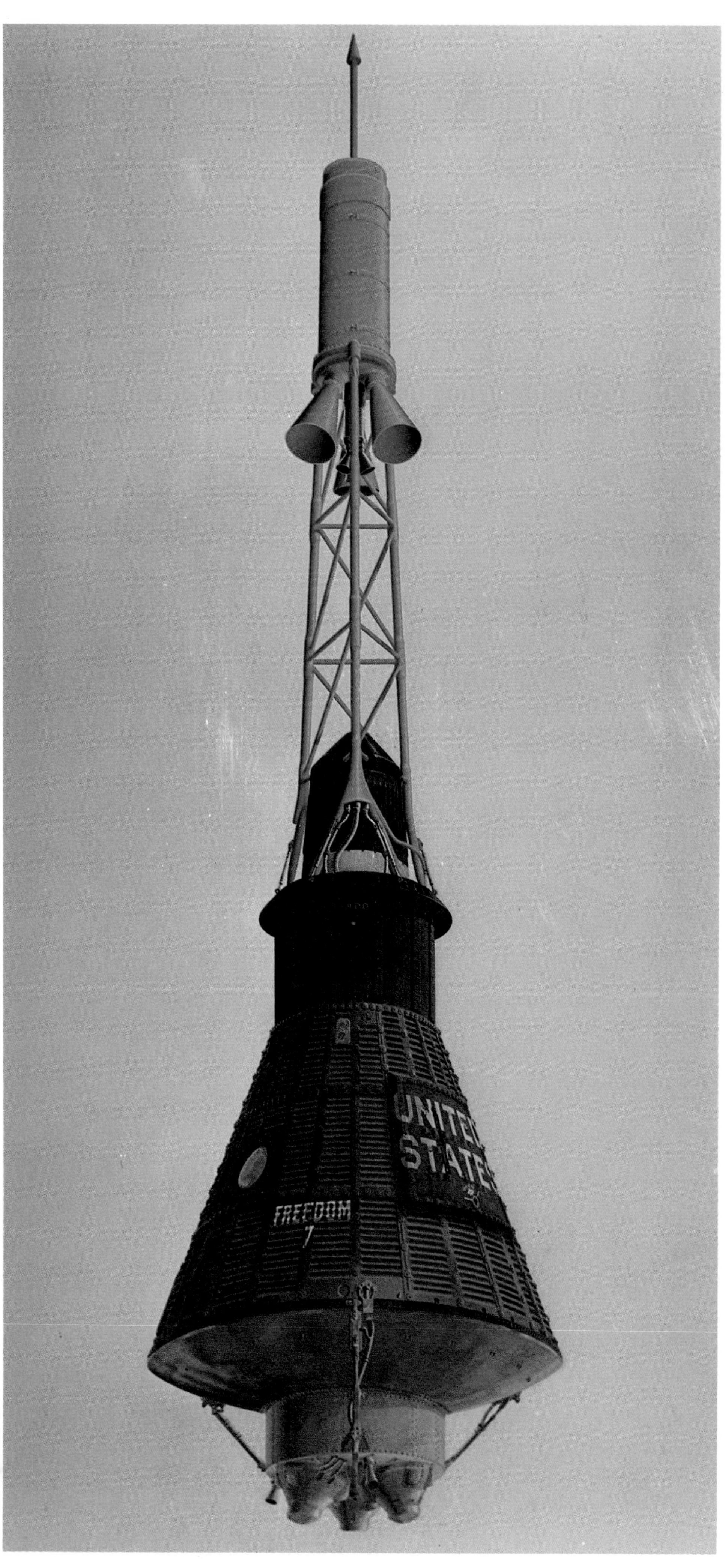

ran on treadmills, endured 160 degree Fahrenheit heat and suffered noise levels of 157 decibels. The Project Mercury planners tried to prepare the men for any eventuality. The heat and pressure that would accompany the return of the Mercury spacecraft into the earth's atmosphere was of special concern. Those planning the training and mission had a unique problem: they were planning for something nobody had ever done before.

MERCURY

The objective of Project Mercury was to get an American into space and return him safely to earth, with an emphasis on the latter. There is little doubt that NASA could have gotten a man into space sooner if it had done away with some of the unmanned Mercury test launches, but there is no way of determining whether an earlier mission would have been a justifiable risk.

The Mercury program began with a series of test launches of the Mercury space capsule between 9 September 1959 and 28 April 1961. These included seven flights in which the Mercury capsule was fired down range into the Atlantic Ocean atop the tiny Little Joe rocket, four with the capsule on top of an Atlas launch vehicle and two with the capsule positioned on top of the Redstone launch vehicle that had originally been developed by Wernher von Braun for the US Army. Of these 13 tests, six experienced failures because of malfunctioning launch vehicles. Of the successful flights, three carried monkeys, including the second of the Redstone rocket tests, which carried the chimpanzee 'Ham' into space on 31 January 1961.

The Mercury program was divided into two phases. In phase one, the suborbital phase, an astronaut was simply launched into space, returning to earth to be recovered in the Atlantic south of the launch site at Cape Canaveral, Florida.

In the second phase, the astronaut actually went into orbit around the earth. In each case, the manned space flight was preceded by a flight of an empty capsule and a flight in which the capsule carried a chimpanzee. As Col John Paul Stapp, director of the Wright-Patterson AFB aeromedical laboratory, pointed out, the ideal way to go into space is with all the hazards overcome in advance.

The Mercury capsule *Freedom 7* (*left*) carried Alan Shepard, Jr (*right*) on America's first manned space flight on 5 May 1961. The orange assembly on top of the capsule was the escape tower, which would be used to rocket *Freedom 7* to safety if the launch vehicle exploded.

The two Redstone tests on 19 December 1960 and 31 January 1961 constituted the full dress rehearsals for the suborbital phase of Project Mercury and received the designations Mercury-Redstone 1 and Mercury-Redstone 2.

The Mercury capsule itself, nicknamed 'garbage can' by the astronauts, was 9 feet, 6 inches long and 6 feet wide at the base, with just enough room for a single astronaut to be strapped into a contoured, shock-absorbing couch. NASA ordered and received 20 flight-rated Mercury capsules from the McDonnell Aircraft Company of St Louis. In the book and later the motion picture *The Right Stuff,* emphasis was placed on the part played by the first seven astronauts in the development of the Mercury capsule. At one point they were depicted as refusing to fly unless a window was placed on the side of the capsule. It is indeed true that input from them helped transform their role in the project from one of objects to be contained within a remotely controlled can to a role of truly piloting the capsule. Though remote control capabilities were present throughout the early years of the American space program, it was the piloting skills of the astronauts that made possible the delicate maneuvers required for the success of the program, especially the Project Apollo moon landings.

By the spring of 1961 NASA had completed tests of the Redstone rocket and had flown further tests with the larger but less reliable Atlas that was to be used on manned orbital flights. Glenn, Grissom and Shepard were picked for the first three manned flights, and tests continued on the escape system. Everyone at NASA knew that the Soviets were close to putting a man into space, but nobody knew how close until 12 April 1961, when Yuri Gagarin became the first man in space as well as the first man to orbit the earth.

A chagrined NASA decided to go ahead with a manned suborbital Mercury launch using the Redstone launch vehicle as soon as possible rather than continue testing the orbital phase of the project. Alan Shepard got the nod to be America's first man in space, and 2 May was selected as the launch date. On that day a rain squall lashed Cape Canaveral and the first flight was canceled 2 hours and 20 minutes before launch time.

On 5 May Shepard was back in the Mercury capsule, which he had nicknamed *Freedom 7.* At 9:34 am the countdown reached 'three, two, one, liftoff' and the big Redstone's engines thundered to life. Five minutes later Shepard was in space at an apogee of 107 miles. Three

minutes after that *Freedom 7* re-entered the earth's atmosphere. Fifteen minutes and 22 seconds after he had left Cape Canaveral and 290 miles down range, the first American in space splashed down in the Atlantic under a huge red, white and blue parachute. Shepard climbed out of his capsule and was quickly reeled into a waiting helicopter and whisked to the aircraft carrier USS *Lake Champlain* that had been prepositioned nearby. America's first space flight had gone flawlessly and had splashed down right on target.

Back in Florida, Shorty Powers, NASA's control room commentator, coined the phrase 'AOK' when reporters asked how the flight had gone. Three days later Shepard met President John F Kennedy, who awarded him NASA's first Distinguished Service Medal in a public ceremony at the White House. On 25 May, less than three weeks after Shepard's flight, Kennedy made a speech before Congress in which he publicly committed the resources of the United States to the goal of landing an American on the moon before the end of the 1960s. The goal that so many at NASA yearned for was now public policy. Everything in the American manned space program was now directed toward that goal and fueled by that enthusiasm.

It was against this backdrop that the second US space flight took place. At 7:20 am on 21 July 1961, Gus Grissom left Cape Canaveral to become the third man in space. Grissom's Mercury capsule was officially designated Mercury-Redstone 4 but nicknamed *Liberty Bell 7.* All of the Mercury astronauts gave their capsules nicknames ending in the numeral '7,' a reference to the original seven Mercury astronauts.

Grissom's suborbital flight ended successfully after 16 minutes, and helicopters quickly located *Liberty Bell 7* in the gentle swells of the Atlantic. Disaster very nearly destroyed the tranquil scene, however, as

***Freedom 7* is hoisted onto the Redstone rocket (*right*) prior to launch of the first American into space. *Left: Liberty Bell 7,* atop a Redstone rocket, carried Gus Grissom on America's second manned space flight, while (*below*) the McDonnell Douglas factory in St Louis readied still more capsules for the program. Of the 20 built, only 6 were used on manned missions.**

STATES
UNITED
STATES
DANGER
EXPLOSIVES
INSTALLED

the explosive pins designed to release the hatch miscarried, opening the hatch and allowing sea water to pour in. Grissom scrambled out of the capsule and one of the helicopters managed to get a line attached. The sinking capsule nearly pulled the helicopter into the ocean, but the helicopter won the tug of war and was beginning to reel in the bell-shaped spacecraft when the second mishap occurred. A faulty warning light erroneously indicating engine trouble in the helicopter forced its crew to cut the capsule loose. Gus Grissom was pulled from the water but *Liberty Bell 7* sank.

With two successful suborbital space flights under its belt, NASA was ready to proceed toward an orbital flight. An unmanned, Atlas-launched Mercury capsule was orbited on 13 September 1961, but between that flight and Grissom's in July, the Soviets had orbited a second cosmonaut, Gherman Titov. Like the Soviet Union, the United States had accomplished two space flights, but they were suborbital. Both Gagarin and Titov had orbited the earth and Titov had made 17 orbits for the balance of 1961. The best that the United States could muster was two out of a scheduled three orbits by the chimpanzee 'Enos' on 29 November aboard the Mercury-Atlas 5 mission.

On the early morning of 20 February 1962 John Glenn entered *Friendship 7,* Mercury-Atlas 6, atop the huge Atlas booster at Cape Canaveral. At 9:47 am the huge rocket tore the tiny capsule away from the launch pad and hurled Glenn into space and into history as the first American to orbit the earth. The only malfunction to mar Glenn's historic three orbits of the earth was a malfunctioning warning light that indicated premature release of the heat shield that was designed to prevent *Friendship 7* and its pilot from burning up during re-entry. It was decided that the retro-rocket package located on the top of the heat shield, which was used for maneuvering in space and designed to be jettisoned before re-entry, should be left on in order to hold the shield in place. When the retro-rocket package burned up on re-entry and rolled past Glenn's window, he thought for a moment that it might have been the heat shield disintegrating. But all was well and he landed in the Atlantic south of Bermuda in the predetermined recovery zone after traveling 83,450 miles in 4 hours and 55 minutes.

On 24 May 1962 Scott Carpenter's *Aurora 7,* Mercury-Atlas 7, was launched flawlessly from Cape Canaveral for another three-orbit flight. Carpenter manually maneuvered the spacecraft more than

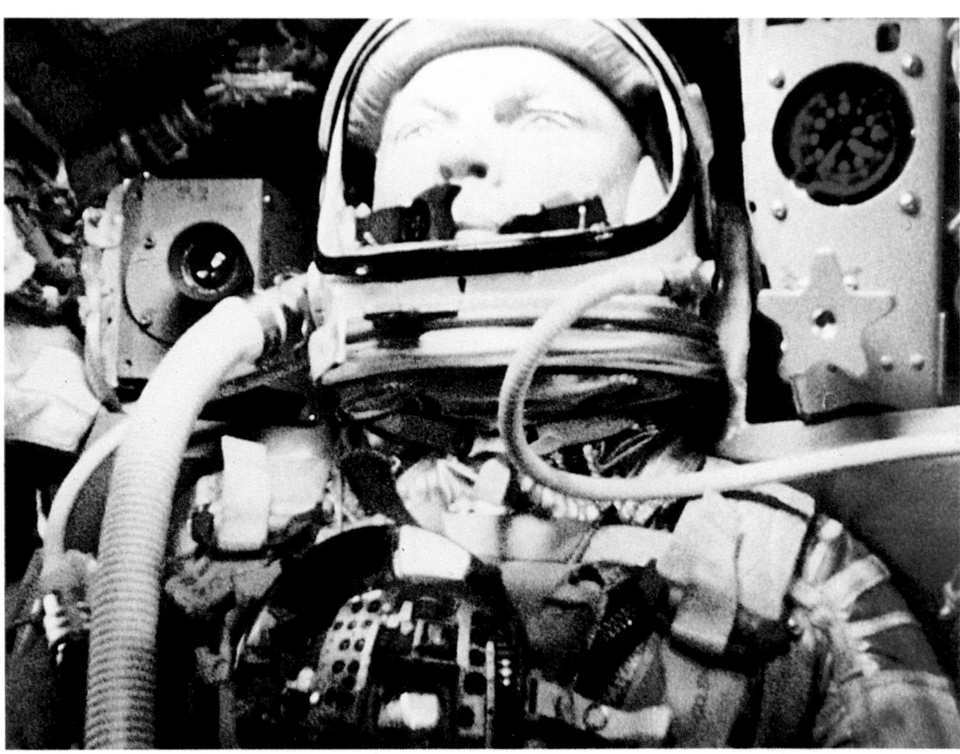

In the wee hours of 20 February 1962, John Glenn, Jr and NASA space suit technician Joe Schmidt (*below*) leave the hangar at Cape Canaveral for the launch area, where the *Friendship 7* Mercury capsule was perched on the big Atlas rocket. The Atlas was more powerful than the Redstone and was used for all Mercury orbital flights, of which Glenn's was the first (*left*). During his flight, Glenn was filmed by a motion picture camera (*above*).

Scott Carpenter and Wally Schirra were the second and third Americans to orbit the earth. *Above:* Carpenter peers inside *Aurora 7* as he prepares for his three-orbit mission. *Right:* Wally Schirra steps from the transfer van shortly before entering the *Sigma 7* spacecraft.

had been done on previous flights and all systems worked perfectly. However, an experiment involving the release of a balloon on a 100-foot cord failed when the balloon did not inflate. Carpenter fired the retro-rockets 3 seconds late at the end of the 4 hour, 56 minute flight and as a result he overshot the landing zone by 250 miles. He quickly scrambled out of *Aurora 7* and inflated his life raft, whereupon he spent 2 hours and 59 minutes adrift in the mid-Atlantic, almost as much time as he'd spent in outer space. Floating all alone in the vastness of the Atlantic must have been a unique counterpoint to being alone in the vastness of space. Previously, Scott Carpenter had spent a peaceful year with his wife Rene high in the Colorado Rockies, cut off purposely from the rest of civilization. Now it was Scott Carpenter who was helping to blaze a path for mankind into a wilderness more spectacular than the Rockies, more vast and empty than a million oceans.

Walter Schirra was the third American to orbit the earth, and his Mercury capsule, *Sigma 7* was scheduled for six orbits, double the number flown by either Glenn or Carpenter. The launch on the morning of 3 October 1962 went almost flawlessly. Schirra spent his first orbit adjusting his pressure suit coolant flow rate to reach a proper temperature and then settled down for a lunch of beef, vegetables and peaches—all squeezed through tubes. The flight took 9 hours and 13 minutes, and there was sufficient fuel left at the end to use automatic control during re-entry. *Sigma 7* was the first Mercury capsule to land in the Pacific and Schirra set it down just 9000 yards, or about 5 miles, from the planned landing point northeast of Midway Island and within sight of the Navy recovery ship USS *Kearsarge.* Schirra stayed with the capsule as it was hoisted aboard the ship, then blew the hatch and emerged saying that he felt 'great.' He commented that his nearly 9 hours in space had been a 'textbook flight.'

With three successful Mercury orbital flights during 1962, NASA felt confident

in planning the longest and most ambitious Mercury flight yet, an 18-orbit flight in April 1963. The space agency was also anxious by this time to get on with the Gemini program, Mercury's successor project. The two-man Gemini capsules were on order and another group of astronauts was being selected. For this reason, it was decided that Mercury-Atlas 9, the sixth manned Mercury flight, would be the last. The long-planned Mercury-Atlas 10, a three-day mission, would be scrubbed.

The astronaut for the sixth and final Mercury mission was Gordon Cooper. The seventh of the Mercury seven, Deke Slayton, was grounded because an erratic heartbeat had been detected.

By the time Gordon Cooper climbed into *Faith 7* at Cape Canaveral, the planned 18 orbits had been confidently extended to 22, and the timing had been pushed from April to 15 May. Cooper's flight took 34 hours and 20 minutes, and during that time he was able to doze off for 7½ hours during the tenth through fourteenth orbits. Two years earlier, an American space flight of 15 minutes had been an epic event, and now Gordon Cooper was sleeping through four complete orbits of the earth.

When it came time for re-entry, however, the automatic system failed, so Cooper had to re-enter the earth's atmosphere under manual control. He was able to land closer to target than any of his predecessors. He came down in the Pacific 7000 yards from the USS *Kearsarge,* the same ship that picked up Schirra, who had re-entered under automatic control but landed 9000 yards from the target.

Even as Gordon Cooper climbed out of *Faith 7* on the flight deck of the *Kearsarge,* plans were under way not only for the two-man Gemini program, but for the subsequent Apollo program that would take the first Americans to the moon.

GEMINI

The objectives of the Gemini program were more complex than those of the Mercury program. Mercury was conceived in a time when space flight was an endeavor shrouded with incalculable, unpredictable unknowns. Mercury's objectives were simply to place Americans into space, into orbit if possible, and return them safely to earth. The Soviets demonstrated that both objectives were possible and Mercury confirmed it.

The Gemini spacecraft had been on McDonnell's drawing boards before the first Mercury capsule went into space, but the program objectives were developed against the background of Mercury's success and the American commitment to reach the moon before 1970. All of the major components of the Gemini program were designed to test procedures that could be utilized in developing the subsequent Apollo program. These included rendezvous and docking in space, extravehicular activity (space walks) and extended-duration flights that would be up to 3 to 10 times as long as the longest Mercury flights. Gemini was to be the first series of manned space flights to take place following the assassination of President Kennedy in November 1963, after which Cape Canaveral was renamed Cape Kennedy. Though the name Cape Canaveral was later readopted, the NASA launch center was permanently renamed Kennedy Space Center (KSC).

Even before the last Mercury flight, NASA began welcoming and training a new 'class' of astronauts to supplement the original group and meet the expanding manpower needs of an expanding space program. The second group of astronauts was selected in September 1962, just three years after the Mercury seven became overnight celebrities. Though considerably less fanfare surrounded the selection of the second group, their number included the first American to walk in space, the two men to set an American space endurance record in a Gemini spacecraft (unmatched until the days of the Skylab space station) and the first human being to set foot on the moon.

Astronaut Group Two, 'class of 1962,' included four US Air Force pilots—Frank Borman, James McDivitt, Tom Stafford and Edward White II—as well as three US Navy pilots—Charles 'Pete' Conrad, Jr; James Lovell, Jr; and John Young. Unlike the first Mercury seven, the second group also contained civilians, an aeronautical engineer named Neil Armstrong and an engineer from the US Maritime Academy, Elliot See.

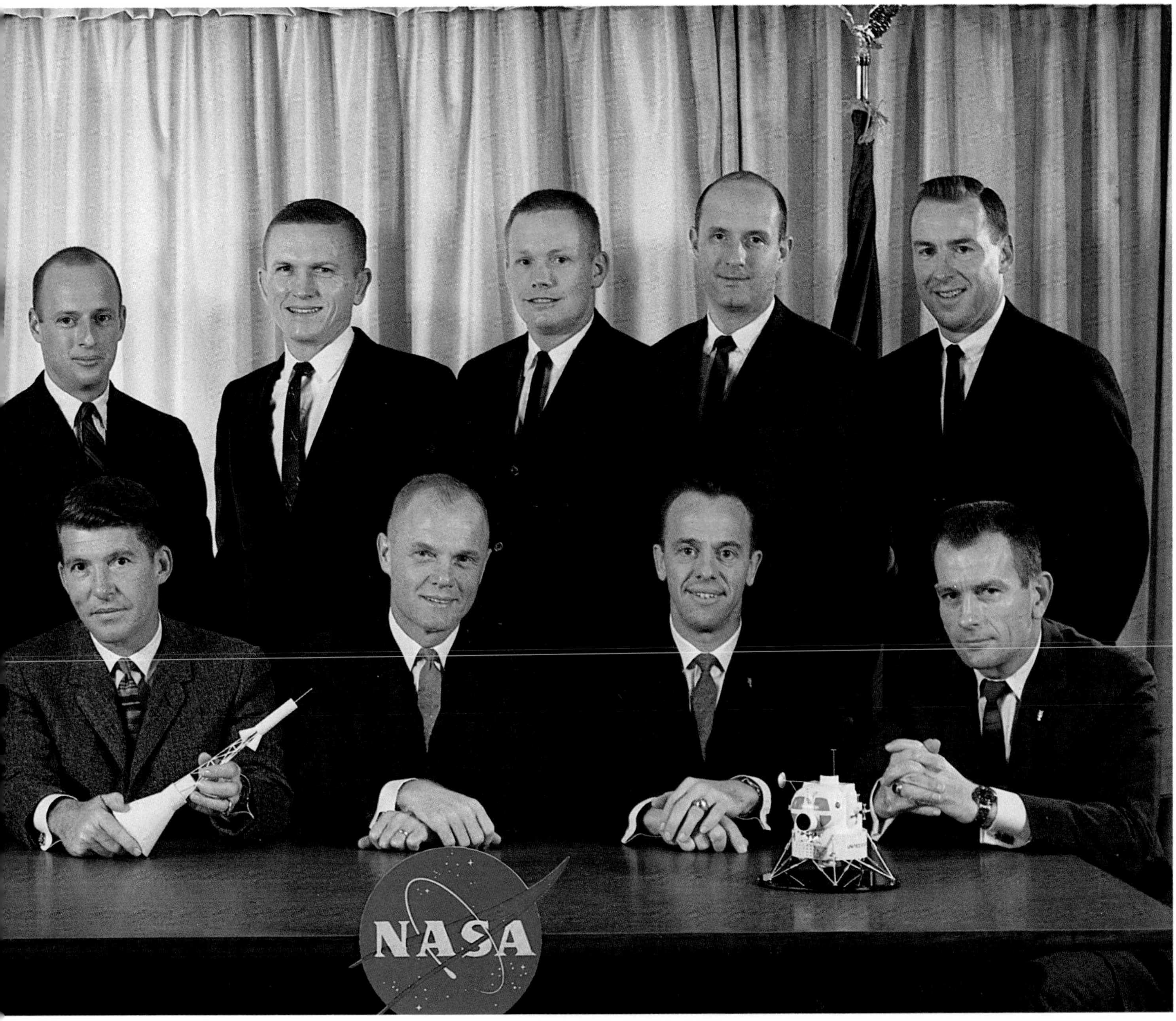

Even before the first manned Gemini spacecraft was launched, a third group of astronauts was selected in October of 1963. Astronaut Group Three included seven US Air Force pilots: Edwin 'Buzz' Aldrin, William Anders, Charles Bassett II, Michael Collins, Donn Eisele, Theodore Freeman and David Scott; plus four US Navy pilots: Alan Bean, Eugene Cernan, Roger Chaffee and Richard Gordon, Jr. There were two US Marines—Walter Cunningham and Clifton Williams, Jr—and one civilian—Russell Schweickart. It was the men of these two groups who formed the majority of the crews for the Gemini and Apollo programs. Only three of the original seven astronauts (Cooper, Grissom and Schirra) took part in Gemini flights and only one (Shepard) went to the moon during the Apollo program.

The first manned Gemini flight came

Above: **Astronaut Groups One (*seated*) and Two (*standing*), photographed in 1963. Group One, selected in April 1959, included (*left to right*) L Gordon Cooper; Virgil Grissom; Scott Carpenter; Walter Schirra; John Glenn; Alan Shepard; and Donald Slayton.**

Group Two, named in September 1962, included (*left to right*) Edward White II, James McDivitt, John Young; Elliot See, Jr; Charles Conrad, Jr; Frank Borman; Neil Armstrong; Thomas Stafford and James Lovell, Jr. The models on the table are the Manned Orbital Laboratory, the Mercury capsule and the Apollo lunar lander.

Glenn was the only Group One astronaut to never make another flight and Shepard was the only one to go to the moon. All of the Group Two astronauts flew aboard both Gemini and Apollo except See, who was killed in an aircraft crash in 1966 without having made a space flight, and White, who flew aboard Gemini 4 but was killed with Gus Grissom in the 1967 Apollo 1 fire. *Left:* Neil Armstrong in his space suit at Edwards AFB after a flight aboard the X-15 research aircraft (*foreground*). *Overleaf:* Group One and Two astronauts participate in tropic survival training in the Canal Zone.

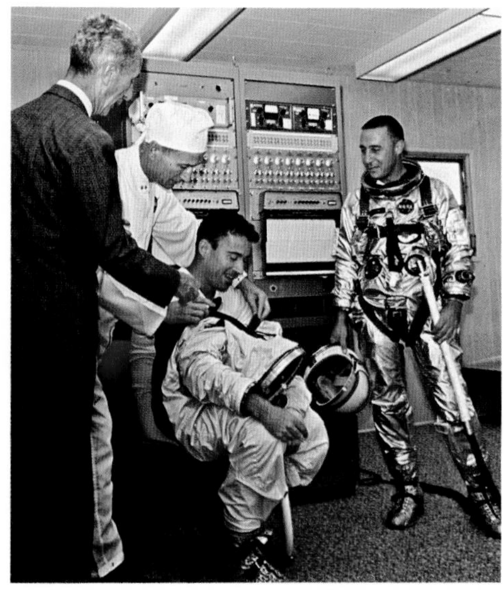

Grissom and Young with the well-known American painter Norman Rockwell before the Gemini 3 mission (*above*) and afloat in the Atlantic (*right*) after the first Gemini flight. Gemini 4 astronaut Edmund White (*far right*) makes the first American space walk in June 1965. *Below:* A powerful Titan put Gordon Cooper and Charles Conrad into space aboard Gemini 5 on 21 August 1965.

on 23 March 1965 with Mercury veteran Gus Grissom and newcomer John Young at the controls. Designated Gemini 3, the mission had been preceded by two unmanned Gemini flights during April 1964 and January 1965. Only three orbits were planned, and Gemini 3 was flown mainly to test the spacecraft's manual controls, which worked perfectly. At 4 hours and 53 minutes, it was almost identical in duration to the third and fourth Mercury flights and much shorter than the last two Mercury flights.

The second manned Gemini flight, Gemini 4, which was launched on 3 June 1965, set several milestones. James McDivitt and Edward White II completed 62 orbits in 97 hours and 56 minutes, making it the longest American space flight to date. During that time a number of medical, engineering and scientific experiments were carried out, but the high point of the flight was White's 21-minute space walk. Known technically as extravehicular activity (EVA) the space walk marked the first time an American had left a spacecraft to move about in space. During the third orbit, White donned special gear and pressurized his suit to 3.7 pounds per square inch while McDivitt depressurized Gemini 4's cabin and opened the hatch. White propelled himself out into the void of space using a compressed gas gun. Its fuel supply was exhausted after 3 minutes, so he spent the remaining 18 minutes maneuvering around the spacecraft by pulling on the tether that kept him firmly attached.

White was connected to Gemini 4 only by the tether and by the 'umbilical cord' that supplied him with oxygen.

The spectacular McDivitt-White Gemini 4 was followed by the 190 hour and 55 minute flight of Gordon Cooper, Jr and Charles Conrad, Jr aboard Gemini 5. Designed to evaluate the performance of both crew and spacecraft on a long-duration mission, the flight was launched on 21 August 1965. The eight days that Cooper and Conrad spent in space were intended to simulate the length of time that it would take for a spacecraft to make a round trip to the moon; hence the mission was an important steppingstone in the long climb to the moon. More than simply an evaluation flight, Gemini 5 was the longest space flight ever undertaken. It was longer than the Soviet's Vostok 5 by half and longer than anything they would accomplish until the Americans were well into their Apollo program. More than anything else, Gemini 5 finally put the Americans ahead of the Soviets in the space race.

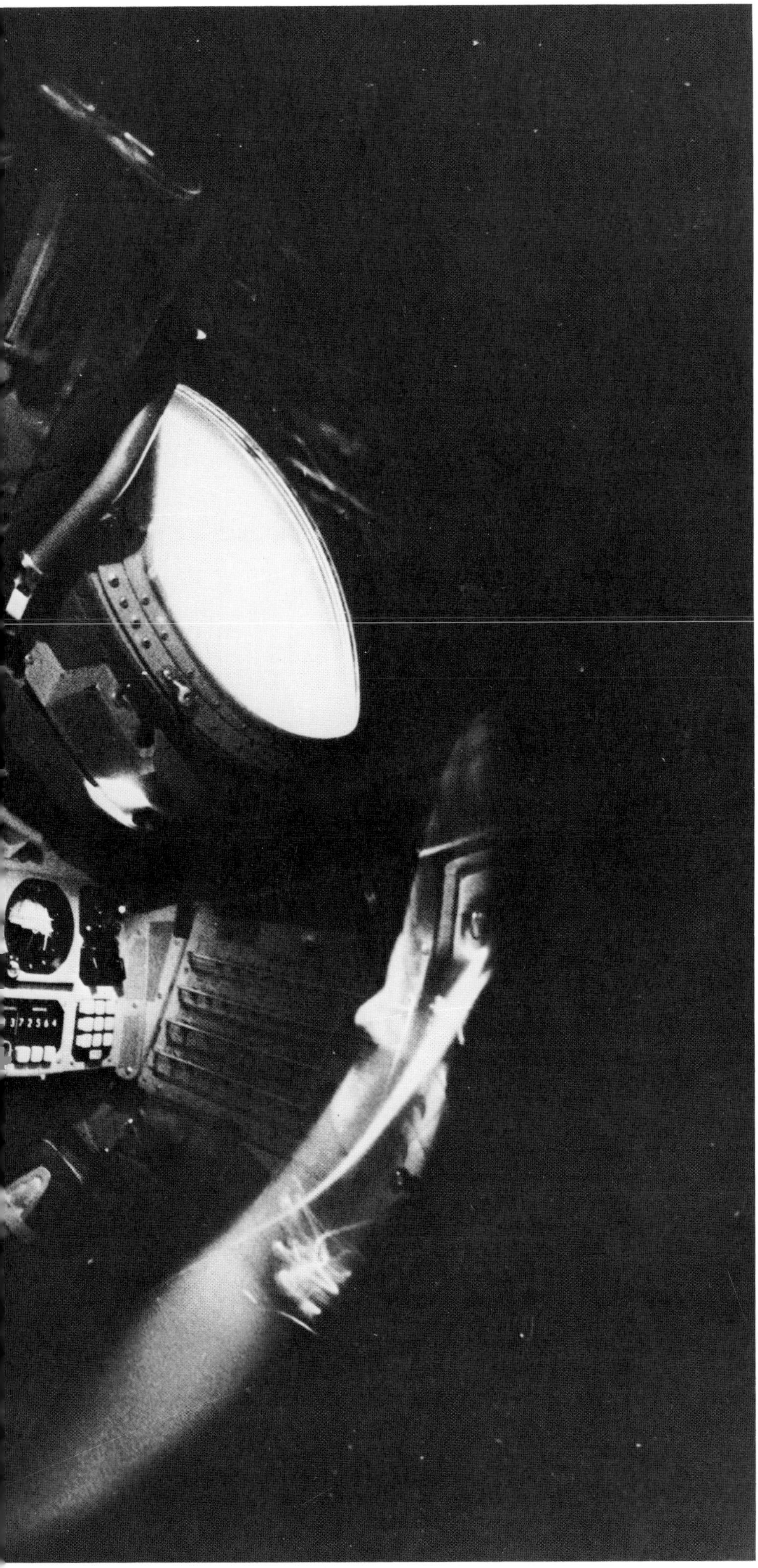

Above: **A Gemini capsule is lifted into position at Cape Canaveral.** ***Left:*** **Gemini cockpit control panels. Unlike Mercury, this craft was designed to be flown by its crew.**

If Gemini 5 was a steppingstone, the dual flights of Gemini 6 and Gemini 7 were milestones. The Soviets had overlapped some of their earlier missions so that two manned spacecraft were in orbit simultaneously, but Gemini 6, flown by Walter Schirra and Tom Stafford, was the first manned spacecraft to locate another manned spacecraft in space and rendezvous with it.

Gemini 7 was actually launched on 4 December 1965, nine days before Gemini 6. Flown by Frank Borman and James Lovell, Gemini 7 was to remain in space for 330 hours and 36 minutes, the longest American space flight until the days on the Skylab space station and the longest American flight aboard a spacecraft (rather than a space station) ever.

During their first five days, Borman and Lovell conducted a variety of experiments and then placed Gemini 7 in a circular orbit 185 miles into space. Gemini 6 was launched on 15 December after a three-day delay due to a launch-vehicle malfunction. Schirra and Stafford reached their orbit roughly 1200 miles distant from Gemini 7 and began to close the gap. At 170 miles they had Borman and Lovell on radar, and after 5 hours and 50 minutes, the two bell-shaped spacecraft were only 40 yards apart. Stafford and Schirra closed to within a foot, then broke

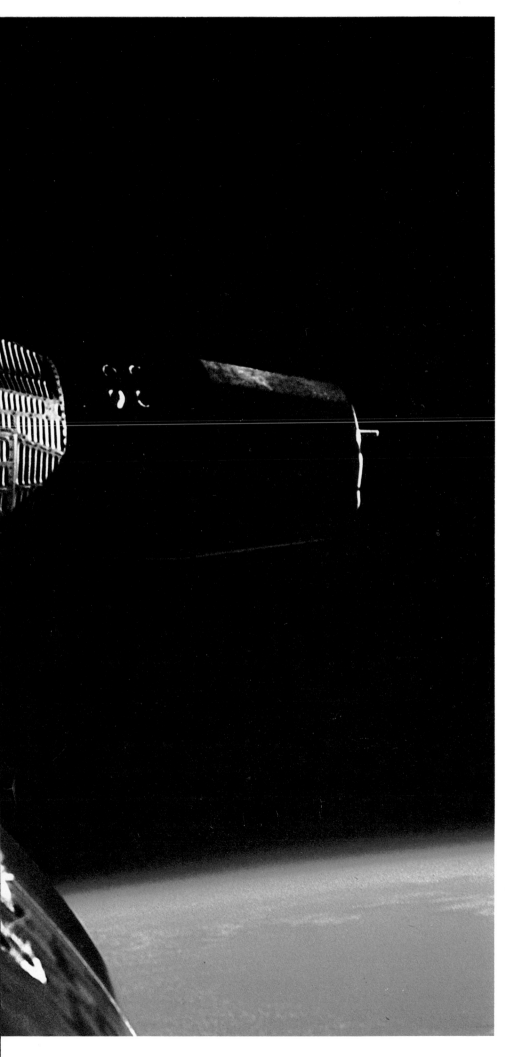

Left: **The view from Gemini 6 as Wally Schirra and Tom Stafford close in on Frank Borman and James Lovell in Gemini 7 for the historic rendezvous on 15 December 1965.** ***Above:*** **Gemini 6, scheduled as a two-day mission, was launched on 13 December.**

away, maneuvering and repeating the procedure many times, clearly demonstrating the capability of two spacecraft to rendezvous in space. For more than 20 hours the two craft remained within 100 feet of one another. On 16 December, after 25 hours and 51 minutes in space, Schirra and Stafford returned to earth, leaving Cooper and Conrad to continue their epic two-week odyssey in space.

Gemini 7 splashed down in the Atlantic two days later on 18 December. The two astronauts had trouble getting used to gravity at first, but after a week the effects of weightlessness had virtually worn off. The long-duration flights of Gemini 5 and Gemini 7 had proven that humans could live in space with a reasonable degree of comfort for longer than a lunar mission would take and readjust fairly quickly on their return. The balance of the Gemini program would be devoted to developing the procedures required for the complex lunar missions that were planned for Apollo.

Gemini 8, with Neil Armstrong and David Scott, was launched on 16 March 1966 for a scheduled three-day mission in which they would not only rendezvous, but dock Gemini 8 with an Agena booster upper stage that had been launched 101 minutes before them. The historic first docking in space was accomplished just 6 hours and 34 minutes into the flight, but when the astronauts attempted to maneu-

Above: **Tom Stafford and Eugene Cernan prepare to egress from Gemini 9 after learning that the Agena target vehicle failed to achieve orbit. Gemini 9 was launched with better results two weeks later on 3 June 1966.** ***Right:*** **Gemini 8 successfully conducted the first docking in space with the Augmented Target Docking Adapter.** ***Left:*** **The space sextant was first used on Gemini 7.**

ver their spacecraft with the Agena, the paired vehicles began to tumble wildly. Armstrong couldn't stop the tumbling, but he was able to disengage from the Agena and bring Gemini 8 under control. However, this used up 75 percent of the spacecraft's fuel, so NASA decided to cancel the balance of the mission and have the two astronauts return to earth. Armstrong and Scott successfully re-entered the atmosphere and splashed down in the Pacific 5 miles from their target after just 10 hours and 41 minutes in space.

Gemini 9 was launched on 3 June 1966, two days (rather than the planned 100 minutes) after its Agena docking target because of a data-transmission malfunction at Cape Kennedy. Aboard the space-

UNITED STATES

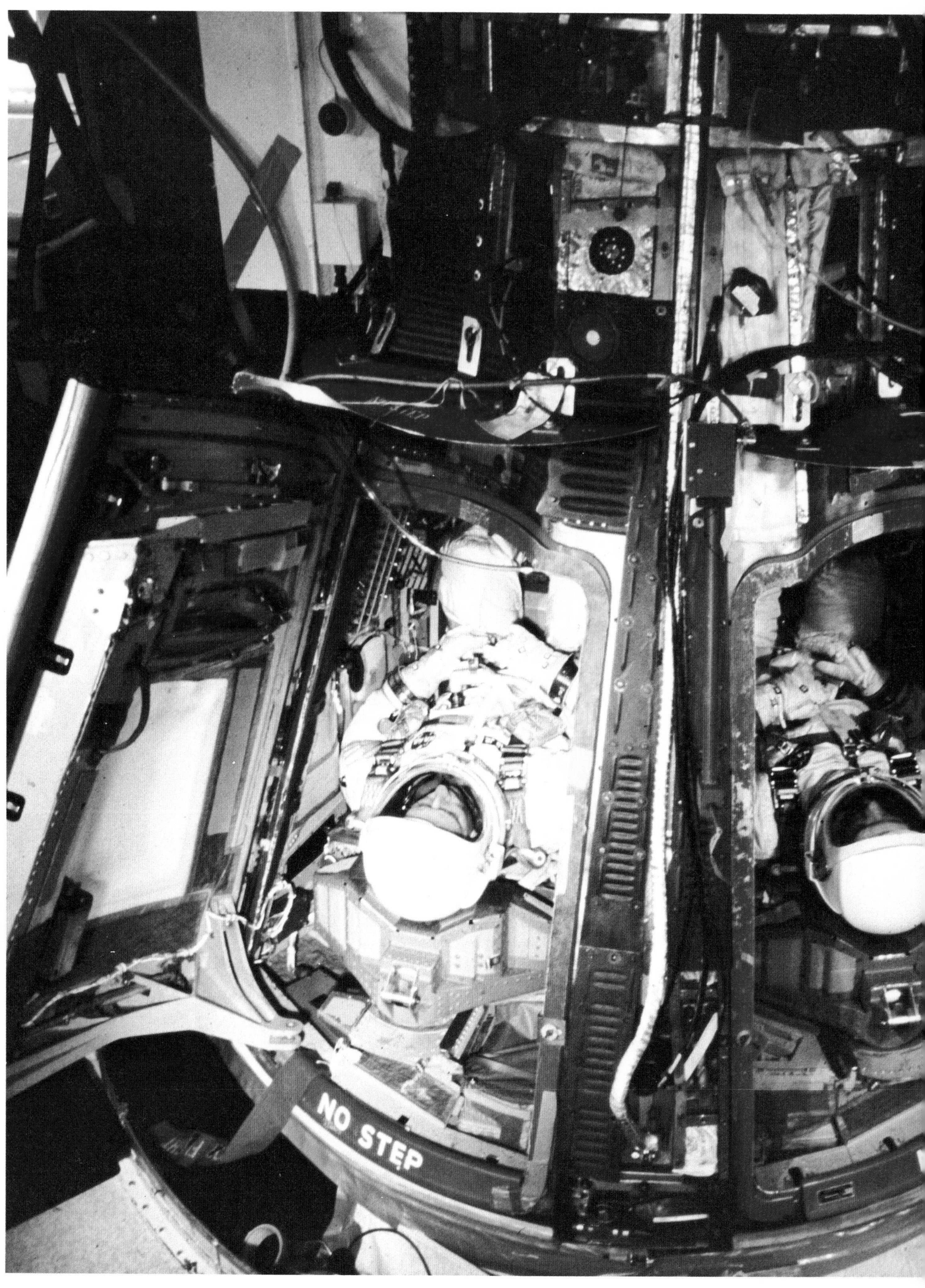
NO STEP

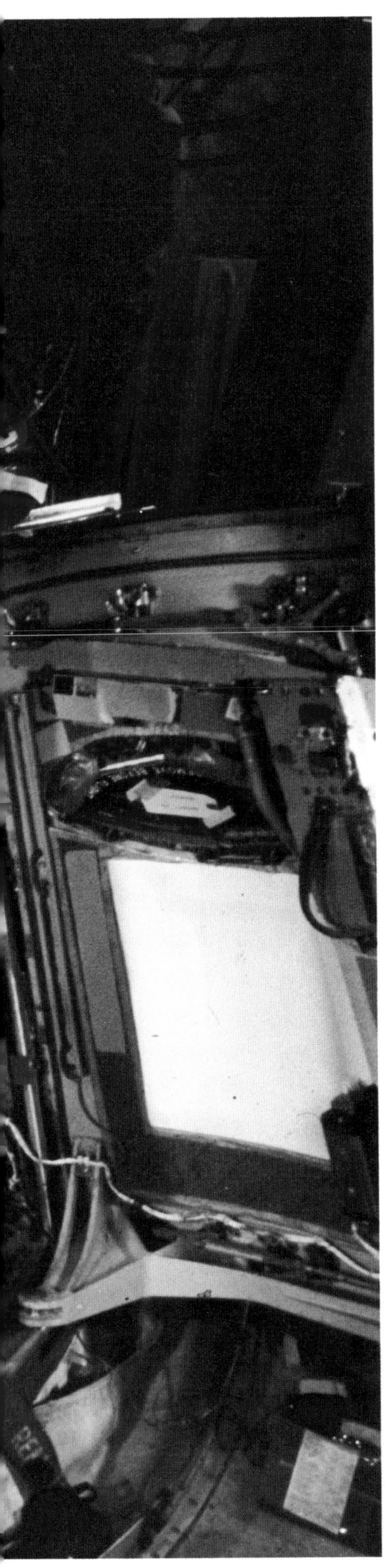

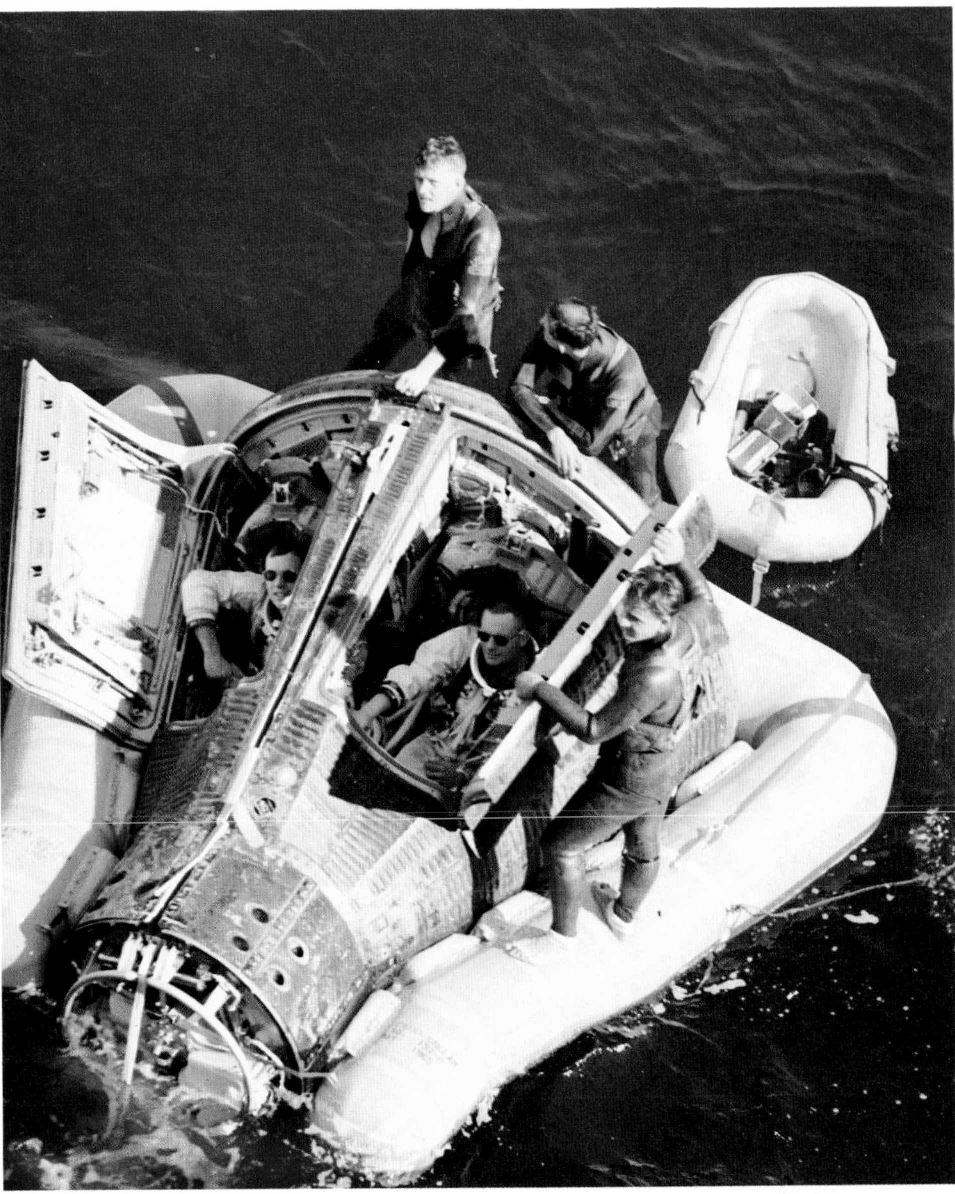

Left: **Astronauts Neil Armstrong and David Scott were helped into the Gemini 8 spacecraft by White Room technicians at Kennedy Space Center prior to liftoff on 16 March 1966. A short circuit in the Orbital Altitude Maneuvering System forced the scheduled three-day mission to return to earth during the sixth orbit.** ***Above:*** **After placing the flotation collar around the spacecraft, pararescue men assisted Armstrong and Scott (*left*) as they waited to be picked up by the destroyer USS *Mason*, some 500 miles east of Okinawa.**

craft were Eugene Cernan, making his first flight, and Tom Stafford (the first non-Mercury astronaut to go into space twice), making his second flight in six months. On the third orbit they easily rendezvoused with the Agena target by means of its Augmented Target-Docking Adapter (ATDA), but the target's shroud was jammed and they were unable to dock with it. Their flight plan was revised to include two more rendezvous with the ATDA and Cernan was able to make a 2-hour space walk. The two astronauts brought Gemini 9 back to earth after 72 hours and 21 minutes in space.

Gemini 10 was launched on 18 July, less than a month after Gemini 9 and the planned 101 minutes after the Agena target. Astronauts Michael Collins and John Young rendezvoused with the target on their fourth orbit, but they used up twice the amount of fuel that was planned. Collins conducted two space walks and retrieved a micrometeoroid detector from the Agena on the second one. The mission returned to earth after 70 hours and 46 minutes in space.

Gemini 11 was launched on 12 September 1966 with Charles Conrad, Jr and Richard Gordon, Jr aboard. They were able to rendezvous and successfully dock with the Agena target vehicle just 94 minutes after launch, consuming less fuel than expected in the most successful rendezvous and docking yet conducted. Gemini 11 was detached from the Agena and each of the astronauts flew the spacecraft in two dockings with it. Gordon conducted two space walks in a total elapsed time of 2 hours and 47 minutes. During their flight the astronauts saw and photo-

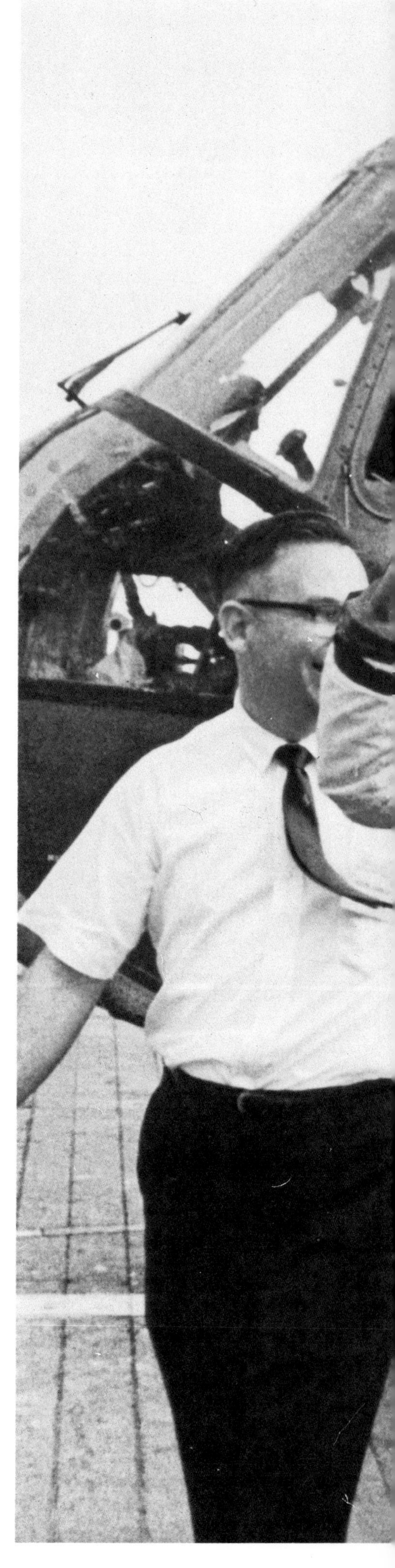

graphed stars and galaxies in deep space, various areas of the earth below them and the Soviet Proton 3 cosmic-ray-detection satellite that passed near them. The mission's total elapsed time was 71 hours and 17 minutes, almost exactly the same as the two preceding Gemini missions.

Gemini 12, the final of the 10 Gemini missions, was launched on 11 November 1966. Astronauts Edwin Aldrin and James Lovell, Jr were able to rendezvous and dock with the Agena on the third orbit using visual sightings. They used the rocket motor of the attached Agena to then boost them to an apogee of 530 miles to view and photograph the 12 November solar eclipse. Aldrin later made a series of three space walks (totaling 5 hours and 37 minutes) in which he carried out a number of manual tasks including installation of a handrail on the Agena. He then used the handrail to reach the work panel on the rear of the ATDA, where he practiced using the specially designed Apollo torque wrench. Gemini 12 returned to earth after 94 hours and 35 minutes in space, landing just 3 miles from the intended impact point.

Above: **John Young (*left*) and Michael Collins aboard the USS *Guadalcanal* after the Gemini 10 splashdown on 21 July 1966.**

Right: **Gemini 12 pilot James Lovell and Edwin Aldrin after splashdown from their four-day mission, the tenth manned and final flight of the Gemini program.**

The 10-mission Gemini program ended on 15 November 1966, having logged 1939 hours and 40 minutes in space over a period of 20 months compared to just 53 hours and 55 minutes for the Mercury program in 24 months. Three of the original Mercury astronauts returned to space aboard Gemini spacecraft and four of the newer astronauts went into space on two Gemini missions. The program had demonstrated that it was possible for long-duration space flights and that astronauts could locate and dock their spacecraft with other objects in space. This provided a huge boost to the overall goal of reaching the moon. While the Gemini astronauts were docking with the Agenas in earth orbit, engineers on earth were busily putting the final touches on the next series of spacecraft, the Apollos.

INTAKE
RESCUE
NASA
NASA

APOLLO

The objective of the Apollo program was clear and simple: to carry out President Kennedy's 1961 commitment to take Americans to the moon and safely back to earth before the end of the 1960s. It is a testament to Yankee ingenuity and the American will to get things done when one considers that the first Apollo spacecraft flew just seven years after an American first went into space and that the first Apollo spacecraft landed on the moon little more than a year after that. It is even more amazing when one considers that this was accomplished while the United States fought its longest and most costly war.

Everything about the Apollo program, from the spacecraft to the launch vehicle to the mission, was larger and more complex than anything that had gone before. The spacecraft was larger than either Mercury or Gemini and was designed for three rather than one or two crewmen. It consisted of three parts, or modules. The first of these was a flattened cone-shaped capsule in which the crew was stationed, called the Command Module (CM). Next came the larger, barrel-shaped Service Module (SM) that carried oxygen, fuel and the rocket motor to propel the spacecraft from earth orbit to lunar orbit and back. These two modules remained attached throughout the entire flight and were abandoned only when it came time for the CM to re-enter the earth's atmosphere. Because of this relationship, the two modules were considered a single unit throughout most of a flight and were referred to as the Command/Service Module or CSM.

The third section of the Apollo spacecraft was the Lunar Module (LM), the spidery contraption that actually landed on the moon. Originally, the lunar landing was to involve a single spacecraft flying from earth orbit to the lunar surface and back. However, this left NASA engineers with the problem of having to carry enough fuel to the lunar surface to later lift the entire spacecraft off the lunar surface. If more fuel were added, it would add weight, requiring yet more fuel and larger engines. Finally, in the midst of the Gemini flights, the idea evolved for the LM (or Lunar Excursion Module as it was first known). It could descend to the lunar surface with just enough fuel for its own needs while the major part of the spacecraft remained in weightless lunar orbit. Because the moon has no atmosphere, the LM had no need for a heavy heat shield or an aerodynamic shape.

The LM consisted of two parts, a Descent Stage and an Ascent Stage, each equipped with a rocket motor. Both stages landed on the moon, with the motor of the Descent Stage cushioning the landing and maneuvering in the landing zone. The LM rested on the Descent Stage's tripod-like legs after landing.

Left: A typical Apollo CM and SM, clearly visible as the CM is mated to the Saturn LEM adapter.

Below: These drawings show the comparative sizes of the launch vehicles (booster rockets) used for the US manned space program. Saturn 5, which launched Apollo, was the largest and most powerful rocket ever used by the US to put humans into space, although the Apollos were smaller than the Space Shuttle.

Far right: Details of the Apollo CM (_both layers, top_), the SM and the LM (_bottom_). During launch the nonaerodynamic LM was carried below the CSM. After launch it was pulled out and attached to the CM nose, feet outward for the trip to the moon. _Bottom far right:_ The Ascent and Descent Stages were both used in lunar landing. The Descent Stage was abandoned on the moon and the Ascent Stage was abandoned after it returned the crew to the CSM.

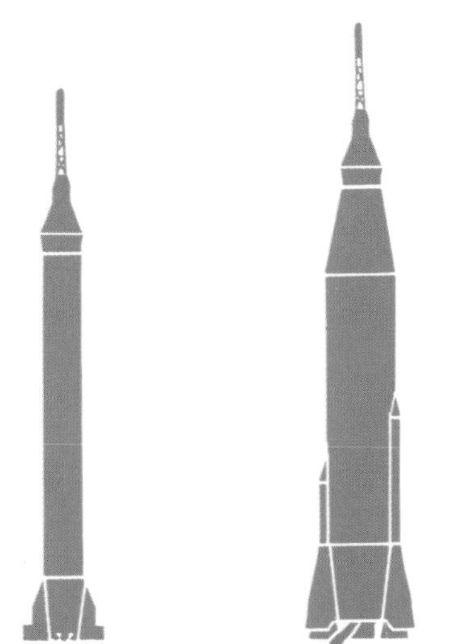

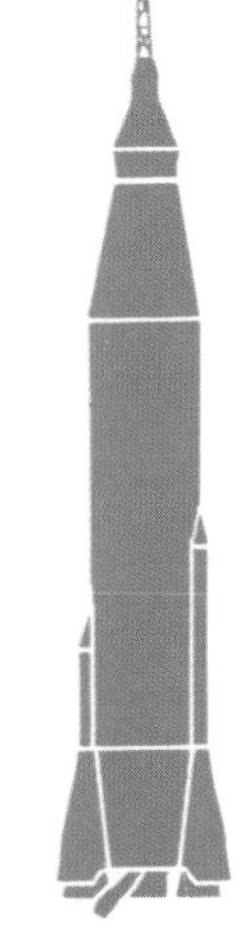

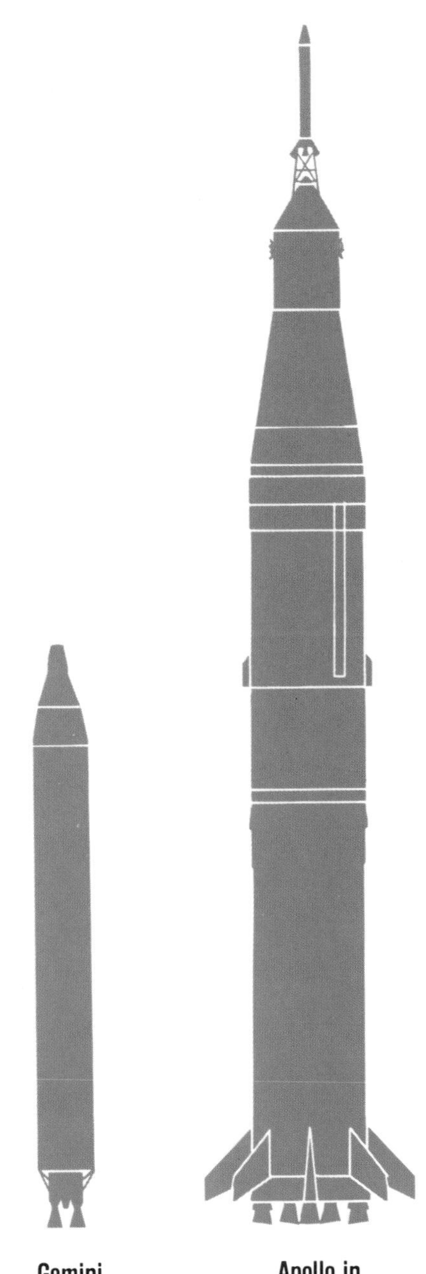

When it came time for the astronauts to leave the lunar surface, they returned to their seats in the Ascent Stage, fired its rocket motor and returned to lunar orbit to rendezvous with the CSM for the return to earth, leaving the Descent Stage on the moon. This required the smallest possible portion of the spacecraft and hence the lightest possible weight to be launched from the gravitational pull of the moon.

Because it had neither the heat shield nor the aerodynamics of the CM, the LM had to be stored below the CM and SM in the upper stage of the launch vehicle. It was designed to be 'unpacked' and attached to the 'nose' of the CM in earth orbit after launch. It was for this and for the lunar-orbit rendezvous that all the rendezvous and docking maneuvers practiced during Gemini were so important.

The Saturn launch vehicles for Apollo were the largest ever launched, dwarfing the Redstone and Atlas used for Mercury and the Titan used for Gemini. The relative thrust of the earlier launch vehicles (cumulative for all stages) had been 78,000 pounds for Mercury-Redstone, 426,000 pounds for Mercury-Atlas and 530,000 pounds for Gemini's Titan 2. By contrast, the Saturn 1B that was used for early earth-orbit Apollo tests had 1,865,000 pounds of thrust and the huge Saturn 5 that was used to carry Apollo astronauts to the moon had a total thrust of 9,038,000 pounds.

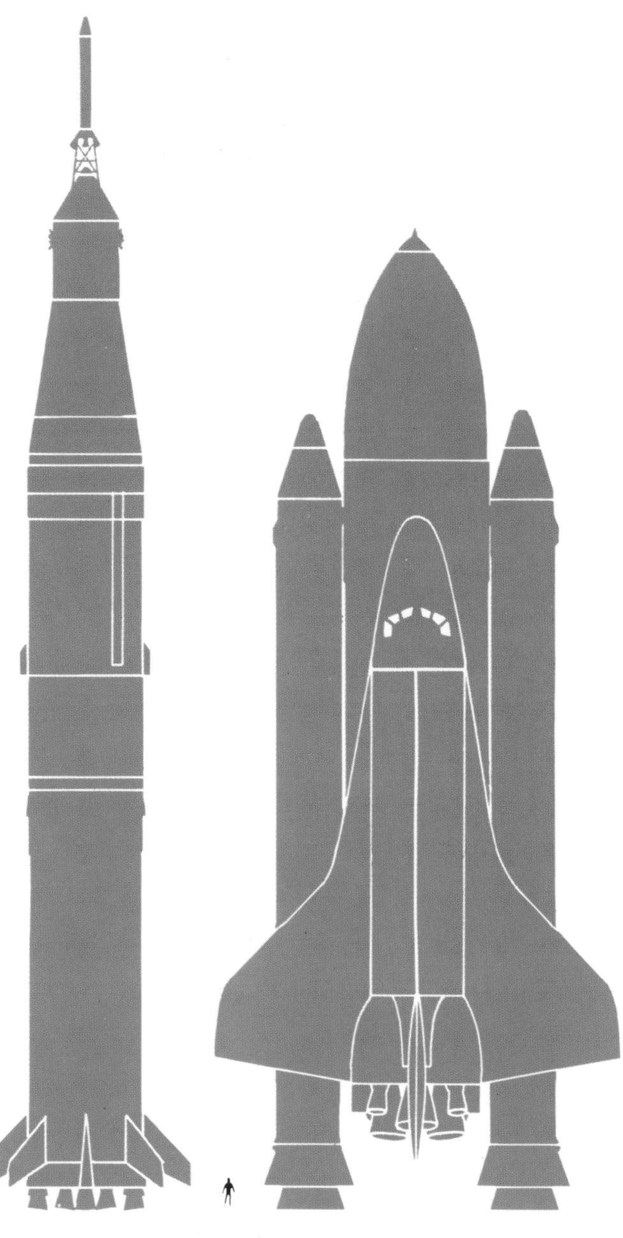

Apollo lunar missions
(Saturn 5 rocket)
1967-72

Apollo to Skylab and Apollo-Soyuz
(Saturn 1B rockets)
1973-75

Space Shuttle Transportation System
1981-present

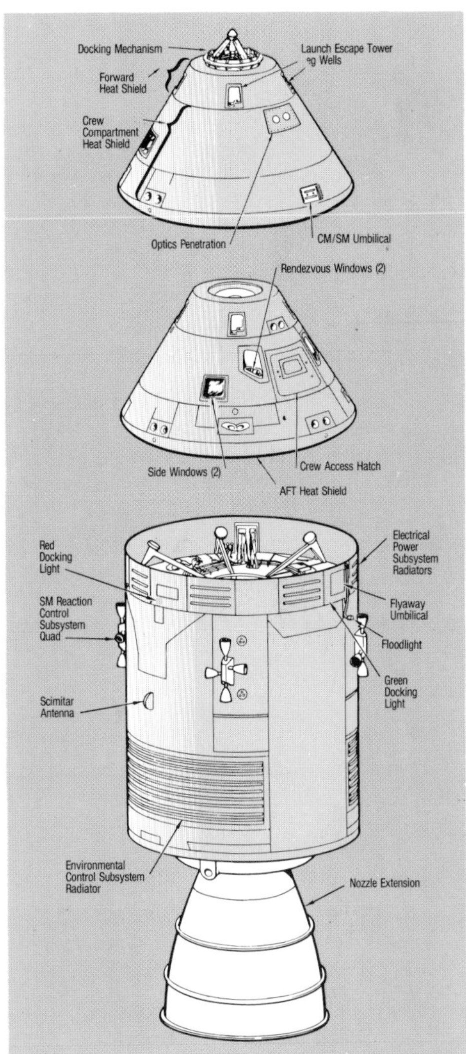

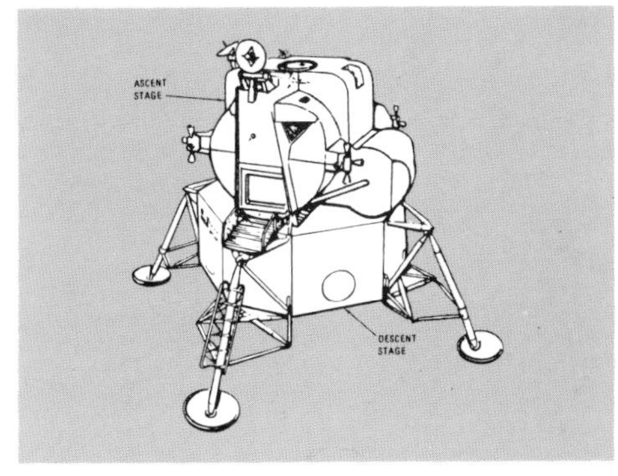

The Apollo program was the biggest single engineering project ever conducted by the United States. It was greater in constant dollar terms than Grand Coulee Dam or even the Panama Canal. Thousands of engineers associated with hundreds of contractors were brought into the project. The major contractors for the Apollo spacecraft were North American Rockwell for the CSM and Grumman for the LM. Boeing, McDonnell Douglas and Rockwell developed and produced the various elements of the huge Saturn 5 under the direction of NASA's Marshall Space Flight Center.

APOLLO TO THE MOON

The Apollo missions were all launched from Pad 39A at NASA's Kennedy Space Center, Cape Canaveral, Florida, and they were monitored and controlled by the NASA Manned Space Flight Center at Houston, Texas. At Houston the director of flight crew operations was Deke Slayton, the only one of the original seven Mercury astronauts not to fly in space during either Mercury or Gemini. Grounded because of a very slight heart condition, Slayton served as flight crew operations director from 1963 to 1972, the tireless voice in Houston's control room through the Apollo years.

As the Gemini were under way and the Apollo spacecraft were being refined, NASA was looking toward its expanding future manpower requirements. To meet these needs, the fourth and fifth groups of astronauts were selected in June 1965 and April 1966. From the US Air Force there were Charles Duke, Jr; Joe Engle; Edward Givens, Jr; James Irwin; William Pogue; Stuart Roosa and Alfred Worden. From the US Navy came John Bull, Ronald Evans, Joseph Kerwin, Thomas Mattingly II, Bruce McCandless II, Edgar

Left: On 29 June 1969 NASA announced the selection of these five scientist-astronauts. In the front row (_left to right_) are F Curtis Michel (physicist), Harrison Schmitt (astrogeologist) and Joseph Kerwin (physician). In the back row (_left to right_) are Owen Garriott (physicist) and Edward Gibson (physicist). Michel resigned two months later.

Below: The 19 pilot astronauts that made up Group Five were selected in April 1966. Seated (_left to right_) are Edward G Givens, Jr; Edgar D Mitchell; Charles M Duke, Jr and Don L Lind. Standing (_left to right_) are John L Swigert, Jr; William R Pogue, Ronald E Evans, Paul J Weitz and James B Irwin. _Below right:_ Seated (_left to right_) are Fred W Haise, Jr; Joe H Engle; Vance D Brand; John S Bull and Bruce McCandless II. Standing (_left to right_) are Gerald P Carr, Stuart A Roosa, Alfred M Worden, Thomas K Mattingly II and Jack R Lousma. A year after this photo was taken Edward Givens, Jr died in an automobile accident and two years later John Bull withdrew from the astronaut program for health reasons.

Mitchell and Paul Weitz. There were also eight civilians, including Owen Garriott, Edward Gibson, Dr Duane Graveline, Curtis Michel and Harrison Schmitt in Group Four and Vance Brand, Fred Haise, Jr; Don Lind and John Swigert, Jr in Group Five. From the US Marine Corps, Gerald Carr and Jack Lousma were selected for Group Five.

Though the Apollo lunar missions were flown mostly by the astronauts from the second and third groups, seven of the new men were also part of these historic flights. The primary role for the men of Astronaut Groups Four and Five was to form the backbone of whatever turn American space flight might take in the 1970s. Indeed, there were to be five of these nine men who would staff the Skylab space station during 1973 and 1974. To prepare for the challenges that lay beyond the lunar missions, NASA was including in the classes of 1965 and 1966 not just pilots, but scientists that it called mission specialists.

The first three flights of unmanned Apollo capsules were launched with Saturn 1B launch vehicles between February and August 1966 as the Gemini program was going through its final phases. Even though Apollo and Saturn together constituted the most complex and sophisticated transportation vehicle ever

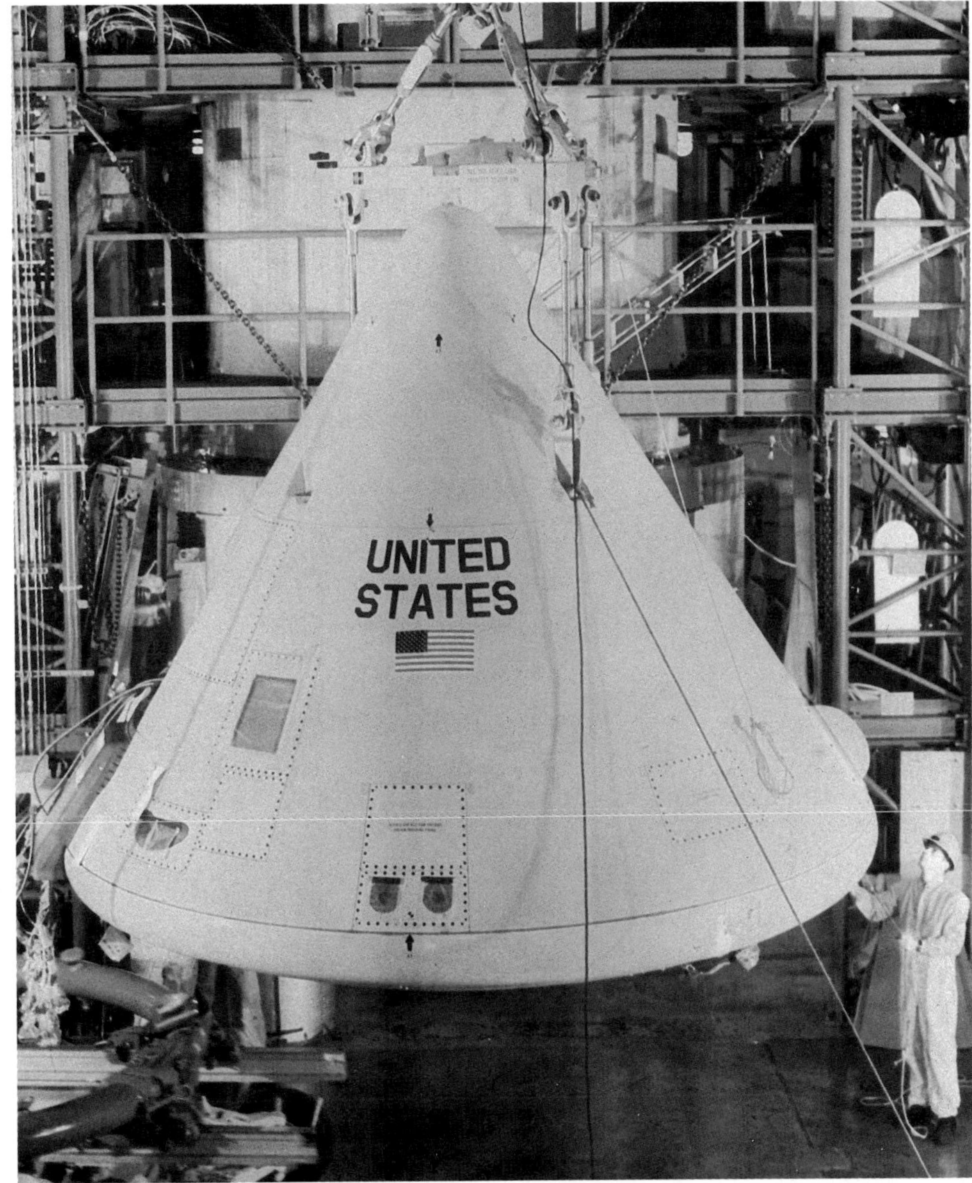

Right: **These men all dreamed of going to the moon aboard one of the new Apollo capsules that began arriving at the Cape in 1966.**

designed by man, NASA was confident that the first manned Apollo flight, a two-week earth-orbit mission, could be made on 21 February 1967, just three months after the last Gemini flight.

The Apollo flight plan for 1967 called for two manned Apollo earth-orbit flights using the Saturn 1B launch vehicle, followed by two unmanned tests of the huge Saturn 5 and finally a manned flight of Apollo atop the Saturn 5. After the success of Gemini, which had seen five manned flights each year in 1965 and 1966, three manned Apollo flights in 1967 seemed reasonable.

The first flight crew was picked and preparations began. The men who were selected to fly 'Apollo 1' were Gus Grissom, the second American in space during Mercury and a member of the first Gemini crew; Edward White, a veteran of Gemini 4 and the first man to walk in space; and Roger Chaffee. On 27 January 1967, the three men were aboard the Apollo spacecraft for a full dress rehearsal for the 21 February flight. At 6:31 pm disaster struck. An electrical fire started inside the capsule and spread quickly in the 100 percent oxygen atmosphere that was used in American spacecraft.

'We've got a fire in the cockpit,' screamed Grissom over the radio as White began to release the hatch. In pure oxygen, fire burns rapidly and soon everything flammable in the capsule was blazing. Fifteen seconds later the pressure of the inferno cracked the capsule and black clouds of acrid smoke rolled out. Chaffee's words were the last recorded from the crew: 'We've got a bad fire, let's get out, we're burning up.'

Fighting their way through the smoke, NASA technicians reached the capsule and finally removed the hatches. Five minutes had passed since the fire had started. All three men were dead. Badly burned by the fire, the three men's fate was sealed by the suffocating smoke.

Even as buglers were blowing taps for Grissom and Chaffee at Arlington's National Cemetery and for White at West Point, NASA was sifting through the charred $35 million capsule looking for answers and trying to pick up the pieces of its derailed lunar program. No one wanted to go ahead with the Apollo program until all the circumstances surrounding the fire were known and everything possible was done to prevent it from happening again.

The interior of the spacecraft from the hatch to the wiring was redesigned. Some thought was given to using an atmosphere of nitrogen plus oxygen like that of the earth's atmosphere and like that used aboard Soviet spacecraft, but the idea was rejected. By redesigning the wiring and fireproofing the interior, it was felt that a future disaster could be avoided. Most important, at least symbolically, was the redesigned hatch that took 5 rather than 90 seconds to open.

Below: The Apollo 1 crew (_top to bottom_) — Gus Grissom, Edward White II and Roger Chaffee, and the charred remains of their craft (_below right_). The Apollo 7 crew (_left, front to back_) — Wally Schirra, Donn Eisele and Walter Cunningham — flew the first manned Apollo.

The fire had cost the Apollo program three of its best astronauts, but it had also cost the program more than a year of delay. Instead of three manned and two unmanned flights during 1967, only one unmanned flight was made—a Saturn 5 launch-vehicle test on 9 November. Only two years remained in the decade. If Kennedy's goal for the American space program was to be met, everything had to move ahead flawlessly.

On 22 January 1968 the unmanned Apollo LM was successfully tested in space, having been launched by a Saturn 1B. On 4 April came a full dress rehearsal with the newly redesigned Apollo CSM launched by a Saturn 5. These two flights were designated Apollo 5 and Apollo 6. Under the original designation system, the Chaffee/Grissom/White manned flight, had it taken place, would have been Apollo 1. The revised designation system began with the first Apollo-Saturn flight, so the Apollo 1 designation was retroactively applied to that flight in 1966 and all other subsequent Apollo-Saturn flights unmanned as well as manned were numbered in sequence.

The long-awaited first manned Apollo flight, designated Apollo 7, was launched on 11 October 1968, 21 months behind schedule. The crew for the flight were Walter Schirra (like the late Grissom, one of the original Mercury seven), Walter Cunningham and Donn Eisele. They conducted a rendezvous with the Saturn 4B upper stage of their Saturn 1B launch vehicle in the same manner that the Gemini astronauts had rendezvoused with the Agena two years earlier. They then carried out exhaustive tests of the spacecraft's system under operational conditions. Schirra came down with a head cold that the others caught, and this led to a decision not to wear helmets during reentry to keep the pressure on their ear drums equalized as cabin pressure changed during descent. The only long-term effect from this was that Schirra showed up in television commercials 17 years later using the incident to help advertise a cold remedy.

With a duration of 260 hours and 9 minutes, Apollo 7 was longer than any American space flight to date except the epic Gemini 7 flight, and it was successful. A disastrous setback had been overcome and the American space program was back on the road to the moon.

By this time, however, the Soviet lunar program was moving ahead rapidly. In September 1968, a month before Apollo 7, the Soviets had sent an unmanned Zond spacecraft, similar to their Soyuz-type manned craft, to the vicinity of the moon and back.

In the meantime, NASA had begun to prepare for the most ambitious and certainly the most dramatic flight to date. The Apollo 8 flight was to see three Americans in orbit around the moon. Apollo 8 was launched atop a Saturn 5 on 21 December 1968, less than two months after the splashdown of Apollo 7. Aboard were Frank Borman, James Lovell and William Anders. Ten hours and 55 minutes after launch they were out of earth orbit and conducting their first midcourse correction enroute to the moon. At 61 hours and 9 minutes a second and final correction was made. Two others that had

Apollo 7 commander Wally Schirra (*left*) relaxes aboard the NASA Motor Vessel Retriever prior to suiting up for water egress training. *Right:* Apollo 8 commander Frank Borman emerges from centrifuge training.

been planned were eliminated as unnecessary because the course they had set was so exact. At 68 hours and 59 minutes Apollo 8 reached and swung around the back side of the moon. Nine minutes later the CSM's engines were fired and the spacecraft was placed into lunar orbit.

It was Christmas Eve as the first television pictures were returned to the United States from the moon. Americans listened to their countrymen speaking from a quarter of a million miles away and watched on their televisions the first pictures of the blue earth rising above the chalky-gray lunar horizon. Borman, who was supposed to have read the Christmas Eve prayer at his church, said he 'couldn't quite make it,' so he read the prayer aloud from lunar orbit.

Apollo 8 made 10 lunar orbits in 20 hours, during which time no one aboard gave any thought to sleep as they photographed the lunar surface and conducted surveys that could be used in planning subsequent landings. The spacecraft conducted a 3 minute and 23 second engine firing at 89 hours and 16 minutes on the tenth lunar orbit. At 146 hours and 31 minutes the CM separated from the SM and plunged into the earth's atmosphere at 24,696 mph. Borman, Lovell and Anders splashed down in the Pacific on 27 December 1968 after a 147-hour, half-million-mile journey. The premier of the USSR sent his congratulations and the Soviet space agency announced that it had no intention of sending a man to the moon. The Soviets had been working feverishly to that end, but they now recognized that the race was lost and it would be better in the long run to drop out rather than come in second. The American space program clearly had momentum. Only two Apollo flights had been flown, but they'd been flown in the period of two months and the second was a Saturn 5-launched lunar-orbital mission.

Apollo 9 was launched atop a Saturn 5 on 3 March 1969 with James McDivitt, David Scott and Russell Schweickart aboard. Although Apollo 9 did not repeat Apollo 8's lunar odyssey, the mission provided several firsts. It was the first manned Apollo mission flown with the LM and hence the first manned flight of the complete Apollo spacecraft. It was also the first mission since Mercury in which the spacecraft were given nick-

This view of the rising earth greeted the Apollo 8 astronauts as they came from behind the moon after lunar orbit insertion burn. They were the first human beings to witness an earthrise. The lunar horizon is about 484 miles from the spacecraft.

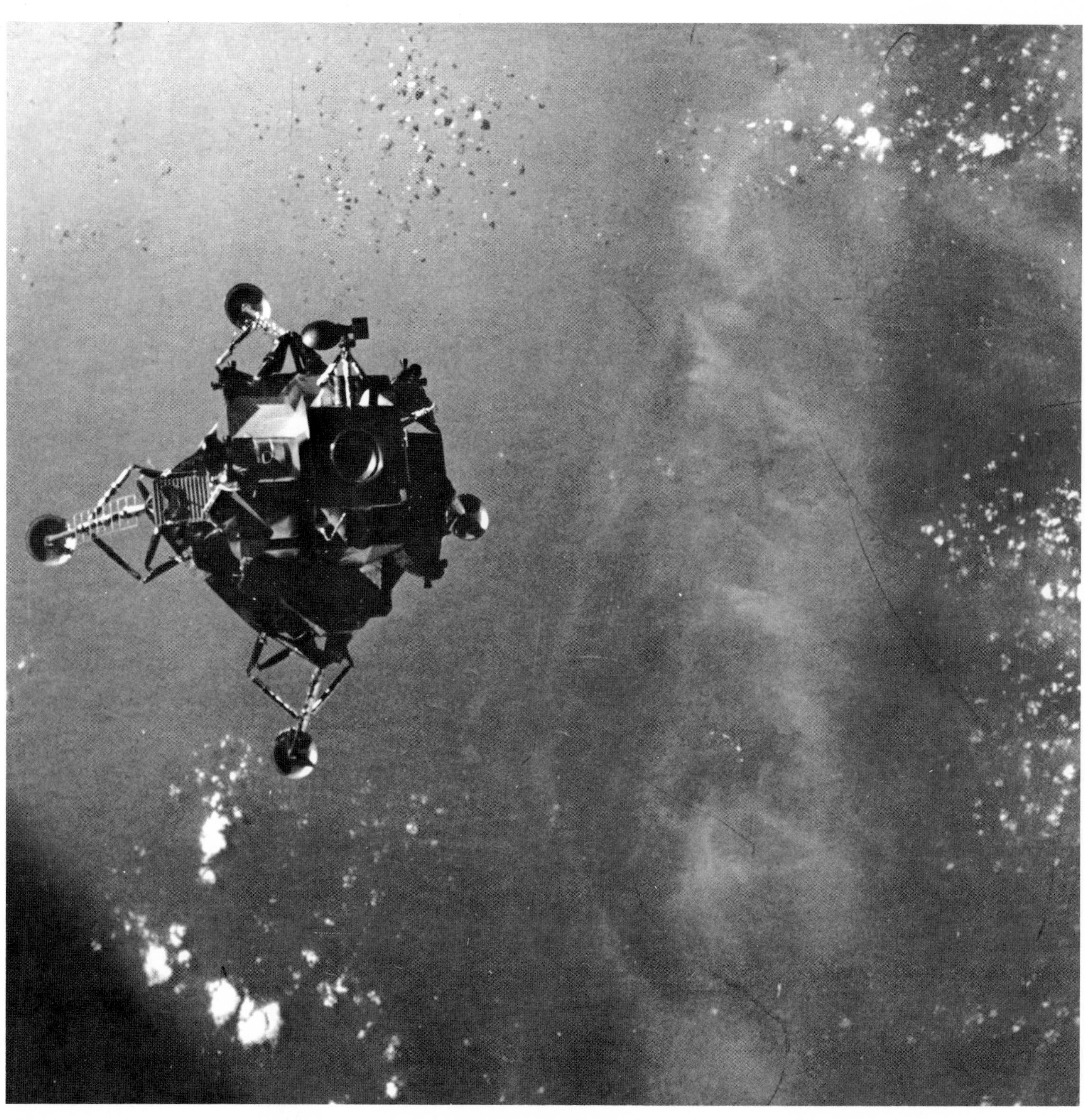

names. The crew of Apollo 9 set a precedent, and thereafter each CSM and LM were given separate names. The names chosen by McDivitt, Scott and Schweickart were particularly descriptive of the shapes of the respective modules. The Apollo 9 CSM was called *Gumdrop* and the LM *Spider*. The mission was to test the entire integrated spacecraft system, including a docking between the CSM and LM. On the third, fourth and fifth days, McDivitt and Schweickart donned space suits and climbed into the LM to conduct systems checks and brief engine firings. On the fifth day they sealed the LM and separated from the CSM. They maneuvered *Spider* to a point 113 miles from

Above: The Apollo 9 LM, _Spider,_ was photographed from the CSM on the fifth day of the earth-orbital mission, poised in landing configuration. James McDivitt and Russell Schweickart were in the LM. _Right:_ A view of the CSM from the LM. Pilot David Scott remained at the controls in the CM _Gumdrop_ while McDivitt and Schweickart checked out the LM.

Gumdrop, jettisoned the Descent Stage and fired the Ascent Stage engine. They flew *Spider* into the proximity of the CSM and conducted the type of rendezvous and docking that would be done by an LM returning from the lunar surface. On 13 March the CM portion of *Gumdrop* returned the astronauts to earth after 241 hours and 1 minute. The mission was the only full-scale rehearsal for the lunar landing that would be held in earth orbit.

Apollo 10 was launched on 18 May 1969 with Tom Stafford, John Young and Eugene Cernan aboard. The mission was similar to that of Apollo 9, except that the dress rehearsal for a lunar landing was to take place in lunar orbit rather than in earth orbit. The crew would be the second group of human beings to travel to the vicinity of the moon. Only one midcourse correction was required and the spacecraft reached lunar orbit 76 hours after launch. Stafford and Cernan left CSM *Charlie Brown,* climbed into the LM nicknamed *Snoopy* and detached themselves 22 hours later. *Snoopy* was lowered into

NASA

an elliptical orbit with an apogee 70 miles above the lunar surface and a perigee of just 9.7 miles, simulating the pattern that was to be flown in a lunar landing mission. Stafford and Cernan rendezvoused with *Charlie Brown* 8 hours after their separation and returned to earth for a splashdown 192 hours and 3 minutes after launch. NASA had now launched four successful manned Apollo missions and two of them (ironically the two shortest) had achieved lunar orbit.

Apollo 11 was by design the culmination of tens of thousands of hours of effort by thousands of personnel and the fulfillment of the goal set by President Kennedy eight years earlier. The comic book nicknames were gone now. The Apollo 11 CSM was *Columbia,* its LM was *Eagle. Columbia* was the third manned spacecraft to enter lunar orbit, and *Eagle* took its crew where no man had gone before.

Left: **Apollo 9 commander James McDivitt stands by to participate in crew compartment fit and function test activity at North American Rockwell. Apollo 9 was the only full-scale dress rehearsal for a lunar landing to be held in earth orbit. Apollo 10 (*above*) was a dress rehearsal in lunar orbit two and a half months later.**

Apollo 11 was launched at 9:32 am on 16 July 1969 in the most widely televised space launch in history. There were 3493 journalists from 56 countries on hand and thousands of spectators camped out for miles up and down the Florida coast north and south of Cape Kennedy. Ex-president Lyndon Johnson, whose presidency had spanned the Gemini program and had included the Apollo 8 Christmas, was in a special box elbow to elbow with Vice President Spiro Agnew, who calmly sipped from a tall iced tumbler as Johnson applauded the launch. Aboard the spacecraft were mission commander Neil

From Cape Canaveral to Tranquility Base, a quarter million miles into history. Apollo rises past the launch tower at Pad 39A (*below*) to begin man's first lunar landing mission, and Neil Armstrong stepped onto the lunar surface four days later (*right*). Edwin Aldrin, Jr (*above*) followed 20 minutes later.

Armstrong, CSM pilot Michael Collins and LM pilot Edwin Aldrin. Aldrin and Collins were US Air Force officers, Armstrong a civilian and all three were spaceflight veterans of the Gemini program. As had been the case with Apollo 10, only a single midcourse correction was needed and the spacecraft reached lunar orbit after 75 hours and 50 minutes. Armstrong and Aldrin entered and checked out the LM and returned to *Columbia*. The following day, they donned space suits, climbed into *Eagle* and sealed themselves in. At 100 hours and 12 minutes, the LM was detached from *Columbia* and began its powered descent toward the lunar surface. Two hours and 17 minutes later the LM was 5 miles from the landing site at 26,000 feet of altitude, using the Descent Stage engine to provide breaking thrust as the LM fell toward the moon. About 60 feet above the surface, Armstrong slowed the LM and began moving laterally, scanning the landing zone in the moon's desolate Sea of Tranquility for a level spot free of boulders.

NASA control in Houston had told the astronauts that they had less than half a minute of fuel left for their landing maneuver when Armstrong brought *Eagle* slowly down to the dusty lunar surface.

Armstrong said, 'Forward . . . drifting right . . . contact light. Okay engine stop . . . descent engine override off. Engine arm off.'

Sensing that history had just been made, Houston replied, 'We copy you down, *Eagle*.'

Over the quarter million miles of space came Armstrong's confirmation, 'Houston, Tranquility Base here . . . the *Eagle* has landed.'

'Roger, Tranquility,' said Houston Control, 'we copy you on the ground. You've got a bunch of guys about to turn blue. We're breathing again. Thanks a lot!'

'Thank you,' replied the crew of the *Eagle* from mankind's first fragile outpost on another celestial body.

The Apollo 11 LM landed in the moon's Sea of Tranquility on 20 July 1969, 102 hours and 45 minutes after leaving the earth. At 109 hours and 19 minutes, Armstrong opened *Eagle*'s hatch and made his way down the LM's ladder toward the

OPEN
COLLINS

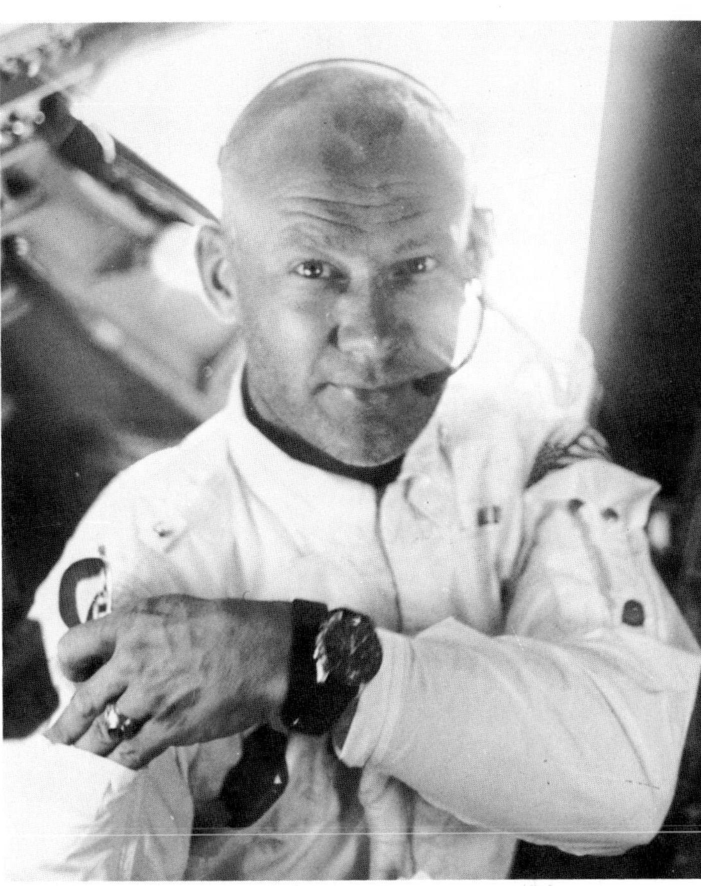

lunar surface. Each measured step was easy in the moon's weak gravity. Armstrong gave a running commentary as he came down.

'I'm at the foot of the ladder. The LM footpads are only depressed in the surface about one or two inches, although the surface appears to be very, very fine grained. As you get close to it, it's almost like powder. I'm going to step off the LM now. That's one small step for man . . . one giant leap for mankind.'

Neil Armstrong was 109 hours and 24 minutes from planet earth, but the dreams of centuries were fulfilled in his single step. Mankind had walked upon the moon.

With the words 'magnificent desolation' on his lips, Edwin Aldrin followed Armstrong down the ladder. They set up a television camera about 30 feet from *Eagle,* gathered samples and walked up to 300 feet from the landing site they'd dubbed Tranquility Base. Their first EVA on the lunar surface lasted about 2½ hours. The entire first visit to the moon lasted 21 hours and 36 minutes and included 7 hours of sleep for the two men.

Eagle's Ascent Stage was fired at 124 hours and 22 minutes into the mission and their rendezvous with Michael Collins in *Columbia* took place 3 hours and 41 minutes later in lunar orbit.

Only a single midcourse correction was required on the return flight, and the Apollo 11 CM splashed down in the blue

The crew of Apollo 11: Michael Collins, CM pilot, practices procedures with the Apollo docking mechanism (*left*) in a CM mockup. *Above:* Commander Neil Armstrong (*left*) and LM pilot Edwin Aldrin, Jr in the LM at Tranquility base. *Below:* Assisted by frogmen, the entire crew in biological isolation garb awaits helicopter pickup after splashdown.

Pacific on 24 July 1969, 195 hours and 19 minutes after its launch. President Kennedy's goal of placing an American on the moon and returning him safely to earth by the end of the 1960s had been met with half a year to spare.

Apollo 12 was launched on 14 November 1969 with the mission of conducting a second lunar landing and a more extensive exploration of the lunar surface, this time in the region known as the Ocean of Storms. The men aboard CSM *Yankee Clipper* were the all-Navy crew of Charles Conrad, Jr; Richard Gordon, Jr; and Alan Bean. Conrad and Bean were to conduct a lunar landing in the LM *Intrepid.*

After arriving in lunar orbit, the crew detached *Intrepid* from *Yankee Clipper* 109 hours and 23 minutes after launch and began their descent toward the moon. Two hours and 9 minutes later a second American vehicle arrived on the lunar surface. The landing site in the Ocean of Storms was just 535 feet from the spot where the American unmanned probe Surveyor 3 had landed on 20 April 1967. It had been just 2½ years, but to everyone concerned, Surveyor 3 was like a relic of a prehistoric civilization. So much had happened in those 2½ years.

One of the jobs on the docket for Conrad and Bean while on the lunar surface was to hike over to Surveyor 3 to retrieve its television camera and other parts. During their first EVA, however, they deployed the Apollo Lunar Surface Experiments Package (ALSEP) and took some core samples from the lunar soil, but didn't venture too far from the LM. They reached Surveyor during their second EVA on the lunar surface, which took them 1300 feet from *Intrepid* and around the rim of Head Crater, in which Surveyor had landed. The Surveyor television camera was removed, as were the probe's motorized soil scoop and pieces of cable and aluminum tubing. The astronauts returned to *Intrepid* 3 hours and 48 minutes after they had begun their second walk on the lunar surface and they ate their lunch. Six hours later, after 31 hours on the moon, the Ascent Stage was fired and *Intrepid* left the moon with not only the fragments of Surveyor 3, but with 75 pounds of rock that had been part of earth's cold gray moon for billions of years. Apollo 12 returned to earth on 24 November 1969, 244 hours and 36 minutes after launch. Not just one, but four Americans had walked the dusty lunar surface before the dawning of the 1970s.

Apollo 13, launched on 11 April 1970, was intended as an almost routine flight in the shadow of the dramatic successes of its two predecessors. The Apollo 13 LM, *Aquarius,* was intended to land in the Fra Mauro region, deploy the ALSEP and conduct soil-sampling and photographic activities similar to those undertaken by Apollo 12. The 'routine' flight of Apollo 13 turned anything but routine on 13 April as bad luck spelled near disaster.

Left: **Tranquility Base as it appeared in July 1969 just before *Eagle's* departure and as it will appear when man next arrives on the moon.**

Above: **Apollo 12 commander Charles Conrad, Jr went on the first Skylab mission in 1973.**

It was 55 hours and 55 minutes into the mission. John Swigert, Jr and James Lovell, Jr were in the CSM *Odyssey* and Fred Haise, Jr was in the passageway between *Odyssey* and *Aquarius* when a loud explosion suddenly rocked the spacecraft. The Number 2 oxygen tank had just exploded as the result of an electrical short circuit and precious oxygen was leaking into space from both the Number 1 and Number 2 tanks. Had the spark occurred anywhere but in airless outer space, an electrical fire would have resulted that would have destroyed the spacecraft. Because of the loss of oxygen and electrical power to the CSM, the mission and even the survival of the crew was in question. Clearly there was not enough oxygen to sustain a moon landing, and that part of the mission was quickly abandoned. Beyond this, however, lurked the fear that there might not be enough oxygen to get the crew back to earth alive. The crew were forced to essentially turn off the CM and abandon it for the undamaged LM. Using the oxygen stored there, they turned *Aquarius* into a 'lifeboat.'

Because the SM had been severely damaged in the explosion, its power could not be used to slow the spacecraft and turn it around. Therefore, Apollo 13 had to continue to the moon with its then present momentum and use the lunar gravity to swing around and hurl the astronauts back to earth. At 61 hours and 30 minutes into the mission, the Apollo 13 crew

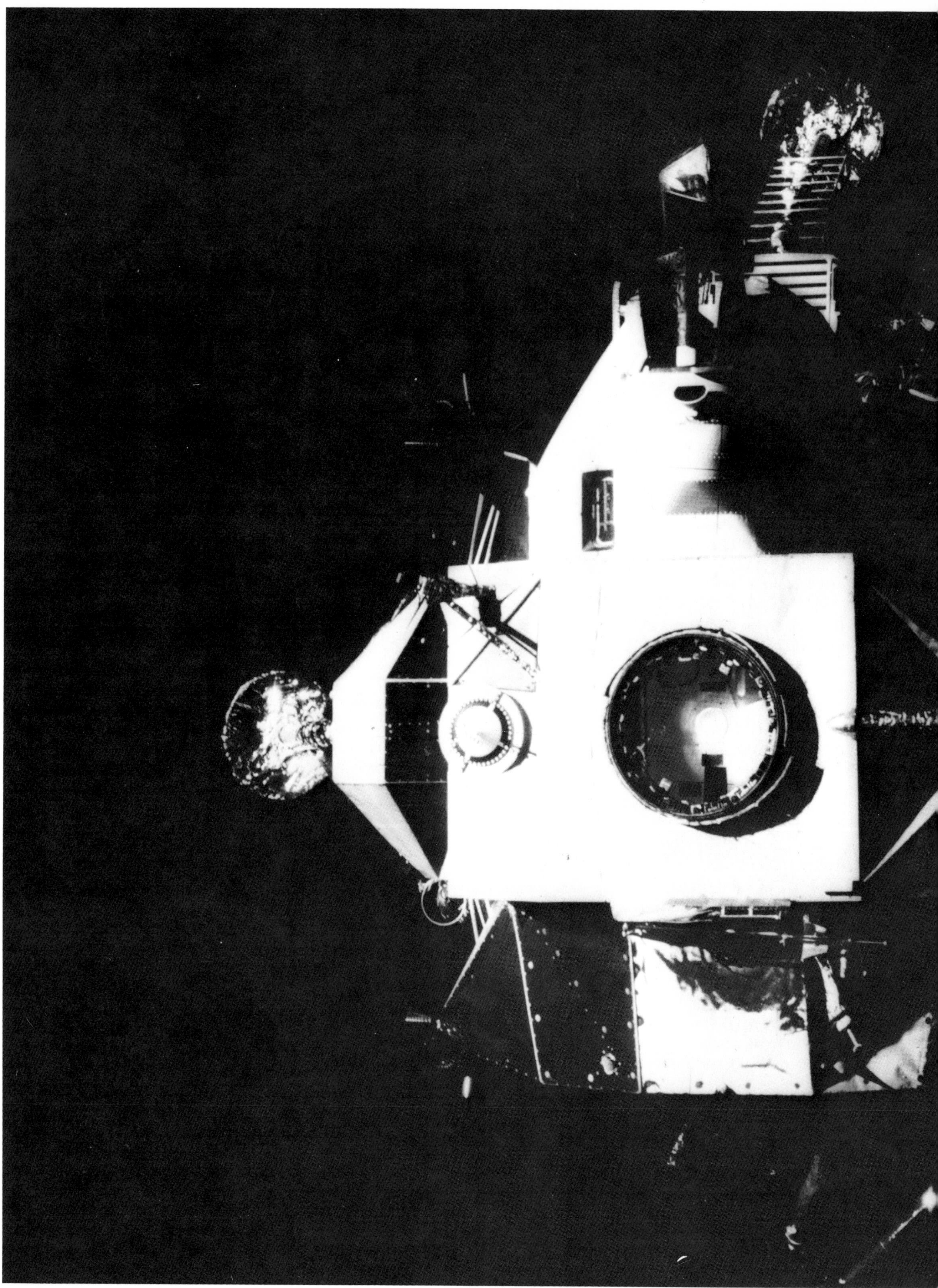

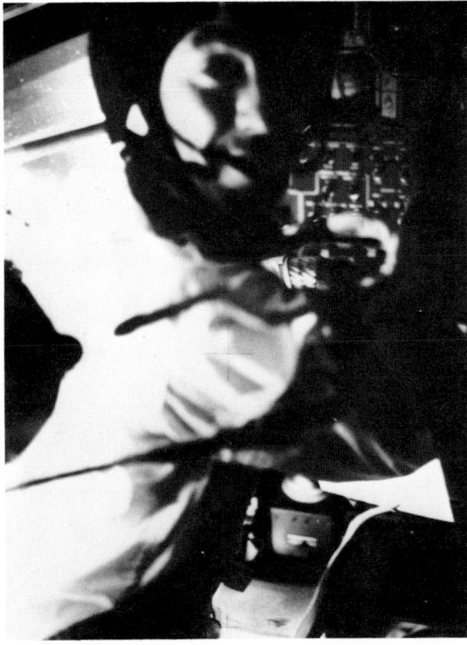

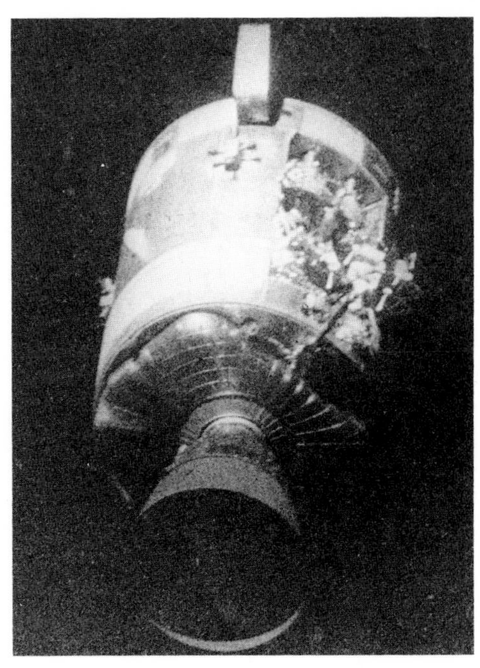

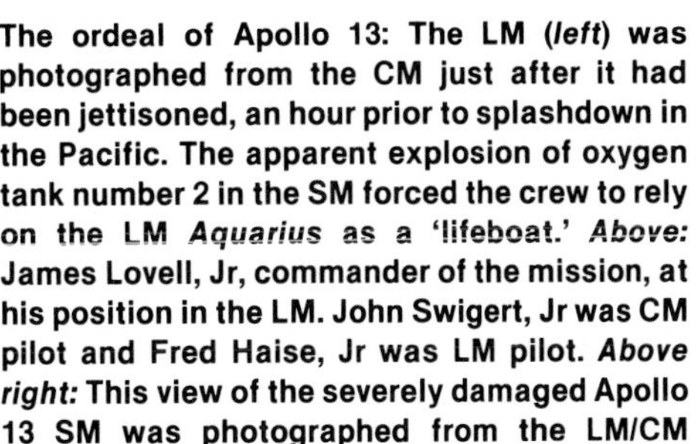

The ordeal of Apollo 13: The LM (*left*) was photographed from the CM just after it had been jettisoned, an hour prior to splashdown in the Pacific. The apparent explosion of oxygen tank number 2 in the SM forced the crew to rely on the LM *Aquarius* as a 'lifeboat.' *Above:* James Lovell, Jr, commander of the mission, at his position in the LM. John Swigert, Jr was CM pilot and Fred Haise, Jr was LM pilot. *Above right:* This view of the severely damaged Apollo 13 SM was photographed from the LM/CM following SM jettisoning. As shown here, an entire panel was blown away by the explosion in Section 4. Two of the three fuel cells are visible just above the heavily damaged area. *Overleaf:* John Swigert, Jr holds the 'mailbox,' a jerry-rigged arrangement that the Apollo 13 astronauts built to use the CM lithium hydroxide canisters to purge carbon dioxide from the LM. The mailbox was designed and tested on the ground before it was suggested to the problem-plagued crew.

reached the moon, completed a half orbit turn around it and set a course for home, praying that the oxygen in the *Aquarius* would be enough.

Back on earth, people around the world watched and prayed as NASA's engineers worked out the calculations that they hoped would give the crew the margin they would need to get home alive. No one was monitoring their progress with more keenness than Deke Slayton, flight crew operations director.

Any number of things could have gone wrong. The men in the *Aquarius* could have simply run out of oxygen. *Aquarius* was designed to support two men on the moon for a day and a half, but now it had to support three men for more than three days. If the oxygen was ample, then there was the problem of the electricity failing and the men freezing to death. Finally, and in many ways most frightening of all, was the prospect of the engines malfunctioning during the required midcourse correction. If that happened, the crew could miss the earth and hurtle into the emptiness of space, lost forever among the stars.

The midcourse correction went smoothly after all, but the powered-down spacecraft got colder and colder. The craft was still 18 hours from earth orbit and near freezing when calculations determined that it was close enough to earth for the astronauts to return to *Odyssey* and begin bringing the power back up. The astronauts had conserved the resources of the *Odyssey* by tapping into the oxygen supply for the LM's rocket engines; by doing this they had ensured enough electrical power for 24 hours and enough water for drinking and cooling the spacecraft's systems for 8 hours after that.

The last major potential source of problems was separating the CM from the explosion-damaged SM in preparation for re-entry. At 138 hours and 2 minutes into the mission, four long days after the explosion, the crew fired the thrusters and they worked. They sealed the passageway between *Aquarius* and *Odyssey* and said their farewell to the lifeboat that had saved their lives. Less than an hour later the CM plunged into earth's atmosphere and 142 hours and 55 minutes after they'd left the earth, Lovell, Haise and Swigert were bobbing in the Pacific Ocean and savoring the sweet smell of earth's atmosphere.

The Apollo 14 lunar landing was postponed. There would be no more attempts to reach the moon in 1970. When it was launched on 31 January 1971, the CSM *Kitty Hawk* was 994 pounds heavier than *Odyssey* because of modifications prompted by the near-disaster of Apollo

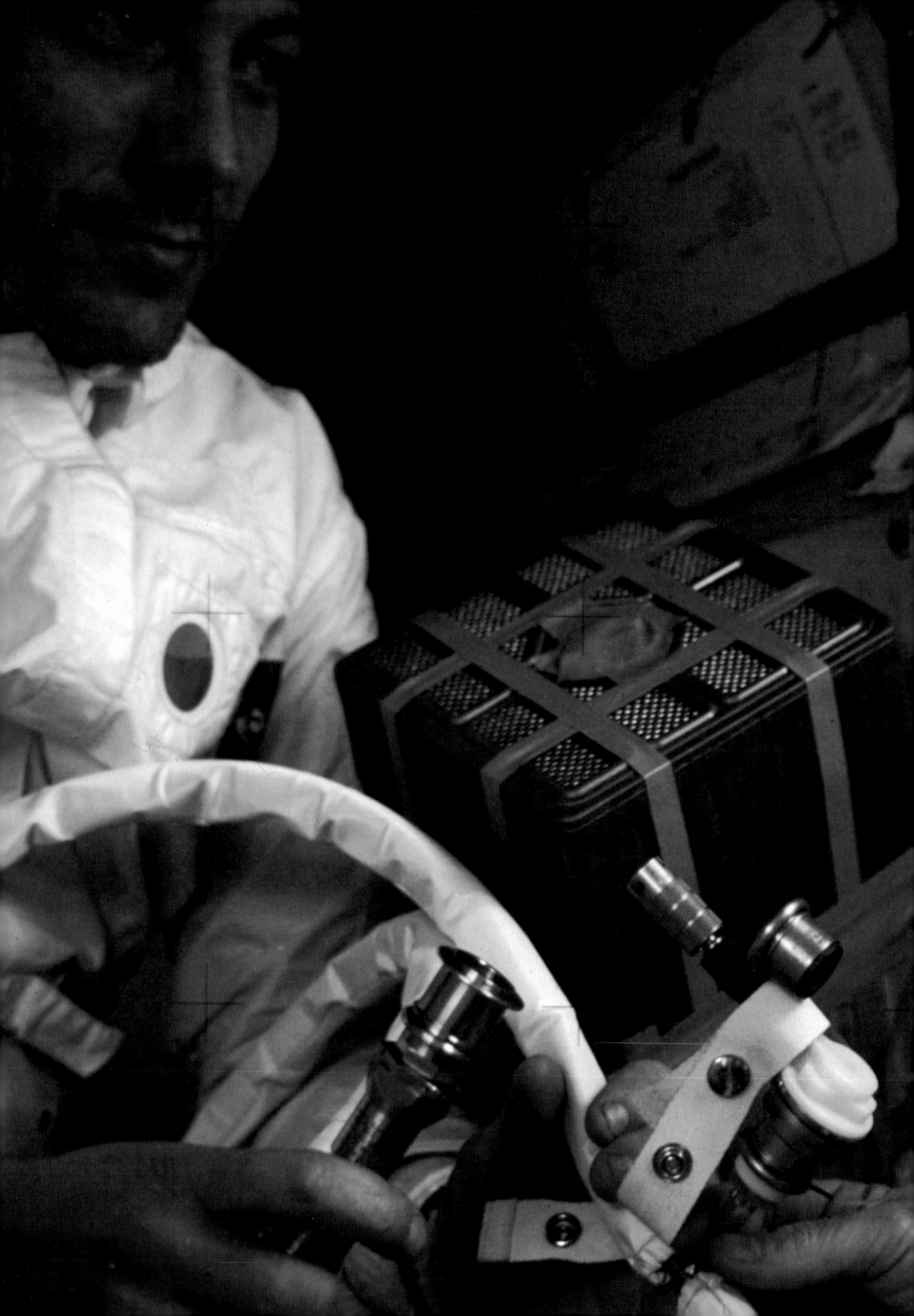

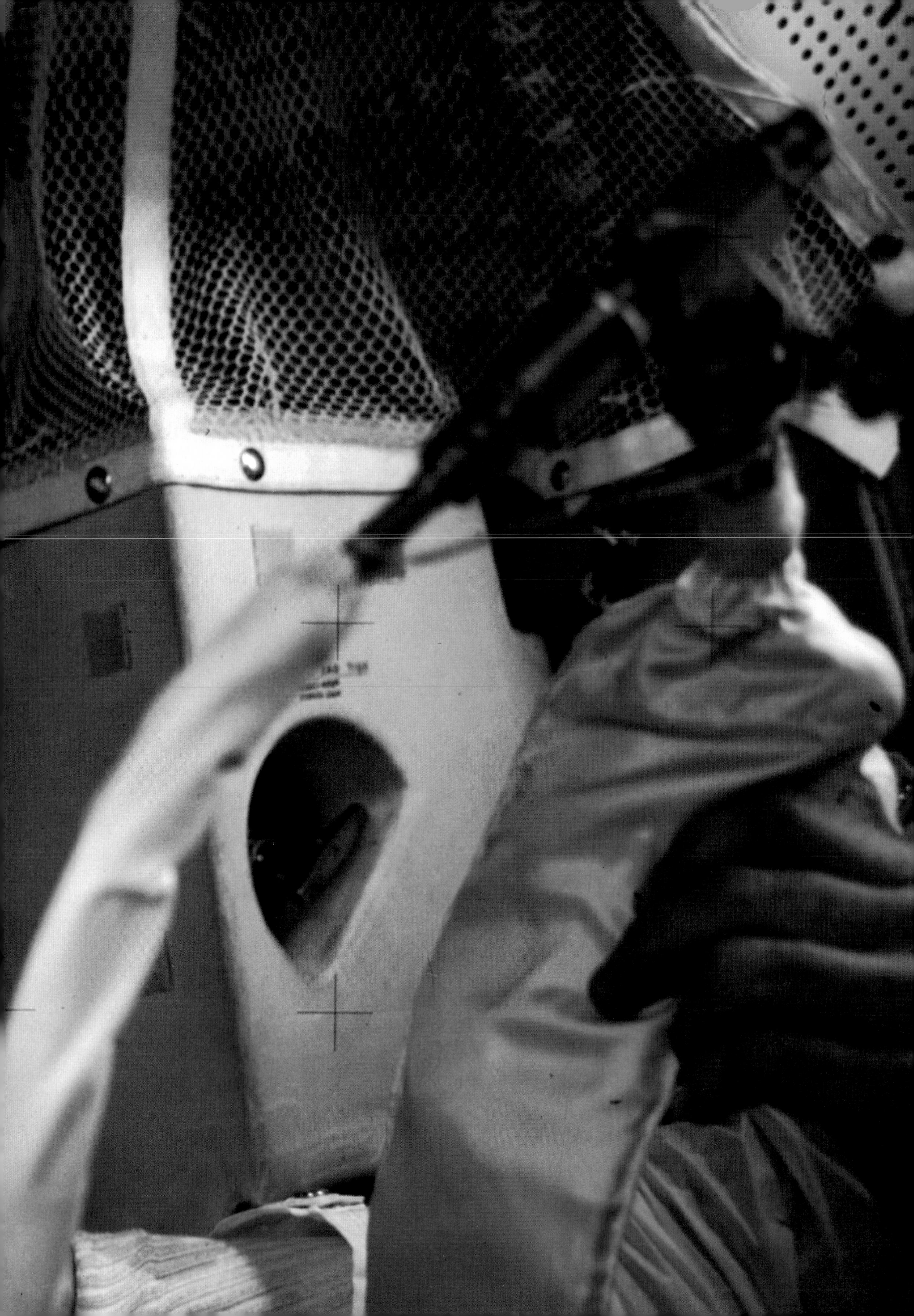

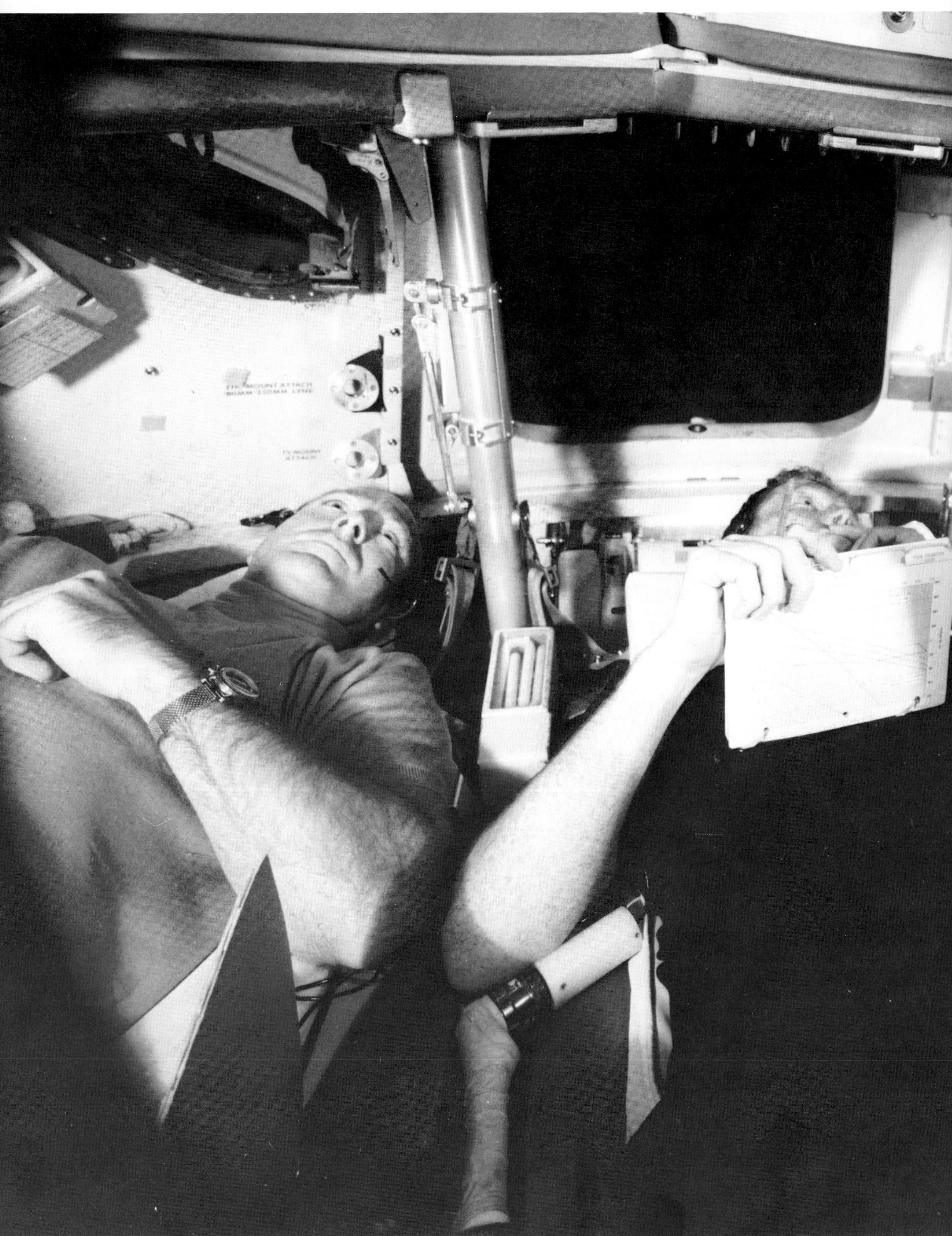
MOUNT ATTACH
80MM 250MM LENS
TV MOUNT
ATTACH

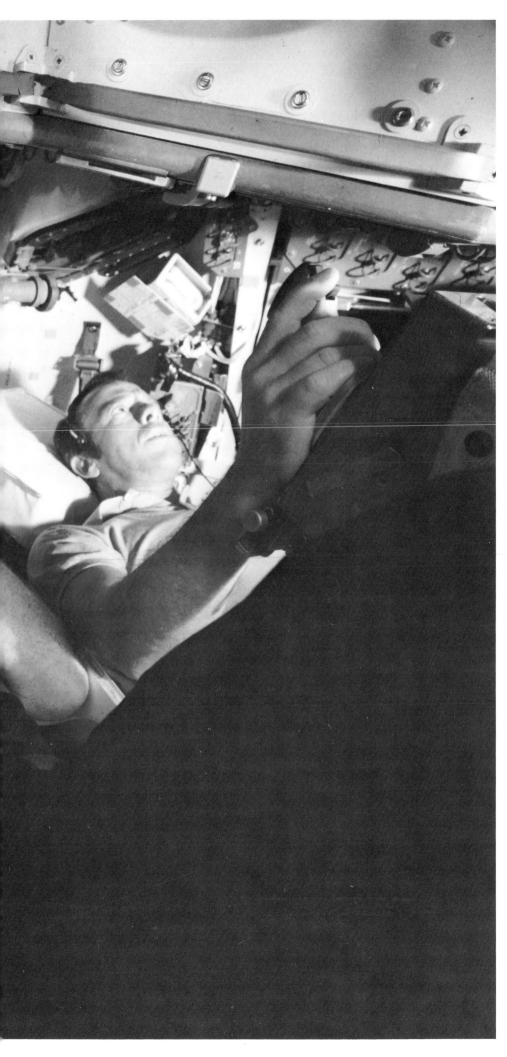

Above: **Alan Shepard, Jr looks over the terrain during training in northwestern Sonora, Mexico that included geological and lunar surface simulation activity. He was the first American in space and the only one of the original Mercury 7 to set foot on the moon.** ***Left:*** **The crew of the Apollo 14 lunar landing mission (*****left to right*****) were LM pilot Edgar Mitchell, CM pilot Stuart Roosa and commander Alan Shepard, Jr, shown in the cramped interior of a simulation CSM** ***Kitty Hawk*** **during training.**

13. The crew included two men who had never flown in space, Edgar Mitchell and Stuart Roosa. The mission commander was Alan Shepard, the first American to fly in space 10 years before.

The landing site for Shepard and Mitchell was the Fra Mauro Crater, 110 miles east of where Apollo 12 had landed and near where Apollo 13 would have landed. The landing went well and Shepard stepped off the ladder on the LM *Antares* 114 hours and 31 minutes after he had left the earth. Shepard and Mitchell deployed the ALSEP and began a nearly 5-hour exploration of the lunar surface. The following day (earth time) they ventured outside again. This time they hiked almost two miles in the Fra Mauro area. They spent 9 hours and 24 minutes outside the LM on the surface, and they collected 94 pounds of rocks and soil for 187 scientific teams back on earth. While he waited in *Kitty Hawk* for the return of *Antares,* Stu

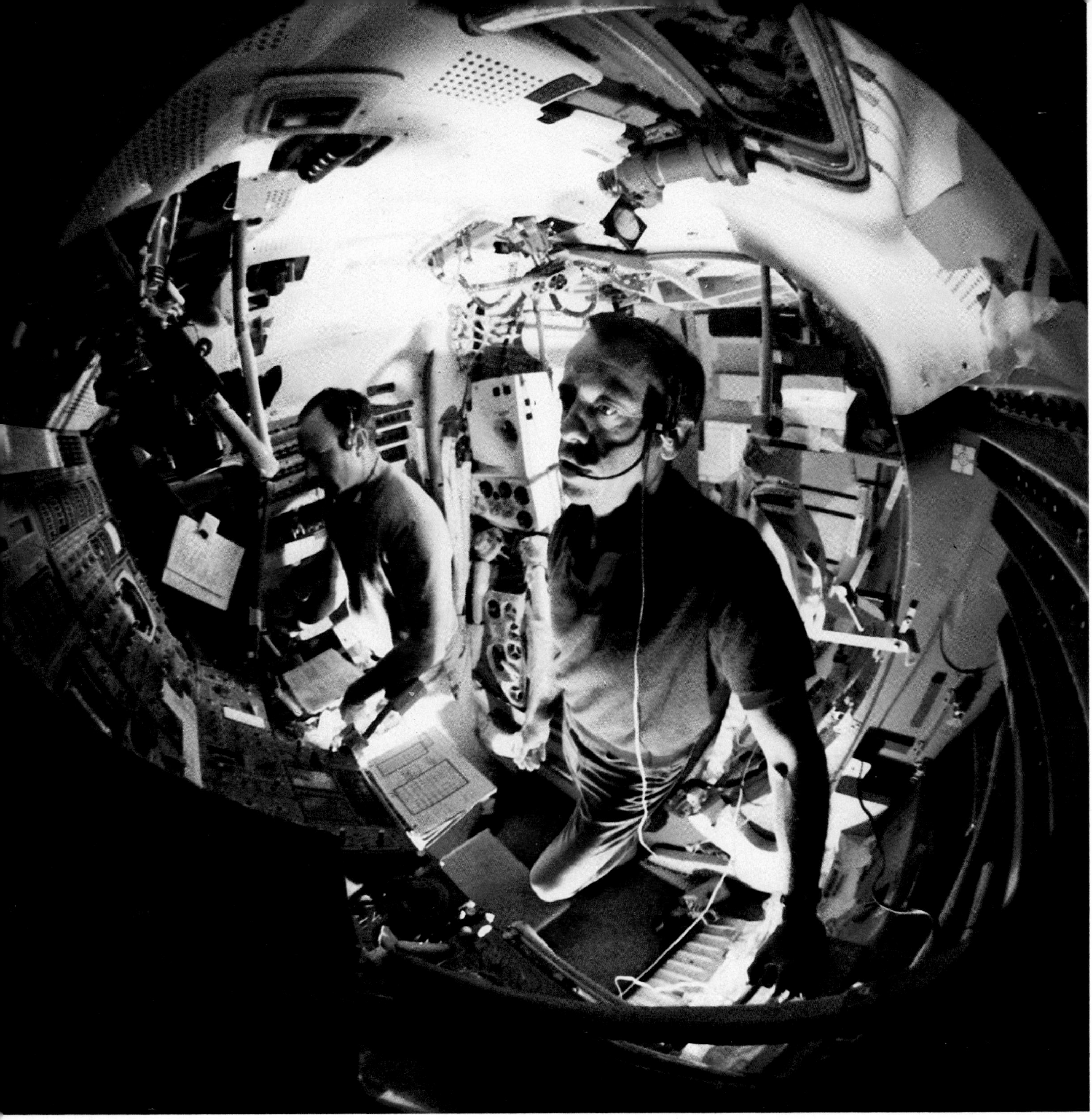

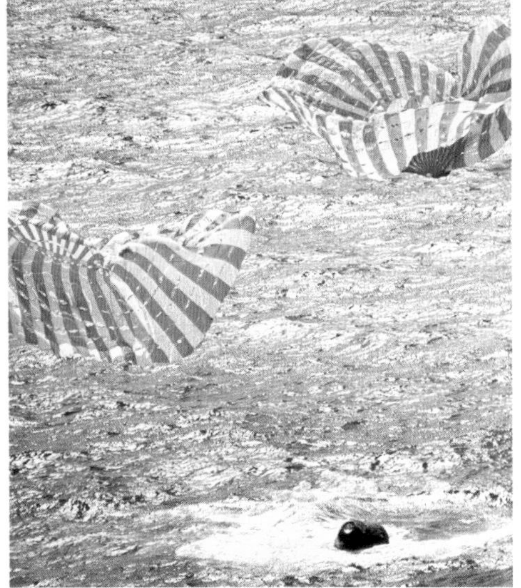

A fish-eye view (*above*) of Alan Shepard, Jr (*foreground*) and Edgar Mitchell in the LM mission simulator during Apollo 14 preflight training. *Left:* The two landing parachutes billow in the wind as *Kitty Hawk* splashed down in the Pacific on 9 February 1971.

***Above right:* Apollo 15 LM pilot James Irwin with the revolutionary, electrically powered Lunar Roving Vehicle that proved invaluable for exploring the lunar surface. Apollo 15 was launched 26 July 1971 and touched down at the Hadley-Apennine site on 30 July. Alfred Worden was CM pilot and Dave Scott was commander of the mission.**

***Right:* The Lunar Rover, looking north. The astronauts collected 173 pounds of lunar samples and drilled for a core sample 10 feet below the lunar surface. Three rovers were carried to the moon by Apollo spacecraft and left there for future use.**

Roosa photographed the lunar surface, including the Descartes area, the planned landing zone for Apollo 16.

Apollo 14 splashed down in the Pacific on 9 February 1971 after 216 hours and 2 minutes. It had been the kind of success that NASA needed after Apollo 13's near brush with death.

Apollo 15, launched on 26 July 1971, was the first of the Apollo J-series missions. It was capable of staying longer on the lunar surface and equipped for more extensive scientific studies in the areas of lunar surface science, lunar orbital science and operational engineering. In the equipment bay of the LM, this new spacecraft carried a simple piece of equipment that revolutionized the exploration of the lunar surface. It was the Lunar Roving Vehicle (LRV), called Lunar Rover for short. This four-wheeled 462 pound vehicle was capable of carrying two astronauts for up to 50 miles at speeds of 8.7 mph. While this was not the kind of speed that would amaze the drivers on earthly freeways, it greatly expanded the areas of the lunar surface that could be explored.

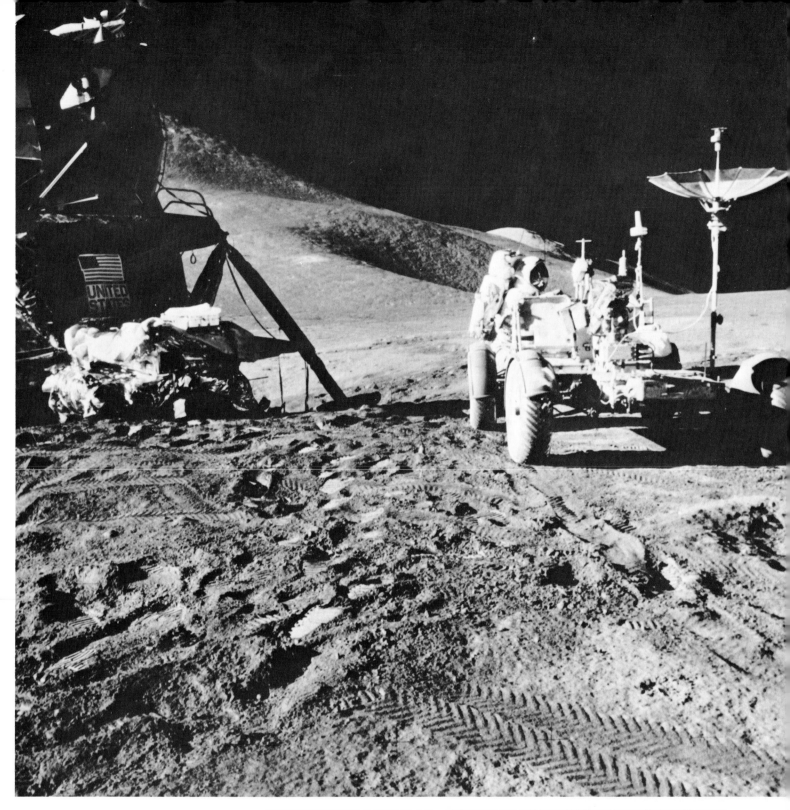

Aboard the CSM *Endeavor* for the first flight of a J-series Apollo were Alfred Worden, James Irwin and the Apollo 15 commander, David Scott, a veteran of Gemini 8 and Apollo 9. After a landing approach with an angle of 26 degrees, the steepest yet flown by an LM, Scott and

Above: **The Ascent Stage of the Apollo 16 LM hovers over the Sea of Fertility prior to docking, carrying LM pilot Charles Duke, Jr and commander John Young. New lunar terrain data was obtained during the 20 hours of EVA.** ***Left:*** **Apollo 15 splashes down in the Pacific after completing the fourth manned lunar landing mission for the United States.**

Irwin brought LM *Falcon* in for a safe landing at Hadley Rille just 1500 feet from their intended landing site. The seventh and eighth men to walk upon the moon unpacked the Rover and deployed the ALSEP. In three excursions, totaling a record 18 hours and 37 minutes, they drove 17.5 miles in the Lunar Rover and collected 170 pounds of lunar material. After 66 hours and 55 minutes Scott and Irwin returned to *Endeavor* and flew home to a Pacific splashdown 335 miles north of Honolulu on 7 August, ending a flight of 295 hours and 12 minutes.

Apollo 16, the second of the Apollo J-series, was launched on 16 April 1972. Aboard the CSM *Casper* were Charles Duke, Jr; Ken Mattingly II and their commander John Young, a veteran of two Gemini flights as well as the earlier Apollo 10 flight that was the second to have orbited the moon. Young was the first man to visit the moon twice, but the Apollo 16 flight was his first trip to its surface.

Young, along with Charles Duke, Jr set the LM *Orion* down on the lunar surface in the Descartes area photographed by Apollo 14 and began a record 71 hour and 2 minute stay. In their first venture out on the moon's surface, they spent 7 hours and 11 minutes visiting Flag Crater for rock samples and a place called Spook Crater, where they took the first measurements with a portable lunar magnetometer. The two returned to *Orion* with 2.5 miles on the Rover's odometer.

The second Apollo 16 EVA began with a drive south to Stone Mountain to collect surface and core samples, and ended after 7 hours and 23 minutes and 6.9 miles in the Rover. Their final exploration of the

Top: **Charles Duke, Jr, Apollo 16 LM pilot, joined commander John Young and CM pilot Thomas Mattingly II for the April 1972 lunar landing mission. *Above:* LM *Orion* Ascent Stage during lunar liftoff, as transmitted by the RCA TV camera mounted on the Lunar Roving Vehicle that was remotely controlled from the Mission Control Center. John Young and Charles Duke, Jr explored the Descartes landing site. *Right:* The Apollo 16 CSM as seen from the LM just after the two spacecraft undocked.**

lunar surface included stops at North Ray Crater, where they took samples at places called House Rock and Shadow Rock. Young and Duke left the moon with 206 pounds of lunar material after a total of 20 hours and 14 minutes of active surface exploration, more time than had been spent on the lunar surface in the first three landings combined. The liftoff of *Orion's* Ascent Stage was photographed by the television camera of the Lunar Rover, abandoned on the moon after 16.6 miles of service. *Endeavor* returned to earth on 27 April after 265 hours and 51 minutes and more than a half million miles.

When the Saturn 5 with Apollo 17 rolled out to Pad 39A in December 1972, everyone knew that it would be the last lunar landing. Grumman engineers had set the tone with a big sign in the mobile

service building that enclosed the huge Saturn rocket—'This May Be Our Last, But It Will Be Our Best.'

The CSM *America* crew consisted of Navy Cdr Ronald Evans, civilian geologist and Apollo 17 commander Harrison Schmitt, and Navy Capt Eugene Cernan, veteran of Gemini 9 and Apollo 10. The Saturn roared to life and hurled *America* aloft in the predawn darkness of 7 December 1972. Four days later Cernan and Schmitt eased LM *Challenger* onto the soft sands of the moon's Taurus-Littrow region.

Four hours after their landing, the two astronauts began their first EVA. Cernan accidentally broke the 'eyelid' off the Rover's fender, but they fixed it on the spot. They drove south to Steno Crater, where geologist Schmitt collected some soil samples and chipped a few slivers off a boulder. The following day they drove west, setting a top speed record of 10.6 mph in the Rover. This second excursion took the men to the top of a huge landslide at Nansen Crater on the base of South Massif. At their third stop, Schmitt made a major discovery on the rim of Shorty Crater. Amid the acres and acres of varying shades of gray that constitute the lunar surface, he found orange soil.

Apollo 17 scrapbook: *Above:* The strange deposit of orange soil that geologist Harrison Schmitt found in the rim of Shorty Crater. *Right:* The Apollo 17 lander *Challenger* that placed Eugene Crenan and Harrison Schmitt in the soft sands of the moon's Taurus-Littrow region in December 1972 after four days of traveling through space. Cernan and Schmitt were the last of the Apollo astronauts to feel the crunch of lunar sand beneath their feet.

On the third day Cernan and Schmitt ventured out once again on what was to be the last lunar EVA of the Apollo program. They drove north to the base of the North Massif, southeast to Sculptured Hills and finally on an excursion to determine whether Van Serg Crater was volcanic or whether it was caused by the impact of a meteorite. (It was the latter).

When they returned to *Challenger,* Cernan and Schmitt had concluded more than just a drive across a dusty gray desert. They completed the longest stay on the lunar surface, the longest total EVA time on the moon (22 hours and 5 minutes), the longest single EVA (7 hours and 37 minutes) and the longest distance covered in a Lunar Rover (21 miles). With geologist Schmitt holding the sample bag, they also took home more of the moon (250 pounds) than any previous Apollo crew. They also left behind a long-term

surface exposure experiment that included photographs taken before the flight of selected equipment as well as equipment samples that could be retrieved and returned to earth sometime after 1992 for study.

America's return to earth took in a 67-minute EVA in deep space by Evans to retrieve film and data cannisters from the SM and ended with a splashdown on 19 December, 301 hours and 52 minutes after launch. The splashdown in the Pacific marked the end of the longest space flight of the Apollo program and the end of the program itself. It was also the end of an era.

Just 11 years earlier the United States had sent one man into space for 15 minutes and President John Kennedy had audaciously committed the nation's resources to the impossible goal of landing a man on the moon by the end of the 1960s. Since that time a vast consortium of private enterprise and government bureaucracy had landed four men on the moon by the end of the 1960s and had sent a dozen Americans to the lunar surface.

Left: An excellent view of the CSM _America_ from the LM _Challenger_ during rendezvous and docking maneuvers in lunar orbit. The Apollo 17 LM Ascent Stage, with Eugene Cernan and Harrison Schmitt aboard, had just returned from the Taurus-Littrow landing site on the lunar surface. The Scientific Instrument Module bay is exposed. _Above:_ A helicopter transfers the last men to visit the moon to their recovery vessel, the USS _Ticonderoga._

In just over four years, the Apollo program astronauts had logged more than 7500 hours in space, more than triple the flight time of Mercury and Gemini combined. Harrison Schmitt stated in his postsplashdown conversation with President Richard Nixon: 'As to the historical legacy of Apollo, I have found no reason to change my thoughts as we left the moon and the Valley of the Taurus Littrow; that valley of history has seen mankind complete its first evolutionary steps into the universe. With those steps a tradition of peace and freedom now exists in the solar system. From this larger home we move to greet the future.'

APOLLO TO SKYLAB

The Apollo program didn't actually end with the last flight to the moon in December 1972. There were four more flights, but the emphasis was on sending astronauts to a space station orbiting the earth instead of to the moon.

During the 1960s, the American space program had stressed getting the manned Apollo spacecraft to the moon, but at the same time the concept of a space station was being developed. The concept was as old as that of space flight and one that offered some exciting possibilities, including zero-gravity scientific experimentation as well as long-duration space visits by American astronauts.

The first serious American space station project was the Manned Orbital Laboratory (MOL) that the US Air Force had commissioned from the Douglas Aircraft Company in the early 1960s. It was designed to be compatible with Gemini spacecraft and could accommodate a two-man crew for a month. The MOL was intended to be a military rather than a NASA program, designed principally for high-altitude reconnaissance and to give the Air Force a presence in space.

As it was envisioned in 1963, the MOL could be deployed expeditiously. The crew could travel into space aboard a Gemini capsule. The Geminis were already on the assembly line for NASA, so the Air Force wouldn't have to pay any development costs. If McDonnell kept the assembly line open for a few more capsules, the individual unit cost would be lower for both agencies. The MOL spacecraft was based on a segment of the Titan launch vehicle that was already in use. Compared to the engineering projects that NASA was operating in the mid-1960s, the job of installing living quarters and oxygen tanks in a segment of a Titan shell would be relatively simple.

President Lyndon Johnson gave the go-ahead for the MOL in August 1965 while Gemini 5 was in orbit and in the headlines. At the same time, the US Air Force was moving ahead with a little-known astronaut selection process of its own. With much less fanfare than had been accorded the NASA spacemen, the Air Force began its own manned space program. This group of unheralded astronauts included the Air Force's Lt Col Karol Bobko, Lt Col Charles Fullerton, Col Henry Hartsfield, Jr and Col Donald Peterson, as well as Cdr Robert Crippen and Cdr Richard Truly from the US Navy and Lt Col Robert Overmyer from the Marine Corps.

When the MOL project got under way in earnest in 1965, it was predicted that the first deployment of the Air Force space station would come late in 1968. By 1967, however, the target date had slipped to 1970. The MOL, which seemed like a relatively simple project compared to Apollo, was being developed against the backdrop of a straining United States budget. Lyndon Johnson's disastrous Great Society programs were devouring money and the expanding war in Vietnam was consuming most of the defense side of the budget. The Defense Department, looking for places to cut costs, seized the MOL and its $1.5 billion projected four-year budget, and on 10 June 1969 the Air Force space station program was canceled. Two months later, the seven MOL astronauts were transferred to NASA as the space agency's seventh astronaut group.

Meanwhile, at NASA plans were going forward toward another, larger space station project called Skylab. Like the MOL, Skylab was built to utilize an existing spacecraft (in this case, an Apollo) to carry its crew into orbit. Also like the MOL, Skylab would use a segment of a launch vehicle (in this case, the 4A upper stage of a Saturn 5) to form the basic fuselage of the space station. And, like the MOL, Skylab would be built by the Douglas Aircraft Company (part of McDonnell Douglas after 1967).

Unlike the MOL, however, the objectives set for Skylab were scientific, not military. Therefore, the crews for the Skylab program were drawn mostly from among scientist-astronauts of NASA's fourth and fifth groups rather than from among the MOL astronauts—even though Bobko, Crippen and NASA's William Thorton had spent 56 days in the earth-bound Skylab simulator during the summer of 1972.

Given the budget-cutting mood of the early 1970s, it is amazing that Skylab got off the ground so soon after the conclusion of the Apollo program. Apollo 17 splashed down on 19 December 1972 and the Skylab space station was ready for launch less than five months later. Skylab had, of course, been in the works since 1969, when the MOL was canceled.

Skylab was huge by comparison to American spacecraft, and it was four times the size of the Salyut space station that the Soviets had placed in orbit in 1971. Based on the 4B upper stage of a Saturn 5, Skylab was 84.2 feet long and it weighed 84 tons. Inside, the Orbital Workshop Section (OWS) had a habitable

Right: An overhead view of the Skylab space station cluster in earth orbit photographed from the Skylab 4 CSM. _Below:_ The Skylab space station comprises the following major parts: (1) the Apollo spacecraft, (2) the Apollo docking module, (3) the Apollo telescope mount (no relation to the spacecraft) with windmill-like solar arrays extended, (4) the airlock module and instrument unit and (5) the orbital workshop, showing both of the solar wings. One of the solar wings was destroyed during launch in 1973.

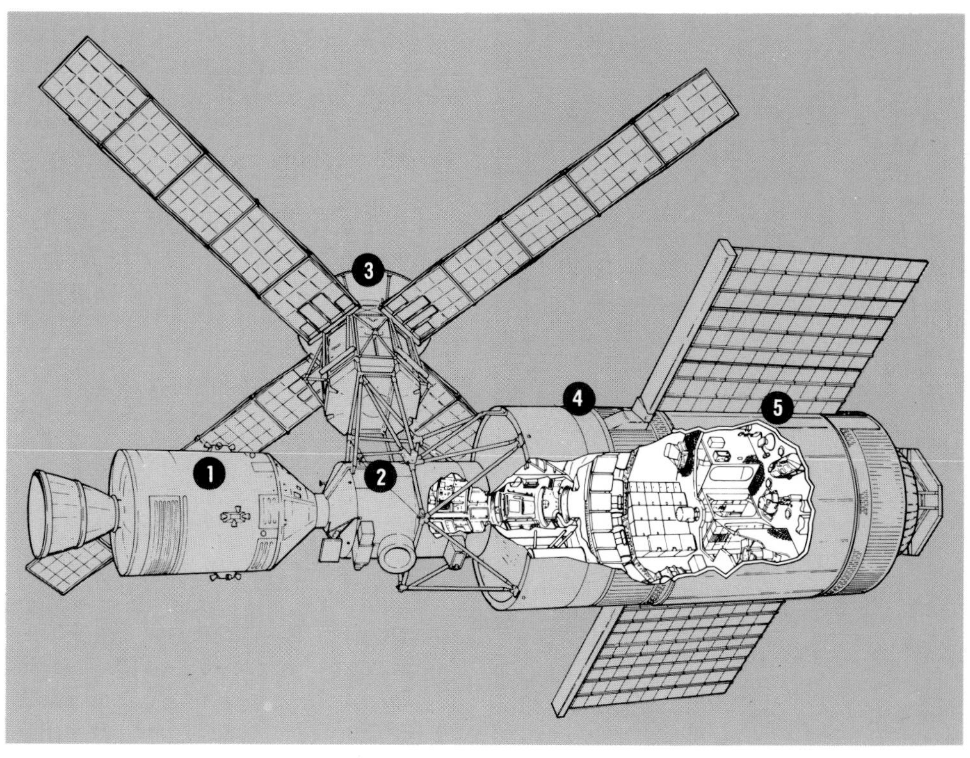

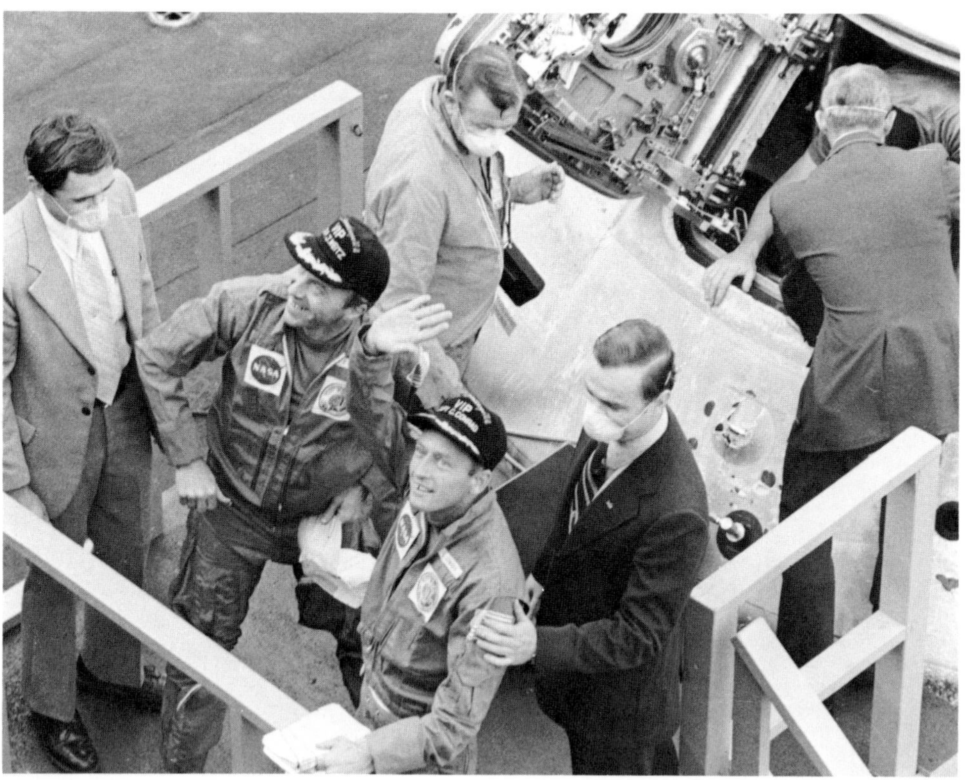

area of more than 10,000 cubic feet, a far cry from the cramped quarters of the Apollo.

The Skylab objective was for three groups of astronauts to live and work in the space station for one, two and three months, respectively, during 1973 and 1974. Skylab would then be left in space to be reopened and used again at a later date, perhaps in the early 1980s.

The massive Skylab space station was placed in earth's orbit on 14 May 1973 in the last launching of a Saturn 5 launch vehicle. The Saturn 5 was the heavy-duty rocket used to launch the Apollo and the only spacecraft capable of lifting a payload as huge as Skylab. Skylab's first crew was to be launched the next day in one of the surplus Apollo capsules atop a smaller Saturn IB, the launch vehicle used for the earlier Apollo earth-orbital missions.

The launch of the first Skylab crew on 15 May 1973 was postponed because the launch of Skylab itself did not take place as planned. During the launch of Skylab a meteoroid/thermal shield tore loose from the OWS, ripping away one of the primary solar 'wings' and jamming the other with debris. Without the thermal shield, temperatures within the space station would soar, and without the solar panels on the wings, electrical power would be less than planned. NASA studied the problem and decided to proceed, to send up the crew, who would attempt to repair the space station and thus salvage the Skylab program. Failing that, the components that existed for a second Skylab space station could have been used.

***Right:* Edging around the globe, the first Skylab crew catches sight of the Skylab 1 space station. The parasol solar shield shades the Orbital Workshop where the micrometeoroid shield is missing. *Above:* Charles Conrad, Joseph Kerwin and Paul Weitz leave the craft with Melvin Richmond, recovery team leader, and NASA doctors Charles Ross and Jerry Hordinsky.**

On 25 May 1973, 10 days later than planned, an Apollo spacecraft was placed into orbit. Aboard this mission, designated Skylab 2, were pilot Paul Weitz and scientist Dr Joseph Kerwin. The flight's commander was to be the Skylab program crew commander, Charles 'Pete' Conrad, Jr. As had been the case through most of the Apollo program, two of the crew were making their first flight, while the commander was a veteran of at least one previous flight. Conrad had flown on Gemini 5 and Gemini 11 before going to the moon as the commander of the Apollo 12 mission.

The astronauts arrived at the space station with the crumpled wing 7 hours after launch and attempted in vain to free it. One of the two wings had been ripped completely off, so it was important to pry the other loose and get it working in order to have enough electricity. A second problem developed in docking the Apollo CSM with Skylab, but the docking was accomplished on the seventh attempt.

Once inside, the crew deployed an umbrella-shaped sunshade outside to protect Skylab from the sun's burning rays. As soon as the shade was in place, the interior of Skylab began to cool to habitable temperatures, although without the solar wings, the station was considerably short of power. On 7 June, 13 days after launch and 12 days after they had taken up residence in Skylab, Conrad and Kerwin put on their space suits and went outside with wire cutters in a dangerous effort to free the crumpled wing. In their 3½ hour space walk they managed to release the solar wing, which began generating electricity immediately, and make several other repairs that would permit Skylab to function as planned for the rest of the three manned missions.

After 23 days in space Conrad, Kerwin and Weitz had surpassed the Soviet Soyuz 11 record duration, and they continued to establish a new record. They returned to earth on 22 June 1973, 28 days after launch, having achieved a new duration record for manned space flight of 672 hours and 50 minutes. This was more than double the record American flight of Gemini 7 and more than triple the duration of half the Apollo flights.

The second manned mission to Skylab was launched on 28 July 1973, just a month after the splashdown of Skylab 2. The crew of the CSM for the Skylab 3 mission included two space rookies, pilot Jack Lousma and scientist Dr Owen Garriott. The Skylab 3 commander was Alan Bean, who had gone to the moon on Apollo 12. The crew docked with Skylab after 8 hours, went inside, and began to start up the station's air-conditioning system. Almost immediately the crew began to suffer from space sickness, a type of nausea that had occasionally afflicted astronauts and cosmonauts in the past. On 2 July things went from bad to worse for the queasy crew of Skylab 3 when a leak was discovered in one of the SM thrusters, a problem that would affect the Apollo spacecraft's maneuverability on the return to earth. Wanting to avoid a possible replay of the Apollo 13 crisis, NASA considered calling for an immediate return to earth or mounting a rescue mission with one of the handful of remaining Apollo capsules. NASA settled on the latter option and the Skylab crew, knowing they would be able to get home (and knowing that they had sufficient supplies to await the rescue should it be necessary), settled down to business. On 7 August Dr Garriott and Jack Lousma spent 6 hours and 31 minutes outside the space station arranging a new, larger sunshade and checking the SM thrusters. By the end of their second week in space, a mission that seemed plagued with problems from the start began to look up. The three men recovered from their space sickness, and NASA engineers calculated that the CSM would be functional for re-entry.

During the remaining six weeks of the flight, the crew conducted unprecedented observations of the sun including monitoring six solar flares and taking 75,000 photographs. They conducted zero-gravity welding tests and watched two spiders, Anita and Arabella, spin webs in zero gravity. Dr Garriott monitored the physical condition of the astronauts and observed that muscular deterioration due to weightlessness observed in earlier long-duration space flights leveled out after 39 days. On 25 September 1973 the crew left Skylab and returned to earth. The Skylab 3 mission had lasted 1427 hours and 9 minutes, a new duration record. Bean, Garriott and Lousma had spent more than twice as much time in space during the mission than had all the astronauts during the entire Gemini program.

The Skylab 4 mission (which used the Saturn 1B and Apollo spacecraft that would have been used to rescue Skylab 3) was launched on 16 November 1973 after a 10-day delay to replace cracked stabilizer fins on the Saturn launch vehicle. For the first time since the Gemini program, an American manned space launch was made with an all-rookie crew—pilot William Pogue, scientist Edward Gibson and commander Gerald Carr.

The Skylab 4 rookies docked with the space station on the third try, and climbed through the airlock into the floating barrel that was to be their home for at least two and perhaps three months. They were shocked to discover what appeared to be three people in space suits sitting in the station, but what turned out to be empty space suits, the previous crew's practical joke.

After the laughing stopped, Pogue became violently ill from space sickness. The crew decided not to say anything about it to NASA's Mission Control, but they inadvertently recorded their discussion and transmitted it back to earth the following day. Their decision to conceal Pogue's getting sick brought a sharp reprimand from Alan Shepard, Jr in the chief astronaut's chair in Houston.

Things seemed to proceed well after that despite the failure of one of Skylab's gyroscopes. The mission was given the job of observing the comet Kohoutek, a comet that was thought to be the brightest since Halley's but instead turned out to be almost invisible from earth and hardly visible from Skylab. Carr and Pogue photographed the comet on Christmas Day during a 7-hour space walk and made more observations three days later as the barely visible comet started on the

LOUSMA
013

80,000-year journey that would bring it back to the sun.

During the first week of January Mission Control gave the crew the go-ahead for a third month in orbit and the crew quietly exceeded Skylab 3's 59-day endurance record on 12 January 1974. The crew left the space station on 8 February, leaving behind a carefully prepared time capsule that could be retrieved should anyone venture out to it in the future. Carr, Gibson and Pogue made a final flyaround of the space station in the Apollo, then headed back for earth's atmosphere. The crew splashed down after 2017 hours and 16 minutes in space.

Each of the four Apollo launches had encountered serious equipment problems that seriously endangered the program and the crews, including the damage to Skylab itself, docking problems, a thrustor leak difficulty in releasing the solar panel and shading the overheated OWS, and cracks in the Saturn's stabilizing fins. The trouble-plagued program was over. It was much less of a public relations sensation than Apollo had been, but all three of the manned missions had gone their full duration and more than 12,000 hours of cumulative man-hours in space had been added to NASA's logs. Beyond that, each of the three crews had been successfully recovered and a wealth of scientific data had been returned. It was clear that the first era in American manned space flight was almost over.

ONE LAST FLIGHT

The early 1970s were bad years for American domestic morale as a result of the Vietnam War, the depressing inconvenience and uncertainty of the oil embargo and finally the shockwaves of the Watergate incident accompanied by the first-ever resignation of an American president. Within NASA morale was hardly better. The end of the Apollo lunar program had brought a tidal wave of layoffs as the greatest manned space-flight support team in history was dismantled. The equipment failures that had hounded Skylab clung to the space agency, awash in the uncertainty of where next to turn in its manned exploration of space.

Amid the uncertainty of the decade's early years, however, one project still glowed within NASA's hope chest. One of the few bright spots in the tarnished legacy of the ill-fated presidency of Richard Nixon had been his foreign policy, particularly his mending of relations with the Soviet Union and the beginning of an era of détente. The 1972 SALT 2 arms

Left: **Skylab 3 pilot Jack Lousma during EVA, with the reflection of the earth on his helmet visor.** ***Above:*** **The Apollo-Soyuz Test Project, a unique example of US-USSR cooperation in space, is launched atop a Saturn 1B on 15 July 1975. It was the last flight of an Apollo capsule.**

limitation treaty had been an important cornerstone of détente, but another more visible part of its foundation had been the idea of a joint US-USSR space flight. On 24 May 1972, less than a month before the Watergate burglary, Richard Nixon signed the agreement with Soviet Premier Kosygin that would ultimately lead to the project. This enterprise was entirely political, and despite the fact that it would give the Soviets a close look at American space hardware, the idea of cooperation between the superpowers in space had a nice ring to it.

For this project the Soviets planned to build another in their continuing series of Soyuz space capsules that had first flown in 1967. The United States planned to use one of its two remaining Apollo capsules launched, predictably, by another Saturn 1B. A joint engineering team from the two countries met to develop a docking system that would permit the two spacecraft to link in space and allow the two crews to travel from one to the other. This system entailed developing a large habitable Docking Module (DM), an airlock to be carried on Apollo's 'nose' to facilitate the joining of two dissimilar spacecraft.

Technical problems, such as the different cabin pressures in the two spacecraft, were discussed and overcome, and joint scientific experiments were developed, including a small electrical furnace mounted in the DM and communications links between the two mission control centers. It was planned for the two crews to meet beforehand and for each crew to learn the other's language.

For the two-man crew of what they would designate Soyuz 19, the Soviets picked Valeri Kubasov, a veteran of Soyuz 6 in 1969, and Gen Alexei Leonov, the first man to walk in space in 1965. NASA chose what might be called an all-star crew. The spacecraft commander was Gen Tom Stafford, a veteran of Gemini 6 and Gemini 9, who had orbited the moon as commander of Apollo 10. Also named was Vance Brand, who had not been into space but who was backup commander of Skylab 3 and Skylab 4. Finally there was Deke Slayton, the only one of the original Mercury seven who had never been into space, grounded because of an irregular heartbeat. He had flown a desk as director of flight crew operations throughout Gemini and Apollo, and was returned to flight status in 1972. The Apollo-Soyuz Test Project (ASTP) got under way with

Above: Apollo commander Thomas Stafford with Soyuz engineer Valeri Kubasov (_left_). _Right:_ Thomas Stafford (_left_) and Deke Slayton with tubes of borscht, pasted over with vodka labels for toasting purposes. _Below:_ A view of Apollo from the Soyuz spacecraft with the DM.

dual launches half a world apart on 15 July 1975. Soyuz was launched from the Baikonur Cosmodrome at 7:20 am (CDT) and the Apollo spacecraft was launched 7 hours and 30 minutes later from Kennedy Space Center. On 17 July, nearly two days after Apollo and Soyuz were launched, the two spacecraft were within sight of one another. The message came up to Apollo from Houston: 'I've got two messages for you: Moscow is go for docking; Houston is go for docking. It's up to you guys. Have fun!'

Carried live to earth television from cameras aboard Apollo (those aboard Soyuz didn't work), the two crews began the docking process with Leonov speaking English to the Apollo crew and Stafford speaking Russian to the Soyuz crew. As the historic international docking was viewed live across the world below, Stafford told Leonov, 'We have capture (meaning the two halves of the docking mechanism were linked), we have succeeded, everything is excellent!' To this, Leonov replied, 'Soyuz and Apollo are shaking hands now!' Said Stafford, 'We agree!'

The actual handshake, however, did not take place until Slayton and Stafford had sealed themselves in the DM and had equalized its pressure to that of Soyuz. When they entered the DM, they recoiled with shock. The interior smelled like an electrical fire, conjuring up memories of Apollo 1 and Apollo 13. Happily, the burning smell was attributable to some velcro that had been stored near the furnace during an earlier test, and the air quickly cleared.

The historic handshake took place 3 hours after docking, amid a tangle of television and electrical cables. Both Soviet Premier Brezhnev and President Ford sent greetings. Flags and commemorative medals were exchanged and the four men (minus Brand, who was sealed behind the DM's doors in Apollo) sat down for lunch in Soyuz. After their lunch of borscht, chicken and turkey, the men settled down for some of the joint experiments, which included work by Slayton at the DM furnace.

The following day Stafford and Brand took Kubasov and Moscow television viewers on a tour of the Apollo spacecraft, pointing out that it was the type that had been used to take Americans to the moon. Kubasov and Brand then toured Soyuz for American television. Over the course of the four days that they were together, the mood became friendly and relaxed. The two crews moved back and forth, taking care that one member of each crew was in his own spacecraft at all times. At last it came time for the final international handshake in space, and the two crews went to their respective spacecraft for an undocking and redocking exercise. This was performed largely by the more maneuverable Apollo. After the final separation, Soyuz remained aloft for

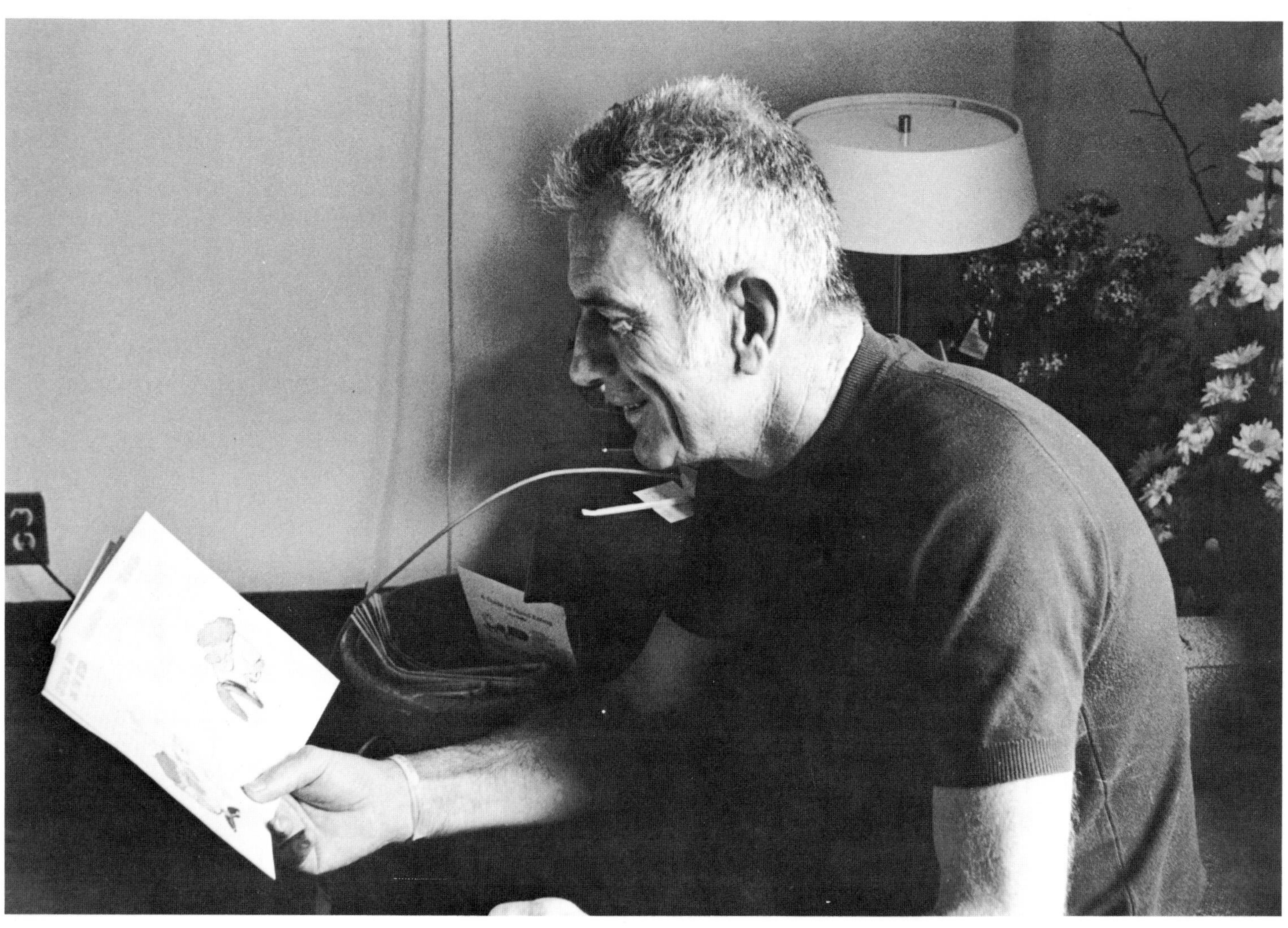

Above: **Group One astronaut Deke Slayton reads a humorous get-well card while recuperating from major surgery for a benign nodule on his lung on 26 August 1975. The surgery was succesful and Slayton remained in the astronaut corps longer than any other Group One colleague. He retired in 1982, having made only a single space flight, the Apollo-Soyuz Test Project.** ***Right:*** **John Glenn, shown with his wife on the presidential campaign trail in 1984, was the first Group One astronaut to retire from NASA. He entered politics instead.**

one more day, Apollo for three and a half.

Stafford, Slayton and Brand re-entered the earth's atmosphere on 24 July 1975, the thirty-first American crew to do so. It should have been a routine re-entry, but a series of events conspired to make it a near fatal experience for the crew. The Earth Landing System (ELS) was not engaged, and as a result the parachutes did not deploy and the thruster engines that kept the spacecraft on a steady course in space did not deactivate. Consequently, they began to fire automatically when the parachutes were deployed manually. Stafford cut off the flow of propellant to the engines to stop them, but in the meantime the pressure relief valves to equalize cabin pressure with earth atmosphere pressure opened. Since the thrusters were shut down, they weren't consuming propellant or oxydizer and the latter, a deadly nitrogen tetroxide gas, was sucked into the capsule through the opened pressure relief valve. Stafford turned the oxygen flow on high and after they plunged into the Pacific Ocean and righted the capsized Apollo, Stafford and Slayton donned oxygen masks and strapped one on Brand, who had lapsed into unconsciousness. They were then able to open the hatch and flood the capsule with fresh air. Disaster had been averted.

The capsule was whisked to the recovery ship, USS *New Orleans,* for celebrations and a phone call from President Ford. A quarter of an hour elapsed before the crew had a chance to tell the doctors what had happened. A two-week stay in Honolulu for recuperation cleared the men of any possible complications. A lesion was noted on one of Slayton's lungs, but a comparison with preflight X-rays showed that it had not been caused by the gas and surgery determined that it was not malignant.

THE MIDDLE YEARS

Skylab marked the real end of the first American manned space program, and ASTP was its triumphant postscript. Beyond 1973, the United States no longer had the capability to put a man on the moon. The huge ground-support system that had been built up in the 1960s was dismantled. Rockwell no longer had an assembly line to build CSMs or Grumman the LMs. The hardware that did exist was committed to Skylab or stored. After ASTP, the United States manned space flight capability was gone. The United States probably could not have put a man into space in 1976 if it had wanted to. Between 1961 and 1976, the only years in which an American space flight did not take place were 1964 and 1967. Through the years of Mercury, Gemini and Apollo spacecraft had been developed as part of a sequence, with each program evolving naturally out of the one before. Now that was over.

A number of programs had been planned for the 1970s that would have continued that evolutionary cycle and made use of the astronauts that came to NASA in Groups Four, Five, Six and Seven between June 1965 and August 1969. Apollo 18, Apollo 19 and Apollo 20 were to have been further J-series lunar explorations through 1974, but they were clipped from the budget in 1970, and

Apollo 15 and Apollo 16 were upgraded to J-series configuration. Another less developed project was to establish a 6-man lunar base by the mid-1970s that could be expanded to a 24-man base by 1980. A possible two-year manned mission to the planet Mars was the object of still another program. The plan was for launch on 12 November 1981, and would entail reaching Mars on 9 August 1982, putting a team on the Martian surface until 28 October and returning to earth on 14 August 1983. This program would have pressed the limits of the available technology, and, as planned, would have depended upon a nuclear propulsion system program that was canceled in the meantime. This, like the other envisioned programs would have required budgets far more vast than Congress was willing to appropriate in the post-Vietnam/post-Watergate years.

Thus it came to pass that NASA had a cadre of trained astronauts, many of whom had actual experience in space, and no manned space program.

Astronaut Group One, selected in April 1959, included the original Mercury seven astronauts. Gus Grissom made one Mercury and one Gemini flight, but was killed in the Apollo 1 fire in 1967. John Glenn, Jr quit the program in 1964 after one Mercury flight and the shortest total flight time of any astronaut. Glenn was elected to the US Senate from Ohio in 1974 and made a serious but unsuccessful bid for the Democratic presidential nomination in 1984. Scott Carpenter flew only in the Mercury program, left NASA in 1967 and the US Navy in 1969. Gordon Cooper, Jr flew with both Mercury and Gemini, served as backup for Apollo 10 and retired from both NASA and the US Air Force in 1970 to go into private industry. Wally Schirra, Jr, the only man to fly during all three of the early manned space programs, retired from NASA and the Navy in 1969 to head up his own consulting firm. Alan Shepard, the first American in space, was also the only Mercury astronaut to go to the moon, although he did not fly during Gemini. Shepard retired from NASA and from the US Navy as a rear admiral in 1974 to go into private industry. Deke Slayton, the Mercury astronaut who didn't go into space until the last Apollo flight, served as manager for Space Shuttle Program Orbital Test Flights until his retirement in 1982 to join Space Services, Incorporated, a private aerospace firm.

Astronaut Group Two consisted of nine test pilots selected in September 1962 to augment the original seven in Gemini and

later Apollo. Neil Armstrong flew aboard Gemini 8 and was the first man on the moon as the commander of Apollo 11. He went on to serve as deputy associate administrator for aeronautics at NASA's Headquarters Office of Advanced Research and Technology until he retired in 1971 to join Cardwell International in Lebanon, Ohio. Frank Borman flew once on both Gemini and Apollo, but resigned from NASA and the Air Force in 1970. He went on to become chairman and president of Eastern Airlines, one of the three largest airline companies in the world. Pete Conrad flew on two Gemini missions, made one trip to the moon on Apollo and commanded the first Skylab crew. He resigned from NASA and the Navy in 1973 and became senior vice president for marketing with McDonnell Douglas in Long Beach, California. James Lovell, Jr made two Gemini and two Apollo flights including the ill-fated Apollo 13. He retired from NASA and from the Navy in 1973 to serve as group vice president with Centel Corporation in Chicago. James McDivitt flew on Gemini 4 and Apollo 9, and after 1969 he served as manager of the Apollo Spacecraft Program at NASA. He retired from NASA and from the US Air Force as a brigadier general in June 1972 in order to serve as senior vice president for strategic management with Rockwell International in Pittsburg, Pennsylvania. Elliot See was the only member of either of the first two astronaut groups to never make a space flight. He died along with Group 3 astronaut Charles Bassett in a T-38 crash on 28 February 1966 at Lambert Airport, St Louis, Missouri. Thomas Stafford flew on Gemini 6, then went on to command Gemini 9, Apollo 10 and the ASTP mission. He resigned from NASA in 1975 to go back into active service with the US Air Force. Stafford retired from the Air Force as a lieutenant general in 1979 and became vice chairman of Gibralter Exploration Ltd in Oklahoma City. He reached the highest military rank of any American astronaut. Edward White II came to the manned space flight program from the US Air Force X-15 program and made the first American space walk from Gemini 4. White had been picked for the first manned Apollo flight but was killed in the Apollo 1 fire in 1967. John Young flew in Gemini 6 and Apollo 10, and commanded Gemini 10 and Apollo 16. He resigned from the Navy but stayed on with NASA to command the first and ninth Space Shuttle flights before becoming chief of

NASA's Astronaut Office. Through 1985, only three American astronauts had made four space flights, none had made five, but John Young had made six.

Astronaut Group Three included 14 pilots selected in October 1963 to supplement the first two groups in anticipation of the needs of the Apollo program. Those who had already made space flights included Buzz Aldrin, who flew on Gemini 12 and the Apollo 11 first lunar landing before resigning from NASA in 1971. He retired from the Air Force in 1972 and went on to serve as science consultant for the Beverly Hills Oil Company in Los Angeles. William Anders flew on Apollo 8 and resigned from NASA in 1969. Still a USAF reserve major general, Anders is general manager of General Electric's Aircraft Equipment Division in Dewitt, New York. Alan Bean flew aboard Apollo 12 and Skylab 3. He left the Navy in October 1975 but stayed with NASA until 1981, when he retired to devote his full time to painting. Eugene Cernan flew on Gemini 9, Apollo 10 and Apollo 17 before resigning from NASA. He now heads Cernan Energy Corporation in Houston, Texas. Michael Collins resigned from NASA in 1970, having flown on Gemini 10 and Apollo 11, and he is currently president of the Vought Corporation in Arlington, Virginia. Walter Cunningham flew on Apollo 7, resigned from NASA in 1971 and joined the Capital Group in Houston, Texas. Donn Eisele flew on Apollo 7, left the Air Force and NASA in 1972 and later joined Oppenheimer and Company of Ft Lauderdale, Florida. Richard Gordon, Jr flew on Gemini 11 and Apollo 12, left the Air Force and NASA in 1972 and went on to become president of Astro Systems in Los Angeles. Russell Schweickart flew on Apollo 9 before going to NASA headquarters in 1974. He left NASA in 1979 to become chairman of the California State Energy Commission. David Scott flew on Gemini 3, Apollo 9 and Apollo 15 before being assigned to Mission Operations for the Apollo-Soyuz project in 1972. Scott was first deputy director, then director of the US Air Force Dryden Flight Research Center from 1973 to 1975. He left NASA in 1977 and to become president of Scott Science and Technology Inc.

Four of the men selected in Astronaut Group Three died before they could make any space flights. Roger Chaffee was killed along with Gus Grissom and Ed White in the 1967 Apollo 1 fire, while the others all died in crashes involving the T-38 trainer aircraft that the astronauts flew to hone their piloting skills. Charles Bassett II and Group Two astronaut Elliot See were killed in St Louis in 1966, Theodore Freeman was killed at Ellington AFB in 1964, and Clifton Williams, Jr was killed near Tallahassee, Florida in 1967.

Astronaut Group Four, selected in June 1965, was unique. It was the smallest group ever chosen, and the six crew members were the first nonpilot, scientist astronauts. Owen Garriott (PhD, electrical engineering) flew on Skylab 3, Edward Gibson (PhD, engineering and physics) flew on Skylab 4, Joseph Kerwin flew on Skylab 2 and Harrison Schmitt (PhD, geology) flew on Apollo 17, the only Group Four astronaut to fly an Apollo mission.

Two other Group Four astronauts resigned without making a space flight, Duane Graveline (MD) after two months and Curtis Michel (PhD, physics) after three years. Of the four men who made space flights, Gibson left NASA between 1974 and 1977 and resigned permanently in 1980 to join TRW in Redondo Beach, California. Schmitt became NASA assistant administrator for Energy Programs in 1974, but resigned a year later to run for the US Senate from New Mexico, where he served one term before his defeat in 1982. Both Kerwin and Garriott stayed with NASA into the Space Shuttle era, Kerwin as director of Space and Life Sciences and Garriott as scientist astronaut aboard the Shuttle missions of the 1980s.

Astronaut Group Five was the largest group yet chosen. All pilot astronauts, the 19 men were selected in April 1966 to augment Group Three for the Apollo program. Vance Brand flew in the ASTP mission and stayed with NASA to fly the Space Shuttle in the 1980s. John Bull withdrew after two years because of pulmonary disease, but he stayed with NASA. Gerald Carr flew in Skylab 4 and left NASA for private industry in 1977. Charles Duke, Jr flew in Apollo 16 and left NASA, then the Air Force, to start his own company in 1976. Joe Engle flew no Apollo missions but stayed with NASA to fly the Space Shuttle. Ronald Evans flew in Apollo 17 and left NASA in 1977 to work for Sperry Flight Systems. Edward Givens, Jr died in a 1967 car crash near Houston before making a flight. Fred Haise, Jr flew on Apollo 13 and stayed with NASA through the early Space Shuttle development, but left in 1979 to join Grumman Aerospace. James Irwin flew on Apollo 15 and left the Air Force and NASA in 1972 to become chairman of the High Flight Foundation. Don Lind made no Apollo flights but stayed with NASA

as a mission specialist into the Space Shuttle era. Jack Lousma flew on Skylab 3 and STS-3 and later resigned from NASA. Thomas Mattingly II flew on Apollo 16 and stayed with NASA as a pilot during the Space Shuttle program. Bruce McCandless II flew on mission 41-B and is still active in the space program as a pilot. Edgar Mitchell flew on Apollo 14 and left NASA and the Navy in 1972 to join Forecast Systems. William Pogue flew on Skylab 5 and left NASA to become an independent consultant. Stuart Roosa flew on Apollo 14 and left NASA and the Air Force to establish his own company, Gulf Coast Coors. John Swigert, Jr flew on Apollo 13 and left NASA in July 1978. He won a new seat for Colorado's Sixth Congressional District in November 1982, but died of cancer on 27 December, a week before taking office. Paul Weitz flew on Skylab 2 and retired from the Navy in 1976, but stayed on with NASA as a pilot in the Space Shuttle program. Alfred Worden flew on Apollo 15 and left NASA and the Air Force in 1975 to become president of his own company in Palm Beach Gardens in Florida.

Astronaut Group Six was composed of 11 scientist astronauts picked in July 1967 to augment the scientists in Group Four during the Apollo applications programs like Skylab that were planned to use Apollo technology for future scientific projects. The scientists and their areas of specialty were Joseph Allen (PhD, physics), Philip Chapman (DSc, instrumentation), Anthony England (PhD, geophysics), Karl Henize (PhD, astronomy), Donald Holmquest (MD, PhD, physiology), William Lenoir (PhD, electrical engineering), John Llewellyn (PhD, chemistry), Story Musgrave (MD), Brian O'Leary (PhD, astronomy), Robert Parker (PhD, astronomy) and William Thornton (MD). Six members of the group, Allen, England, Henize, Musgrave, Park-

Above left: **The 14 Group Three astronauts, announced on 18 October 1963, were (*seated, left to right*) Edwin Aldrin, Jr; William Anders; Charles Bassett II; Alan Bean; Eugene Cernan; Roger Chaffee and (*standing, left to right*) Michael Collins; R Walter Cunningham; Donn Eisele, Theodore Freeman; Richard Gordon, Jr; Russell Schweickart; David Scott and Clifton Williams, Jr. They all made space flights except Bassett, Chaffee, Freeman and Williams. Chaffee died in Apollo 1 and the other three were killed in airplane crashes.**

Above: **The sixth group of astronauts was made up entirely of civilians, and was the second group selected specifically for scientific education rather than for pilot background. The four seated at the table (*left to right*) are Philip Chapman, Robert Parker, William Thornton and John Llewellyn. Standing (*left to right*) are Joseph Allen, Karl Henize, Anthony England, Donald Holmquest, Story Musgrave, William Lenoir and Brian O'Leary. Even though they are posing with various Apollo modules, none of the 11 flew an Apollo mission.**

Below: **The Group 7 astronauts were (*left to right*) Karol Bobko; Charles Fullerton; Henry Hartsfield, Jr; Robert Crippen; Donald Peterson; Richard Truly and Robert Overmyer.**

NASA 916

Joe Engle joined the astronaut program with Group Five in April 1966. While many of his classmates flew aboard Apollo to the moon, he had to wait until 1981 for his first space flight, on Space Shuttle *Columbia*. He is shown here at the controls of a T-38 jet en route to Kennedy Space Center to join Group Seven astronaut Richard Truly for the STS-2 launch on 12 November. Engle and Truly had experienced working together aboard *Enterprise* during earth-atmosphere tests. Engle made his second space flight at the controls of *Discovery* in 1985.

er and Thornton, remained with NASA into the Space Shuttle era, but the others resigned without ever flying a mission.

Astronaut Group Seven comprised the seven pilot astronauts who joined NASA in August 1969 when the US Air Force Manned Orbiting Laboratory (MOL) program was canceled. None of them flew during the Apollo program, which was at its peak when they joined NASA, but they all stayed with the space agency into the Space Shuttle era. They were Col Karol Bobko, USAF; Capt Robert Crippin, USN; Col Charles Fullerton, USAF; Col Henry Hartsfield, Jr, USAF (retired); Col Robert Overmyer, USMC; Col Donald Peterson, USAF (retired); and Capt Richard Truly, USN. Hartsfield and Peterson both later left the Air Force but stayed to fly the Shuttle, and Truly left NASA after two Shuttle flights to head the US Navy Space Command. The middle years after the end of America's first era of manned space flight saw many men leave NASA's astronaut corps before the Space Shuttle program got into space in 1981. From Group One, only Slayton remained, but not on flight status. From Group Two, only Young remained; from Group Three, no one remained. From Group Four, Garriott and Kerwin remained; from Group Five, Brand, Engle, Lind, Mattingly and Weitz remained, and from Group Six, Allen, England, Henize, Musgrave, Parker and Thornton remained.

In 1981, of the 49 pilot astronauts that NASA trained between 1959 and 1966, 38 were still alive and had space flight experience, but only 6 remained on flight status. Of the 17 scientist astronauts chosen in 1965 and 1967, only 4 had made space flights and only 2 of them remained on flight status.

When the Space Shuttle program began it was planned to be more than just a new piece of hardware. It had a new emphasis and a fresh corps of astronauts, and it opened a whole new era in America's exploration of space.

THE SPACE SHUTTLE ERA

The idea of a reusable spacecraft dates back to the early days of manned space flight. Ballistic return capsules got men into space, but for any vehicle to be practical over the long run it would have to be reusable. The family tree that sprouted the Mercury, Gemini and Apollo capsules was only an expedient first step in the evolution of spacecraft. They were designed simply to get Americans into space and to the moon, at the same time answering many basic questions about the nature and practice of manned space flight.

The idea of an aircraft that could be launched into space, return to the atmosphere and land on a runway can be traced to the Antipodal Rocket Bomber designed in Germany during World War II by Dr Eugen Sanger, but never built. In the postwar world there was a series of rocket-lane concepts developed by the US Air Force that led to the X-15 rocket research plane. The X-15 was built by North American Aviation, a company that evolved into Rockwell International and along the way was the prime contractor for both the Apollo CSM and the Space Shuttle. The X-15 was first flown in 1959 by Air Force test pilot Scott Crossfield, who ultimately earned his astronaut wings flying it to the edge of space. (Another X-15 test pilot, Ed White, later flew in Gemini 4 and was picked for the first Apollo crew.) The X-15 made 199 flights between 1959 and 1968, during which time it reached an altitude of 67 miles, only half way to the recognized edge of space but well above 99 percent of the mass of the earth's atmosphere.

The X-15 design was followed by Boeing's X-20, the real forerunner of the Space Shuttle. The X-20 was blessed, or perhaps cursed, by the nickname Dyna-Soar. The basic idea was the same as that of the Space Shuttle: a reusable aerodynamic powered glider that would be launched into space atop a conventional rocket then return into the atmosphere to perform an airplane-type landing. Technically, the concept was much more complicated than a ballistic re-entry capsule like Mercury, Gemini and Apollo, and it would take longer to develop. NASA decided to go ahead with the capsules, and the Air Force proceeded with Dyna-Soar. The final configuration of the X-20 was settled in March 1960, more than a year before the first manned Mercury launch. Dyna-Soar was scheduled for its first manned space flights in 1966 and expected to be fully operational within three years after that. In September 1962 the first Air Force astronauts, Albert Crews, Henry Gordon, William Knight, Russell Rogers and James Wood, were selected amid fanfare that emulated the selection of the Mercury seven three years before. By the end of 1963, however, the budget axe had fallen, and the Dyna-Soar was extinct.

Six years after Dyna-Soar faded from the scene and three months before the first Apollo LM reached the lunar surface, NASA went to work on the Space

Tucked under the wing of a B-52 aircraft from which it was launched, this sleek X-15 research plane is poised for another of its many experimental missions. By late 1968 the rocket-propelled plane had made nearly 200 flights for NASA. Both Ed White of Gemini 4 and Neil Armstrong of Gemini 8 and Apollo 11 flew the X-15 before they took the controls of a spacecraft.

U.S. AIR FORCE X-15
RESCUE
NORTH AMERICAN AVIATION INC.
NASA

The Space Shuttle Orbiter *Enterprise* is mated to a NASA 747 at Edwards AFB. On 12 August 1977, Group Five astronaut Fred Haise, Jr and Group Seven astronaut Gordon Fullerton guided the Orbiter on its first free flight in earth-atmosphere.

Shuttle. By definition, it was to be a reusable powered glider that could land like an airplane. However, many additional refinements were made, like including a tailor-made launch vehicle in the system rather than an adaptation of an earlier Titan or Gemini.

The final Space Shuttle design was approved in March 1972, and Rockwell International was given the go-ahead to begin construction of the spacecraft portion of the system. It was America's largest spacecraft, with a specially developed launch vehicle system consisting of two enormous Martin Marietta solid rocket boosters and an even larger external fuel tank. The boosters were designed to parachute into the ocean and be retrieved for later use. The spacecraft portion, called the Orbiting Vehicle (Orbiter), was 122 feet long and had a wingspan of 78 feet. It was the size of a small airliner, weighing 75 tons. It had a 15-by-60-foot cargo bay capable of carrying up to five satellites to be launched in space.

The Space Shuttle Orbiter was designed to be piloted by a flight crew of two but capable of routinely carrying seven or more 'mission specialists' or 'payload specialists' to help launch satellites or operate scientific experiments. It was the first US spacecraft to utilize an oxygen-nitrogen atmosphere (like the atmosphere on earth or in Soviet spacecraft) rather than pure oxygen like Mercury, Gemini or Apollo. It was designed for an optimal mission of seven days but was capable of remaining in space for a month. As originally conceived, the Space Shuttle was to make its maiden voyage in 1979, restoring a manned space flight capability to the United States just five years after Skylab and only four years after the Apollo-Soyuz flight. In early 1980 the Space Shuttle was supposed to fly into space to rescue Skylab, which had been floating untouched for six years. By the end of 1981 the Shuttle was scheduled to have made as many as 22 flights.

None of this came to pass, however. The year 1979 came and went without the first Shuttle flight, but it did witness the final anticlimactic chapter in Skylab's odyssey. Still crippled by damage done at its launch in 1973, Skylab's orbit began to decay gradually until finally on 11 July 1979 it re-entered the earth's atmosphere over Australia as a blizzard of burning debris. NASA stood by helpless, bereft of a manned spacecraft program that might have been able to save what was at least an important relic from a bygone era and at best a useful scientific platform for research in the 1980s.

In the meantime, the Space Shuttle Transportation System (STS), as the Shuttle was known, was being put together. The first Shuttle Orbiter was delivered for testing at Edwards AFB, California in February 1977. The first Orbiter, nicknamed *Enterprise,* and designated OV-101, was used only within the earth's atmosphere for testing its ability to fly and land. Space flight was a privilege reserved for *Enterprise*'s successors such as *Columbia* (OV-102), *Discovery* (OV-103) and *Atlantis* (OV-104). A predecessor, *Challenger* (OV-99), had not been scheduled for space flight either, but was converted to flight status. By the time of its disastrous accident on 28 January 1986, *Challenger* had flown nine successful space missions, more than any of the others.

Throughout early 1977, *Enterprise* was flown piggyback aboard a former American Airlines Boeing 747 jetliner while NASA engineers carefully monitored its vital signs in anticipation of the day when it would fly alone. That day came at last on 12 August 1977, when the big Orbiter lifted off aboard the 747, destined this time to land on its own. At the controls were Fred Haise, Jr, a NASA astronaut since 1966 and a veteran of the nightmare flight of Apollo 13. With Haise was Charles Fullerton, one of the original Air Force MOL astronauts, inherited by NASA in 1969. Haise and Fullerton reported that the huge spacecraft handled like an agile fighter plane and soon brought it in for a perfect landing at Edwards AFB. Four more tests followed over the next two years, with Haise and Fullerton back in the cockpit for flights number three and five. The second and fourth atmospheric test flights were flown by Joe Engle and Richard Truly, two other former MOL astronauts who had never had a chance to fly with Apollo. After the successful atmospheric flight tests, *Enterprise* was flown to Kennedy Space Center at Cape Canaveral for static testing in the company of its launch vehicle.

Meanwhile, NASA was selecting its first group of new astronauts since the scientists of Group Six in 1967. The first new group of American astronauts in a dozen years also included the first American women to be selected for astronaut training. The women knew that none of them would be the first woman in space, but they knew that among them would be the second, third and fourth. The first had been Valentina Tereshkova, launched by the Soviets for 48 orbits in 1963. After nearly 20 years, the Soviet Union had

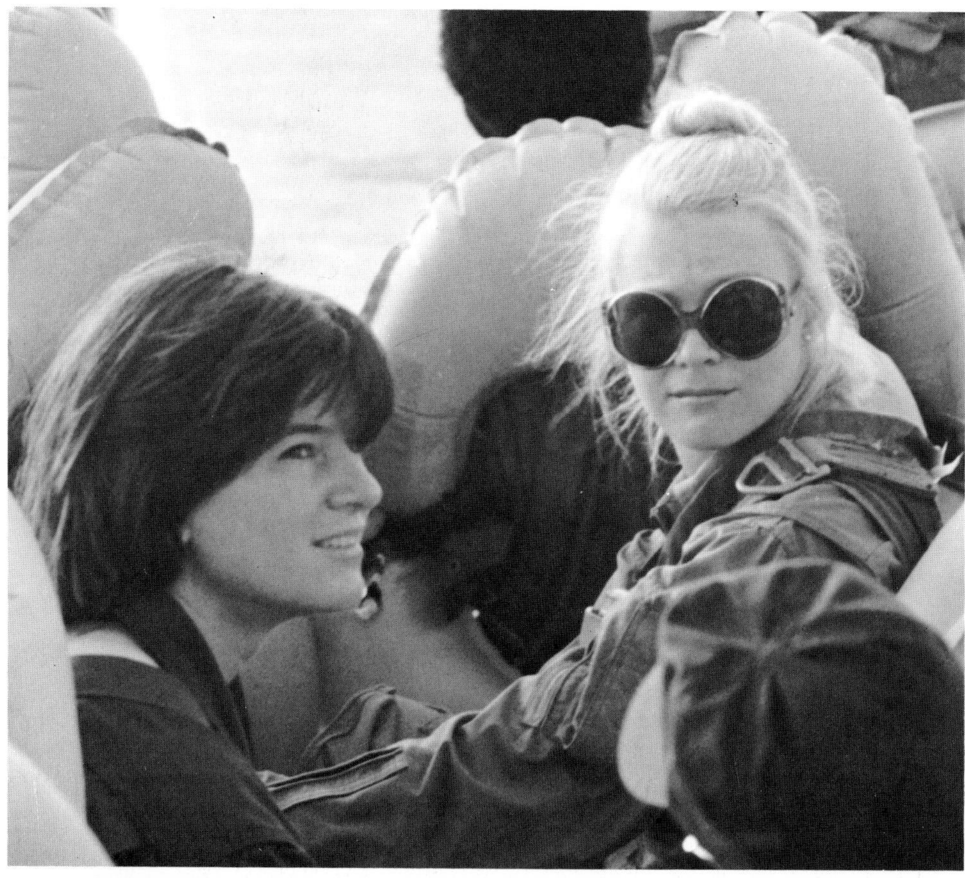

shown no intention of sending a second woman into space.

Astronaut Group Eight was the largest ever. With 35 persons, it was almost as big the first four groups combined. It included Col Guion Bluford, Jr, USAF; Capt Daniel Brandenstein, USN; Lt Col James Buchli, USMC; Cdr Michael Coats, USN; Lt Col Richard Covey, USAF; Cdr John Creighton, USN; Col John Fabian, USN; Anna Fisher, MD; Cdr Dale Gardner, USN; Cdr Robert Gibson, USN; Col Frederick Gregory, USAF; David Griggs; Terry Hart; Capt Frederick Hauck, USN; Steven Hawley, PhD, astronomy; Jeffrey Hoffman, PhD, astrophysics; Shannon Lucid, PhD, biochemistry; Cdr Jon McBride, USN; Ronald McNair, PhD, physics; Lt Col Richard Mullane, USAF; Lt Col Steven Nagel, USAF; George Nelson, PhD, astronomy; Maj Ellison Onizuka, USAF; Judith Resnik, PhD, electrical engineering; Sally Ride, PhD, physics; Maj Francis Scobee, USAF; Margaret Rhea Seddon, MD; Lt Col Brewster Shaw, USAF; Lt Col Loren Shriver, USAF; Col Robert Stewart, US Army; Kathryn Sullivan, PhD, geology; Norman Thagard, MD; James van Hoften, PhD, hydraulic engineering; Cdr David Walker, USN; and Cdr Donald Williams, USN.

Of the 35 people in Astronaut Group Eight, 13 were selected as pilots: Brandenstein, Coats, Covey, Creighton, Gibson, Gregory, Hauck, McBride, Scobee, Shaw, Shriver, Walker and Williams. The others

Above: Along with other astronaut candidates, Group Eight astronauts Sally Ride (_left_) and Rhea Seddon (_right_) take part in a water survival training exercise. _Below:_ Group Eight astronauts, named in January 1978, attend a familiarization session. _Clockwise, around the outside row,_ are Steven Nagel; Ellison Onizuka; David Walker; Jeffrey Hoffman; Shannon Lucid; Richard (Mike) Mullane; Brewster Shaw, Jr; Judith Resnik; Daniel Brandenstein; James Buchli; two unidentified Rockwell personnel; Loren Shriver; Kathryn Sullivan; Anna Fisher; Dale Gardner and Frederick Hauck (out of frame). _Clockwise on the inside_ are John Creighton, Michael Coats, Norman Thagard, George Nelson, Frederick Gregory, Steven Hawley, Sally Ride, Ronald McNair, Francis Scobee, astronaut Alan Bean, Rhea Seddon and David Griggs. _Right:_ Apollo 13 veteran Fred Haise, Jr suits up for a test in August 1978 prior to the resumption of American manned space flight.

F. HAISE

Above: The first American manned space flight in six years. The launch of the first Space Shuttle on 12 April 1981 carried John Young and Robert Crippen into an earth-orbit mission scheduled to last for 54 hours. *Below:* STS-1 pilot Robert Crippen addresses greeters at Ellington AFB after *Columbia's* return to Edwards AFB. John Young is next to his wife at right.

were selected as mission specialists, the people who would run the equipment and perform the experiments while the Shuttle Orbiter was in space.

Astronaut Group Nine followed in January 1980, two years after Group Eight, and still prior to the first Shuttle launch. This time eight pilots were chosen: Col John Blaha, USAF; Lt Col Charles Bolden, Jr, USMC; Col Roy Bridges, Jr, USAF; Lt Col Guy Gardner, USAF; Lt Col Ronald Grabe, USAF; Lt Col Bryan O'Conner, USMC; Cdr Richard Richards, USN and Cdr Michael Smith, USN. Accompanying them were mission specialists: James Bagian, MD; Franklin Chang-Diaz, PhD, applied plasma physics; Mary Cleave, PhD, civil and environmental engineering; Bonnie Dunbar, PhD, biomedical engineering; William Fisher, MD, husband of Anna Fisher; Maj David Hilmers, USMC; Lt Cdr David Leetsma, USN; John Lounge, MS, astrogeophysics; Maj Jerry Ross, USAF; Lt Col Sherwood Spring, US Army; and Lt Col Robert Springer, USMC.

By December 1980, the Shuttle Orbiter *Columbia* was at Kennedy Space Center being attached to its external tank and solid rocket boosters. On 29 December it went to Pad 39A, the historic Apollo/Saturn pad, and prepared for launch. On 20 February the three main engines were fired and checked, and during March launch verification runs and countdown demonstration tests were made to ensure that *Columbia* was ready for its first flight into space, scheduled for 10 April. The crew for that first flight consisted of just the pilot and spacecraft commander. The pilot was Robert Crippen, one of the Group Seven astronauts who had waited more than a dozen years for his first space flight. The spacecraft commander was John Young, who had flown on both Gemini and Apollo twice, and who was about to become the first man to go into space five times.

Seven hours and 4 seconds after midnight on 12 April 1981, the Space Shuttle *Columbia* thundered into the sky, six years after the last American space flight. *Columbia* was two days late because of a minor computer malfunction, but America was back in space. Young and Crippen spent 54 hours and 21 minutes in space, checking out *Columbia*'s systems before gliding back into the atmosphere for a safe and normal landing at Edwards AFB in California on 14 April. It was the first time an American spacecraft had touched down on land, and there were thousands of people on hand to witness the historic event. Thousands of camera shutters were tripped as John Young and Robert Crippen stepped out of *Columbia* on the Edwards salt flats. It was a far cry from the days of the ballistic re-entry capsules splashing into the ocean, miles from the target.

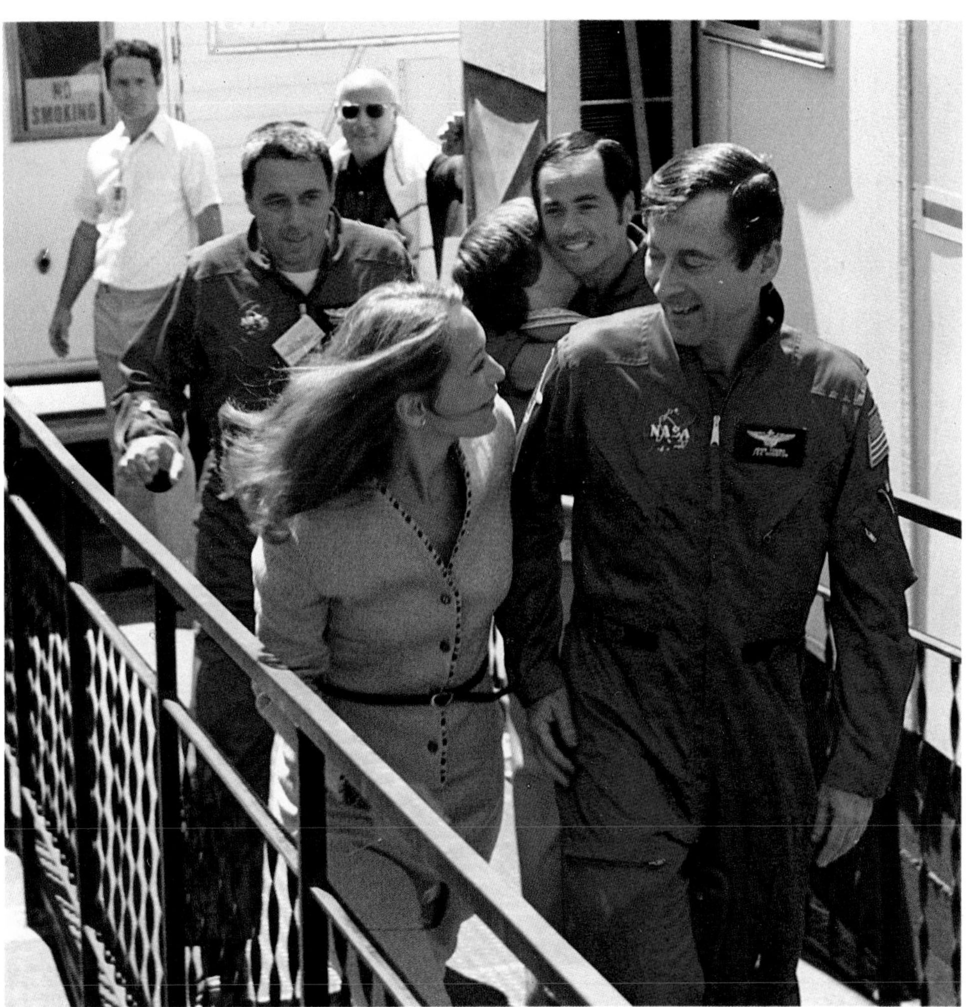

Above: **Astronauts John Young (*right*) and Robert Crippen (*center*) are greeted by their wives, Susy and Virginia, after completing the successful first STS mission on 14 April 1981.**

STS-2 astronaut Richard Truly arrives at Pad 39A after completing a 'dry' Countdown Demonstration Test with Joe Engle, a full dress rehearsal for launch on 9 October 1981.

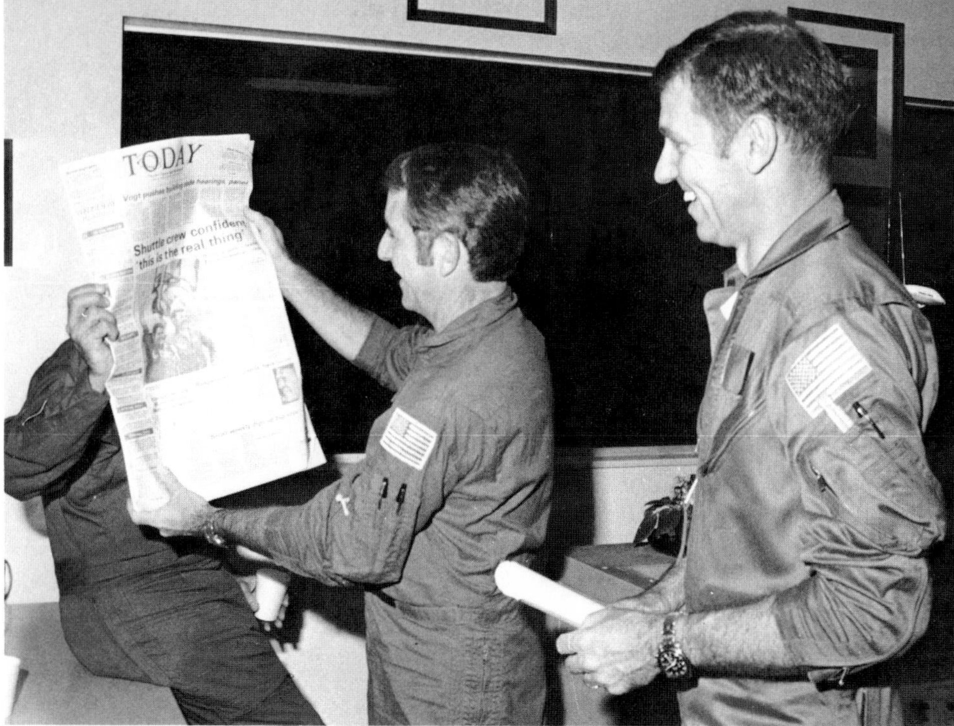

Above: STS-3 commander Jack Lousma poses with his family at Patrick Air Force Base where he will prepare for his 22 March 1982 flight aboard *Columbia* with Gordon Fullerton. To Lousma's left are his wife, Gratia, and son Matthew. At his right is his daughter, Mary. Two other sons, Timothy and Joseph, are not pictured. *Left:* STS-2 mission pilot Richard Truly (*center*) uses George Abbey, director of flight operations, as a good-natured prop for his newspaper as mission commander Joe Engle looks on.

The astronauts were at the Landing Aids Control Building, adjacent to the Shuttle landing facility, for morning 'touch and go' landing practice in a Shuttle Simulator on the eve of the scheduled 12 November 1981 second attempt to launch the second Space Shuttle mission. *Right: Columbia* climbs into space for a return visit with STS-2 astronauts Joe Engle and Richard Truly in the cockpit. In addition to a payload of science and applications experiments, *Columbia* carried the Remote Manipulator Arm designed to handle cargo in orbit.

Despite a mission shortened from five to two days, the crew accomplished 90 percent of its objectives. STS-2 was the last flight in which the big external fuel tank was painted white.

Columbia's maiden voyage was marred by the loss of some heat-shield tiles, but this did not seem to impair the spacecraft's re-entry. This first flight, designated STS-1 for Shuttle Transportation System flight 1, was the first of four test flights that *Columbia* was scheduled to make. This first phase of the Shuttle program through STS-4 was designed as a series of test and evaluation missions to iron out any bugs left in the Orbiter itself and precede any scientific or commercial application of the STS. These flights were crewed by just the pilot and commander. Mission specialists joined the crews for the operational flights beginning with STS-5. As originally planned, all four missions were to be flown during 1979, with operational missions starting in 1980. *Columbia*'s first flight was already two years behind schedule, and problems such as the heat-shield tiles caused delays in the subsequent flights.

Columbia's second launch came on 12 November 1981, seven months after the first. At the controls this time were Joe Engle and Richard Truly. Neither of them had made previous space flights, but they had made up one of the two crews that had taken *Enterprise* through her glide, approach and landing tests a couple of years earlier. Like the first flight in April, STS-2 had a two-day duration. The highlight of the mission was the first deployment of the Canadian-designed remote manipulator arm located in *Columbia*'s payload bay.

Rounding out the test phase, the third and fourth flights were each flown for durations to match those of the future operational flights. The third flight, STS-3, was launched on 22 March 1982 and lasted eight days, while STS-4, launched on 27 June, lasted seven. The crews were Charles Fullerton and Jack Lousma aboard STS-3, and Henry Hartsfield, Jr and Thomas Mattingly II aboard STS-4.

The four-flight test phase was concluded in 14 months, with *Columbia* logging 470 hours of flight time, more than any previous American manned spacecraft. Of the eight men who flew the new reusable spaceship, only three had ever gone into space before. The test-phase flights had been manned by a two-man flight crew. During the upcoming operational phase, the Orbiter would have a two-man flight crew, usually military pilots, and between two and five mission or payload specialists. The payload specialists would be non-NASA personnel going along for a single purpose relating to a specific payload.

Columbia's first operational mission, STS-5, was launched on 11 November 1982 with the Shuttle's first four-man crew, which included Joseph Allen, Vance Brand, William Lenoir and Robert Over-

SATELLITE DEPLOYMENT BY
the Ace Moving Co.
FAST AND COURTEOUS SERVICE
"WE DELIVER"
LENOIR
NASA

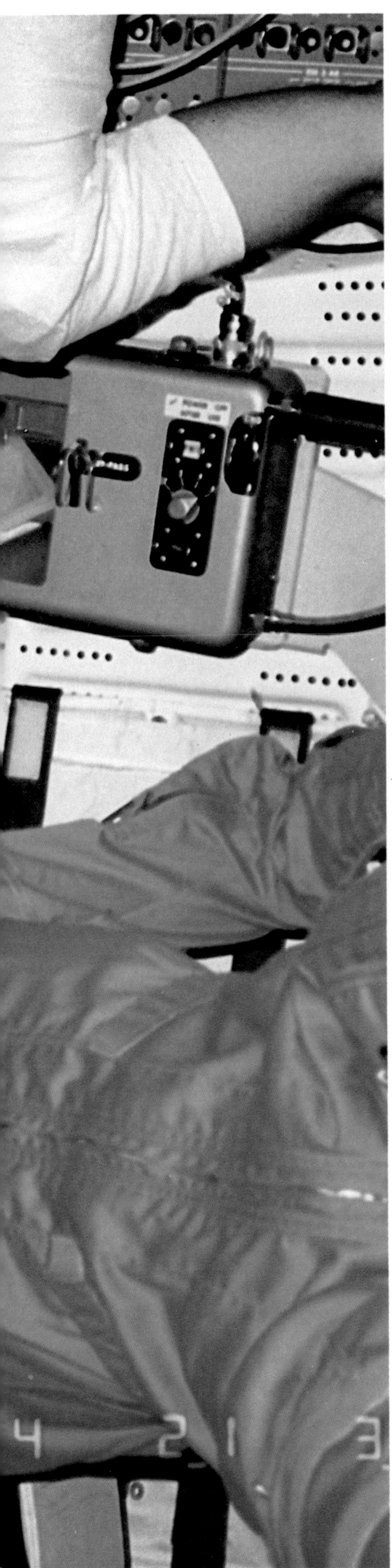

Above: **STS-5 mission specialist Joseph Allen IV photographing the earth from *Columbia*. *Left:* The STS-5 crew: Vance Brand, with the sign, is surrounded (*clockwise from left*) by William Lenoir, Robert Overmyer and Joseph Allen IV. The sign refers to the successful deployment of two commercial satellites. *Below:* STS-4 pilot Henry Hartsfield, Jr demonstrates the sleeping restraint.**

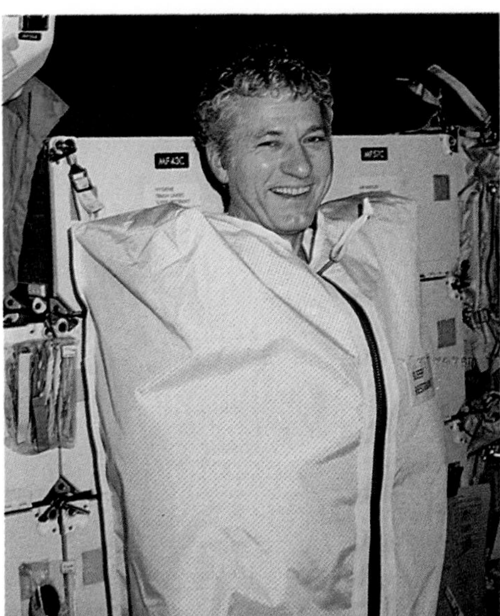

myer. The principal operational element in this first working flight was the launching of two communications satellites, the Canadian Anik-C and the American Small Business Systems SBS-3. Over the next few years, launching satellites proved to be one of the most important and profitable uses for the Space Shuttle.

On 4 April 1983 *Challenger* (OV-99) became the second Space Shuttle Orbiting Vehicle to venture into space. Like *Columbia*'s STS-5, the STS-6 mission lasted five days and carried a crew of four. The crew members included Karol Bobko, Story Musgrave, Donald Peterson and Paul Weitz. During the flight, Musgrave and Peterson made the first EVAs of the Space Shuttle era. It was the first time in more than nine years that an American ventured beyond the comforts of a spacecraft to walk alone in space.

Two months later *Challenger* was ready for its second mission and the sixth of the Space Shuttle program. In many ways STS-6 was a routine Shuttle flight, but in one important way it stood out from all

The first EVA from an STS Orbiter. Donald Peterson (*starboard side*) and Story Musgrave, STS-6 mission specialists, evaluate the handrail system on the starboard longeron and aft bulkhead, respectively. The vertical stabilizer and orbital maneuvering system pods frame a portion of Mexico's state of Jalisco below. Pacific waters make up about half of the backdrop. Pilot Karol Bobko and commander Paul Weitz took the photographs.

FUEL CELL
RCS/OMS PRESS
MISSION TIME
NASA

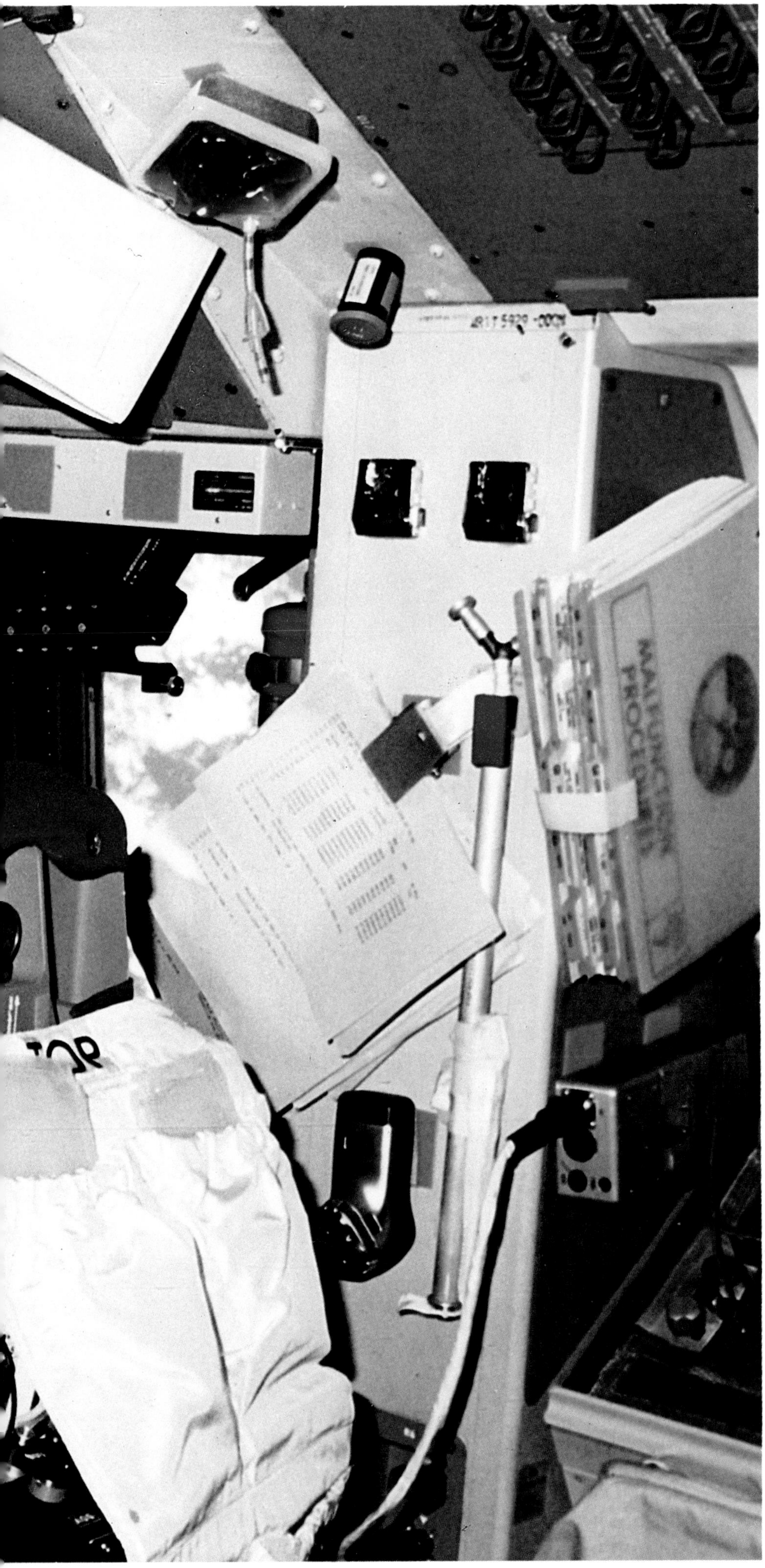

STS-7 was the second flight of *Challenger* (*above*) and the first to take an American woman, Sally Ride, into space (*left*). Floating freely on the flight deck she communicates with ground controllers in Houston, moving within feet of important reference data, hand calculators and other aids. She is one of the team of five that included Frederick Hauck, Robert Crippen, John Fabian and Norman Thagard.

the 37 American space flights that had preceded it. Through all those flights, American manned space flight had included only men, but on 18 June 1983 Sally Ride, a 32-year-old physicist from Encino, California, became the first American woman to fly in space. It had been 20 years and two days since Valentina Tereshkova became the first woman in space, and less than a year after Svetlana Savitskaya had been the second. By the time Sally Ride became the first American woman ever to fly in space twice, just 16 months later, three American women had made space flights aboard the Space Shuttle. Sally Ride was the biggest media star that the American space program had had since Neil Armstrong set foot on the moon and perhaps even since Alan Shepard first went into space. Sally Ride, however, achieved her stardom in an era when television talk shows and personality-oriented magazines abounded to an extent unheard of in the 1960s, and this helped make her number one cover material for the summer of 1983.

Below: This view of *Challenger* over a heavily cloud covered portion of the earth was taken by a camera on board the temporarily free-flying Shuttle pallet satellite (SPAS-01) during the STS-7 mission. The STS-7 crew and RMS arm later retrieved the SPAS and returned it to a stowed position in the payload bay of *Challenger.*

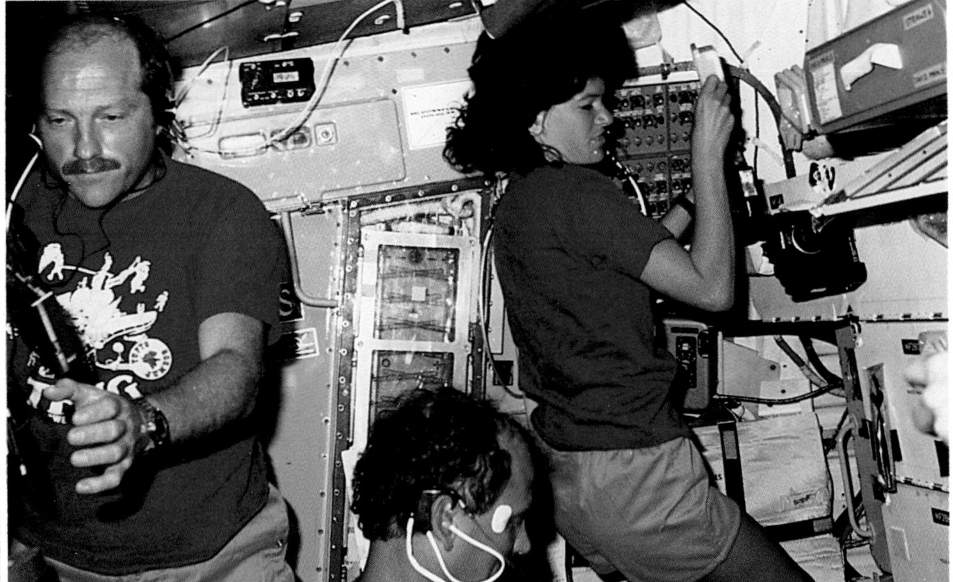

Above right: On board STS-7 astronauts Norman Thagard, Sally Ride, John Fabian and pilot Frederick Hauck in the process of preparing a snack. Hauck's 'TFNG' tee shirt pays tribute to the 'thirty five new guys' of the 1978 class of astronauts. The tall experiment in the background is the continuous flow electrophoresis system. *Below right: Challenger* comes in for a perfect landing, completing the rigorous STS-7 mission. It carried the first five-member crew, launched an Indonesian and Canadian communications satellite experiments platform and used it to get the first pictures of the Shuttle in orbit.

Left: **The Space Shuttle lights up the predawn sky as it begins the STS-8 mission, the first nighttime launch of a Shuttle, carrying Daniel Brandenstein, Dale Gardner, William Thornton, Richard Truly and Guion Bluford, Jr.** ***Above:*** **Mission specialist Guion Bluford, Jr, the first black American astronaut, is shown in early training for STS-8. He is helping to evaluate a self-supporting, controlled environment rescue device that NASA planned to use on Shuttle flights if an emergency should necessitate leaving one spacecraft for another in space.**

Ride was accompanied by four other people during the six-day flight of STS-7. Among them were Robert Crippen, the first person to fly twice aboard a Shuttle Orbiter, as well as John Fabian, Frederick Hauck and Norman Thagard. STS-7 also saw the first deployment of a satellite by using the remote manipulator arm. That satellite, a West German SPAS, used a remotely controlled 70mm camera to take the first full-view photos of a Space Shuttle Orbiter in space.

Challenger made its third flight in a little over four months on 30 August 1983. Like STS-7, this flight lasted six days and had a crew of five. Also like its predecessor, STS-8, it was recognized for a handful of firsts. It was the first time that the Shuttle had been launched at night, and it carried the first black astronaut to make a space flight, Guion Bluford, Jr. The rest of the crew included Daniel Brandenstein, Dale Gardner, William Thornton and Richard Truly, who was the second man to fly twice aboard the Shuttle.

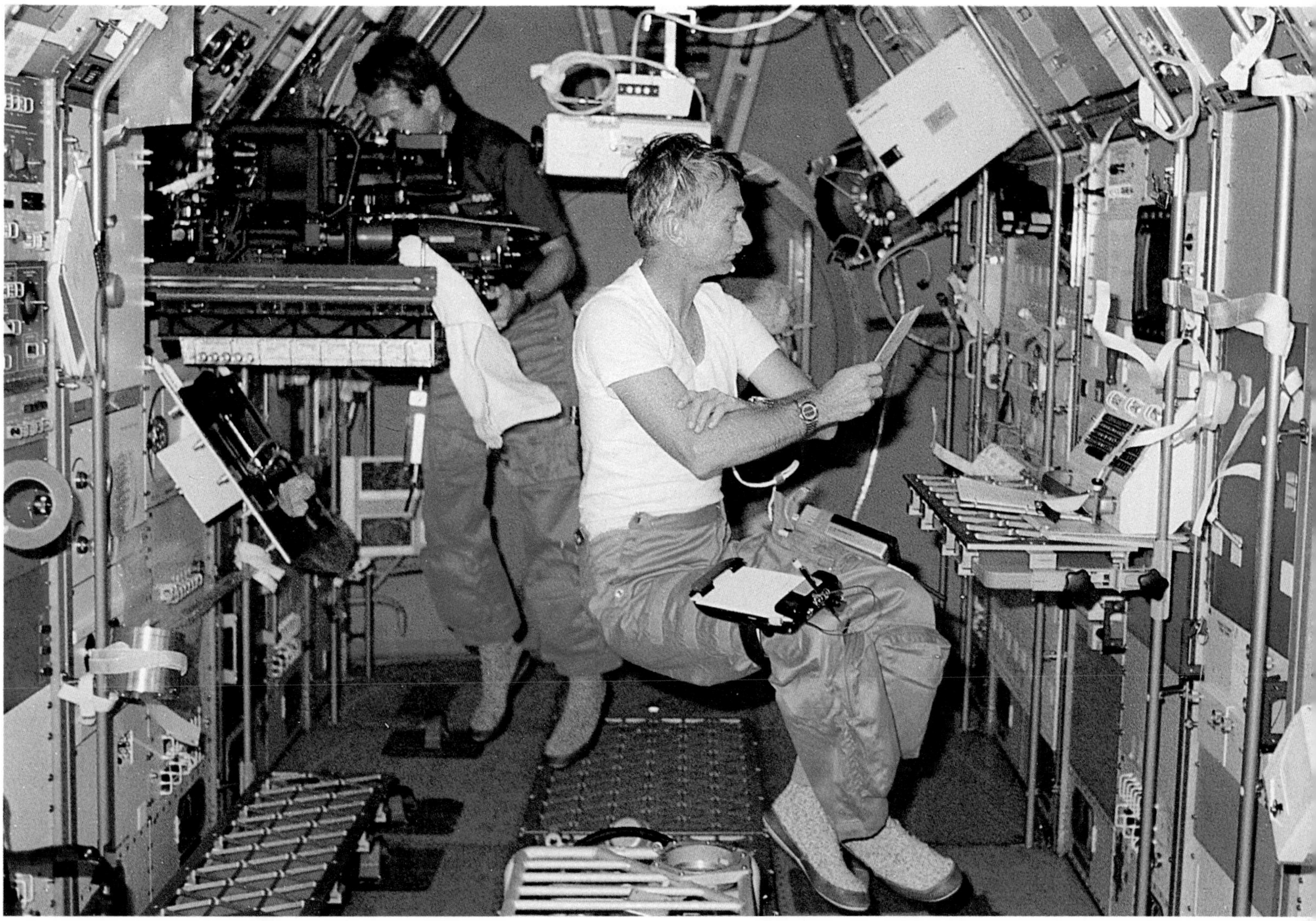

Left: **John Young takes notes in the commander's station on the flight deck of *Columbia* for the STS-9/Spacelab 1 mission. This was his sixth space flight; no Soviet or US astronaut had been in space more than four times.**

Payload specialists Byron Lichtenberg and Owen Garriott at work in Spacelab 1 (*above*) and Byron Lichtenberg positioned at the materials science double rack facility (*below*), pushing buttons related to the fluid physics module.

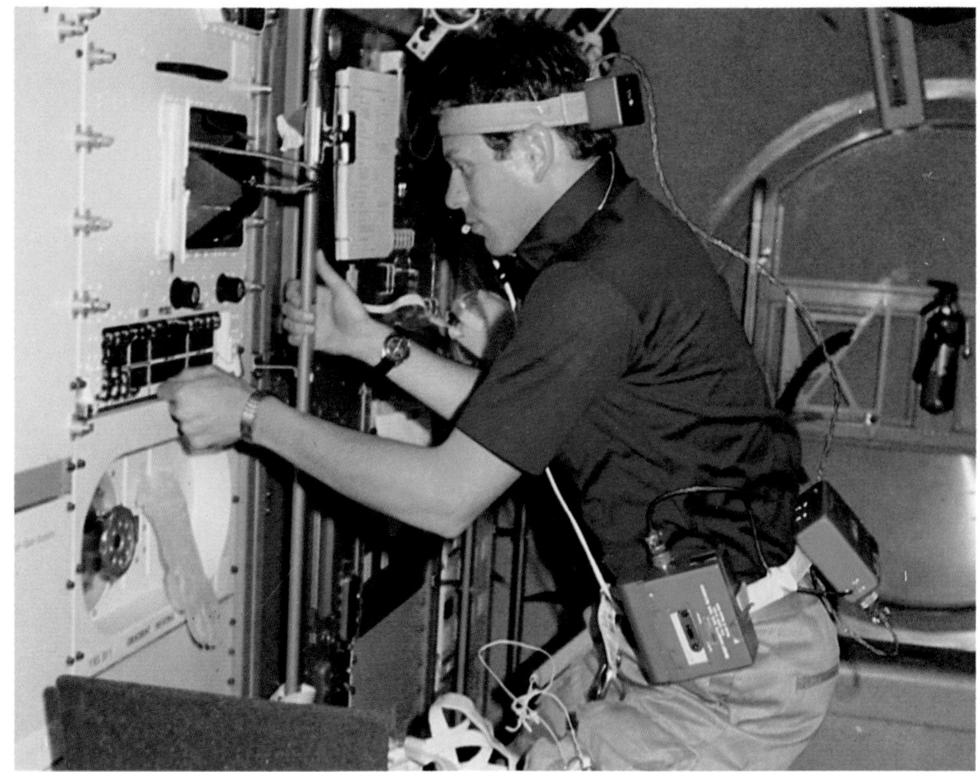

Columbia flew mission STS-9, its first flight in just over a year. Launched on 28 November 1983, the record 10-day mission carried the European-designed Spacelab for the first time. Produced by the European Space Agency (ESA), Spacelab was a zero-gravity laboratory designed to be carried in the Orbiter's payload bay. For STS-9 *Columbia* was flown by Brewster Shaw, Jr and John Young, the first American to make six space flights. Operating the Spacelab hardware were mission and payload specialists Owen Garriott (Skylab 3's scientist astronaut), Byron Lichtenberg and Robert Parker, as well as the first non-American astronaut to fly aboard an American spacecraft. The major payload aboard STS-9 was the ESA Spacelab, and it was clearly appropriate for ESA to send its first astronaut, Ulf Merbold of West Germany, to work with Garriott, Lichtenberg and Parker.

STS-9 was the last mission to receive an STS number and the first to carry a number under NASA's cumbersome new three-digit designation system. The first digit refers to the fiscal year (FY) in which the flight was scheduled, the second to the launch site and the third to the order in

CAL POLY
SAN LUIS OBISPO
NAVY
IT'S NOT JUST A JOB, IT'S A

Above: Mission specialist for 41-B Bruce McCandless II is leaning into space with his feet anchored in the mobile foot restraint of the RSM. ***Left:*** Robert 'Hoot' Gibson, 41-B pilot, reviews some teleprinter copy on the flight deck's starboard station. Mission specialists Vance Brand, Robert McNair and Robert Stewart were also part of the crew. ***Below:*** Rhea Seddon and Hoot Gibson with their infant son in 1982. Both parents were astronaut trainees in Group Eight. She is a mission specialist and first went into space in April 1985.

which the mission was originally scheduled within that fiscal year. Thus it came to be that STS-9 was also 41-A, with the 4 designating FY 1984 (NASA's fiscal years start in October) and the 1 designating Kennedy Space Center (2 is for Vandenberg AFB in California, which was not planned to launch a manned space flight until 1986). The A indicates that it is the first flight scheduled in FY 1984.

The first flight of calendar year 1984 was the launch on 3 February of *Challenger*. Designated 41-B, the mission lasted eight days and carried a crew of five: Vance Brand, Robert Gibson, Bruce McCandless II, Ronald McNair and Robert Stewart. During the mission McCandless made the first EVA using the Manned Maneuvering Unit (MMU), a backpack-type device that permitted an astronaut to walk in space completely independent of the spacecraft. The sight of McCandless floating free high above

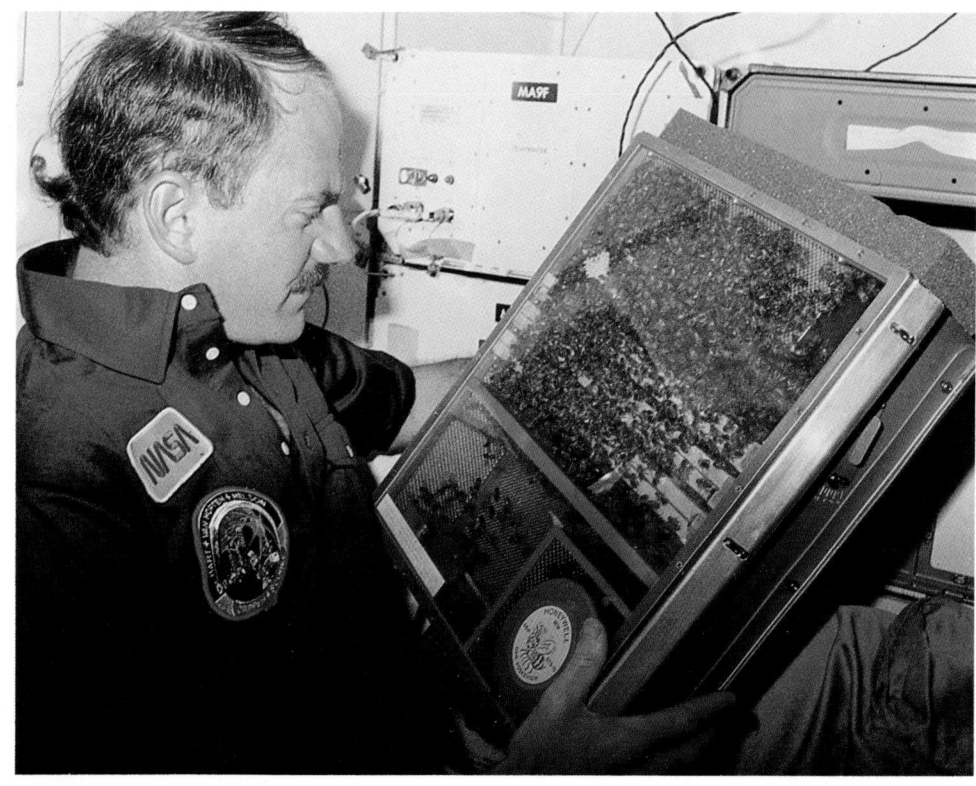

Left: **Using the MMU for the first time during 41-B, Bruce McCandless reaches the maximum distance from *Challenger* before returning.**

Above: **James van Hoften, 41-C mission specialist, holding a honeybee experiment and (*below*) in *Challenger's* payload bay.**

Challenger and above the earth was awe-inspiring. The performance of the Payload Assist Module (PAM) was anything but sensational. The PAM was supposed to launch two communications satellites, the Western Union Westar 6 (USA) and the Palapa B-2 (Indonesia), into useful orbits, but PAM malfunctioned and misplaced both. By the end of the year, however, NASA had returned both satellites to earth for repair.

Mission 41-C was launched on 6 April 1984, with the expressed mission of making repairs, in this case of the Solar Maximum Mission spacecraft. The Solar 'Max' had been launched in February 1980 to observe solar phenomenae during a period of maximum solar flare activity and had malfunctioned in December of that year. During Mission 41-C the satellite was retrieved by *Challenger*'s remote manipulator arm and successfully repaired by astronauts George Nelson and James van Hoften in the longest EVA since Apollo 17. Solar Max was then re-released into space to continue its observations of the sun and later Halley's

NASA
NASA
NASA

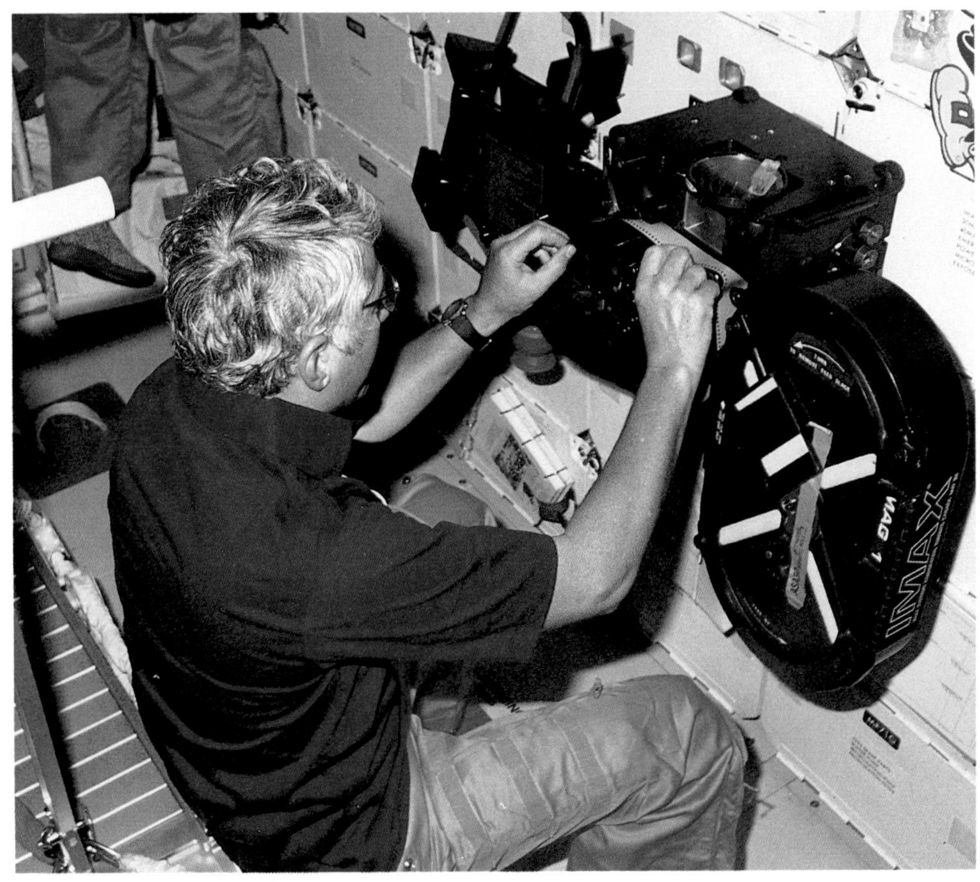

Left: **The six crew members of mission 41-D, the maiden voyage of *Discovery*, having some fun. They are (*counterclockwise from center*) commander Henry Hartsfield, Jr; pilot Michael Coats; mission specialists Steven Hawley and Judith Resnik; payload specialist Charles Walker and mission specialist Richard (Mike) Mullane. *Above:* Henry Hartsfield, Jr loads a roll of film into the IMAX motion picture camera. *Below:* Charles Walker (*left*) and Michael Coats, photographed during a sleep period in the spacecraft's mid deck.**

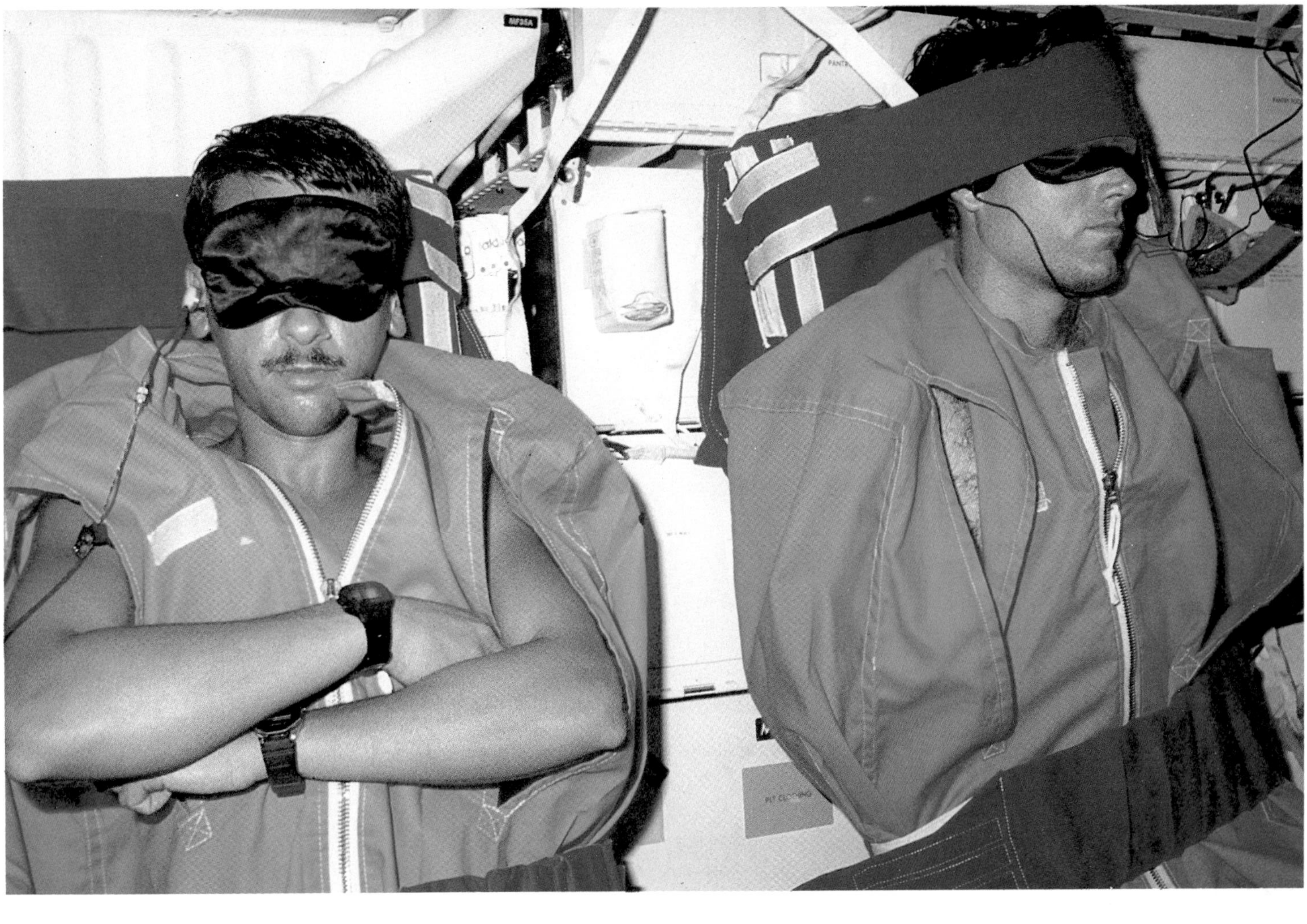

Comet. In addition to Nelson and van Hoften, *Challenger*'s crew included Terry Hart, Francis Scobee and Robert Crippen, piloting the spacecraft for his third flight aboard a Shuttle Orbiter.

Mission 41-D, launched on 30 August 1984 for a five-day flight, was the maiden voyage of the Orbiter *Discovery* (OV-103). The crew included America's second woman in space, Judy Resnik, as well as Michael Coats, Henry Hartsfield, Jr, Steven Hawley, Richard Mullane and Charles Walker, the first American to go into space representing private industry. Walker's job was to operate the McDonnell Douglas Electrophoresis Operations in Space (EOS) project. EOS had been developed by McDonnell Douglas as a means of processing pharmaceutical materials in the weightlessness of space. The separation of certain enzymes and hormones from other materials can be done on earth, but the process is impeded by gravity. McDonnell Douglas had been working on EOS since 1977, and by 1984 commercial production was imminent. They purchased space aboard *Discovery* for the EOS module and for Charles Walker, the first paying passenger in the history of manned space flight. While Charles Walker was at work at the EOS experiment, the NASA mission specialists

Dale Gardner, mission 51-A astronaut, wearing the MMU, approaches the spinning Westar 4 satellite over Bahama banks. The end effector of the RMS, controlled by Anna Fisher inside *Discovery*'s cabin, awaits its duty at right.

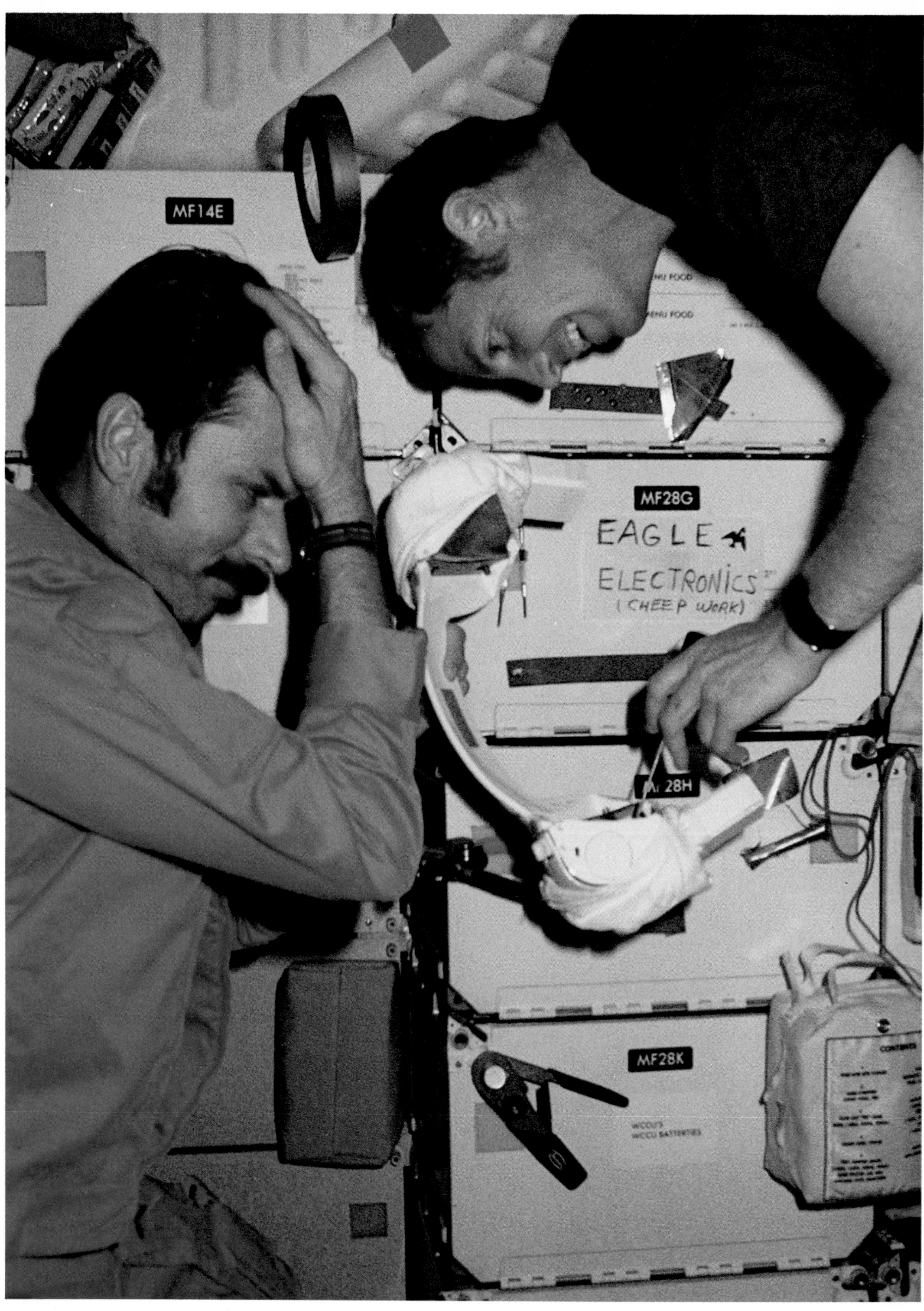
MF14E
MF28G
EAGLE
ELECTRONICS
(CHEEP WORK)
MF28K
WCCU'S
WCCU BATTERIES

were busy launching three American satellites, Leasat 2, Telstar 3 and SBS 4.

A month after *Discovery* returned from 41-D, *Challenger* was launched on 41-G (missions 41-E and 41-F were canceled). The mission was launched on 5 October 1984 and included the first Canadian astronaut, Marc Garneau. The mission was also Sally Ride's second into space and it was the first flight by America's third woman in space, Kathryn Sullivan. Sullivan was also the first woman to walk in space, and Paul Scully-Power became the first oceanographer to scientifically observe the earth's oceans from space. The other members of the record seven-person crew were David Leestma, Jon McBride and Robert Crippen, making his fourth shuttle flight.

The last flight of 1984 and the first of FY 1985, 51-A, was launched on 8 November. For three months running, the United States had launched a manned space flight every month. This time the crew aboard *Discovery* included Joseph Allen, Dale Gardner, Frederick Hauck, David Walker and the fourth American woman in space, Anna Fisher. Even after 14 flights, the STS seemed like it was chalking up new milestones on every flight and 51-A was no different. During this mission, the crew located and retrieved the Palapa B-2 and Westar 6 satellites that had misfired into useless orbit during 41-B nine months before. The

Above: **NASA's 51-A flight crew included (*top row, left to right*) Dale Gardner, mission specialist; Frederick Hauck, crew commander; David Walker, pilot and (*below*) specialists Anna Fisher and Joseph Allen IV. *Left:* Aboard 51-A, Dale Gardner has just discovered that lights designed for mounting on space suit helmets have developed a problem, while David Walker (*right*) uses a screwdriver to inspect the problem area. The lights were later successfully repaired. *Below:* Scientist-astronaut Anna Fisher accompanies her husband, scientist-astronaut Group Nine candidate Bill Fisher, on his initial familiarization flight in a NASA KC-135 aircraft. Anna Fisher made her first space flight in November 1984.**

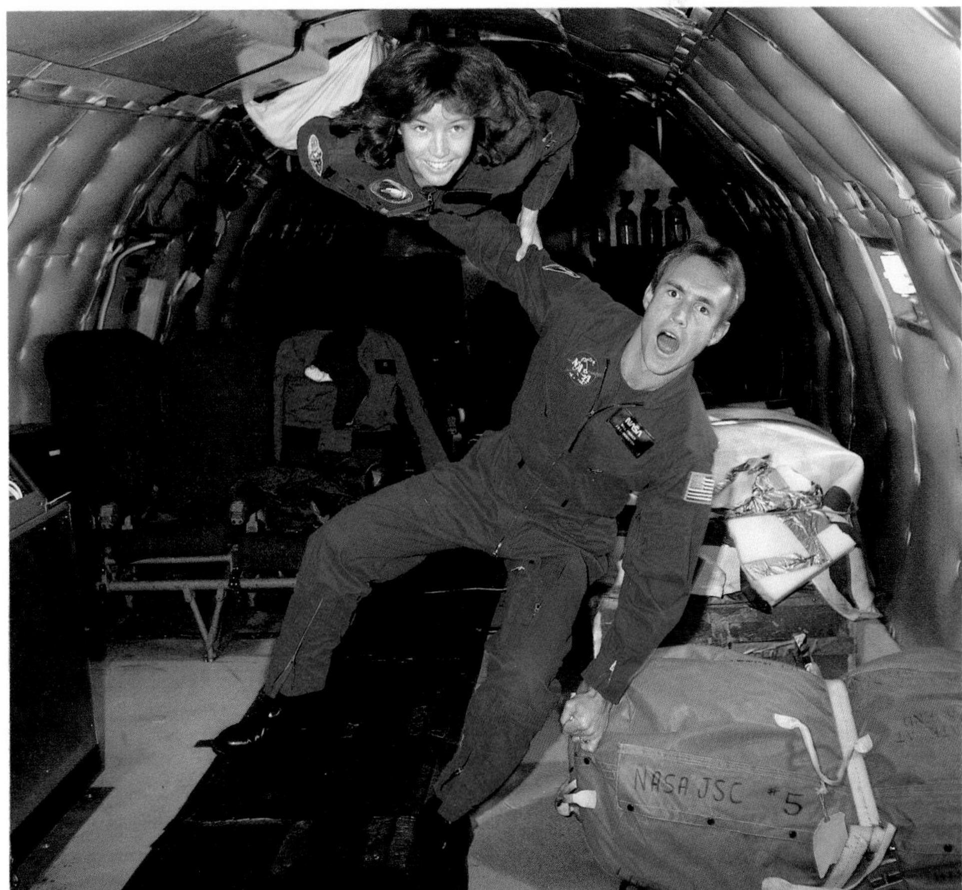

Astronaut Dale Gardner (*left*) holds a For Sale sign, making light reference to the status of the recaptured Westar 6 communications spacecraft that has been stranded since its initial deployment. Joseph Allen IV stands on the mobile foot restraint, which, along with the RMS, was controlled by Anna Fisher from inside *Discovery*'s cabin. Mission 51-A was the first to retrieve wayward satellites.

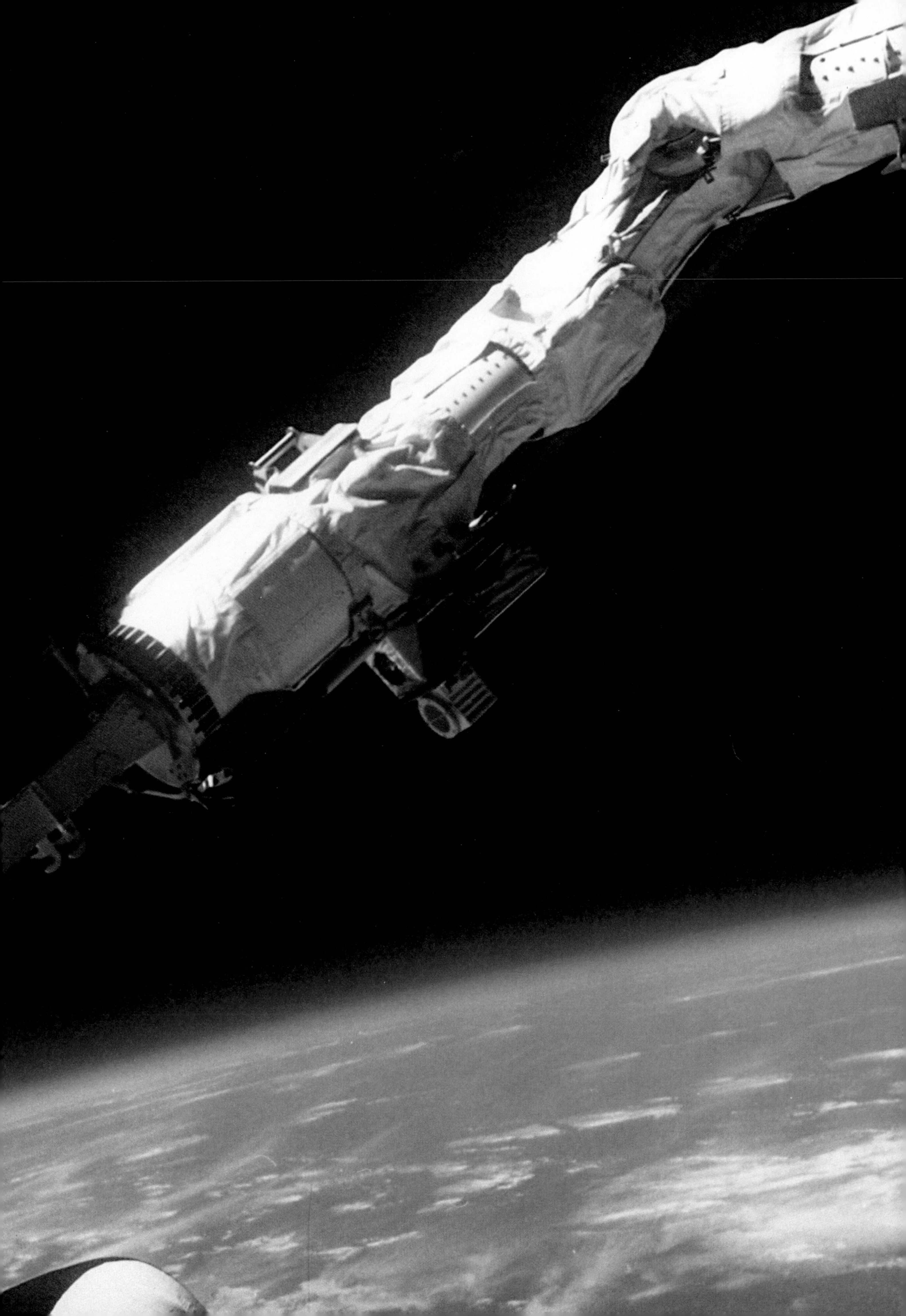

NASA

'rescue' of the two wayward satellites made the commercial potential of the Shuttle seem much greater than ever before.

The year 1985 saw an unprecedented number of American manned space flights. The first was 51-C, *Discovery*'s three-day semiclassified Defense Department mission launched on 24 January. The all-military crew, who launched a Code 647 Defense Support Program Satellite, included astronauts Lt Col James Buchli, USMC; Maj Ellison Onizuka, USAF; Lt Col Loren Shriver, USAF as well as USAF payload specialist Maj Gary Payton. The second flight of the year, 51-D, was the launch of *Discovery* on 12 April, carrying the American space program's first VIP passenger, Senator Jake Garn (Republican, Utah), whose Senate committee oversees NASA's budget. Also on board were Charles Walker, from the McDonnell Douglas EOS project, who had first flown in space less than a year before, and Rhea Seddon, the fifth American woman to fly in space in less than two years. The mission was commanded by Karol Bobko, piloted by Donald Williams, and it included David Griggs and Jeffrey Hoffman.

Mission 51-B, which had first been scheduled earlier in the year, was launched on 29 April, less than two weeks after 51-D landed. Even as *Discovery* was flying the 51-D mission, the ESA Spacelab module was being loaded aboard *Challenger* for 51-B. The 51-B crew included Robert Overmyer and Frederick Gregory

Left: **Mission 51-D carried the first VIP, Senator Jake Garn, to fly aboard a Space Shuttle. He is shown here in flight with Rhea Seddon and Jeffrey Hoffman to his right.** ***Above:*** **On board the 51-B/Spaceslab mission, mission specialist William Thornton observes one of two squirrel monkeys in Cage No. 1 in the research animal holding facility.** ***Below:*** **Astronaut Norman Thagard, mission specialist for the 'silver' team aboard 51-B rests on the mid deck while the 'gold' team is on duty in the science module.**

Gold team member Don Lind (*left*) participates in autogenic feedback training, designed to help flight crew members overcome the effects of zero-gravity adaptation.

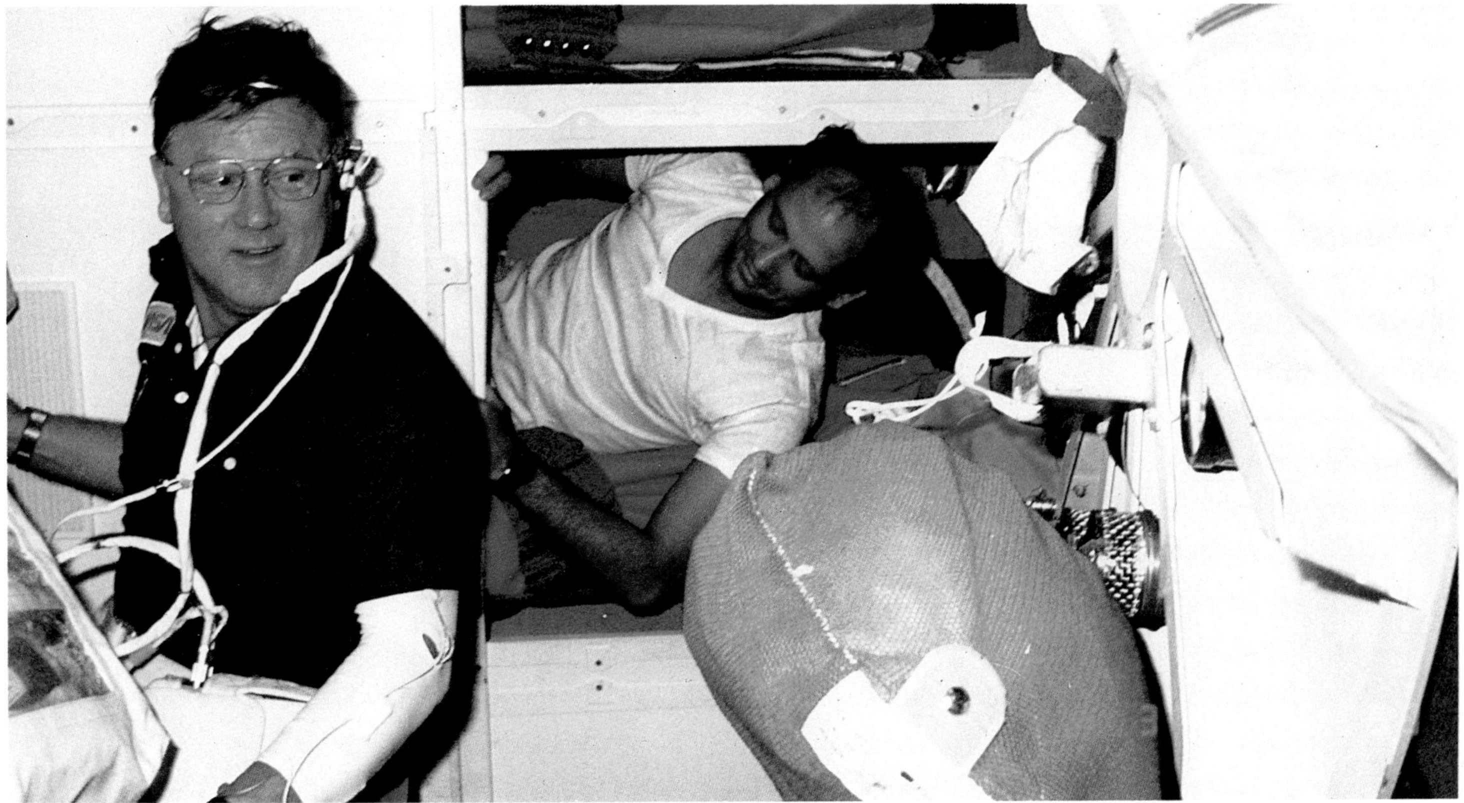

HUGHES

Left and above: **James van Hoften and William Fisher are shown during one of their two extravehicular sessions during the August 1985 51-I mission. Dr Fisher leans over the engine nozzle (*left*) to repair the temporarily 'captured' Leasat communications satellite.**

as commander and pilot, respectively. Also aboard were astronauts Don Lind, Norman Thagard and William Thornton from NASA as well as two payload specialists, Taylor Wang of NASA and the first Dutch astronaut, Lodewijk van den Berg of ESA.

Mission 51-G was launched on 17 June 1985 with Daniel Brandenstein as commander, John Creighton as pilot and three NASA astronauts as mission specialists—John Fabian, Shannon Lucid and Steven Nagel. Also aboard *Discovery* were two non-American astronauts as payload specialists, Patrick Baudry of CNES, the French space agency, and Sultan Salman Abdel-aziz Al-Saud of Saudi Arabia. A member of the Saudi royal family, the sultan, who was the first member of royalty to ever fly in space, was aboard on the seven-day mission to observe the launching of the Arabsat communications satellite. The crew also launched the Telesat 3 and Mexican Morelos satellites.

On 12 July 1985, *Challenger* was set to go on its eighth space flight and the fiftieth of the American manned space program, when a minor engine malfunction forced a delay. The launch of 51-F came 17 days later as *Challenger* carried the ESA Spacelab into orbit for the third time. Spacelab's solar telescopes provided the most detailed observations of the sun and other deep space objects since Skylab, 12 years before. For the first time, Spacelab flew without an ESA astronaut as payload specialist. The commander and pilot for 51-F were Charles G Fullerton and Roy Bridges, Jr, both Air Force colonels. The rest of the crew included astronauts Story Musgrave, Anthony England and Carl Henize as well as payload specialists John David Bartoe of the Naval Research Laboratory and Loren Acton of Lockheed's Palo Alto research laboratory.

Mission 51-I, which saw the 26 August launch of the Orbiter *Discovery,* was the

Bill Fisher, perched on the RMS arm and attached by the mobile foot restraint during 51-I extravehicular activity to repair and redeploy the Leasat satellite in August 1985.

HARTSFIELD
NAGEL
BUCHLI
SPACELAB
D1
BLUFORD
DUNBAR
MESSERSCHMID
OCKELS & FURRER

Above: **The seven member STS 61-B crew were photographed on the flight deck of *Atlantis* with the aid of a fish-eye lens. In the back row (*left to right*) are Jerry Ross; Brewster Shaw, Jr; Mary Cleave, Bryan O'Connor and payload specialist Rodolfo Neri. In the front row (*left to right*) are payload specialist Charles Walker and Sherwood Spring.**

Left: **Five of the eight crew members for STS 61-A. Henry Hartsfield, Jr (*rear left*) was commander of the mission. To his right are ESA payload specialist Reinhard Furrer and pilot Steven Nagel. In front are ESA payload specialist Wubbo Ockels and Bonnie Dunbar. Mission 61-A carried the ESA spacelab, spacebound for the fourth time. During this mission part of the mission control for the spacelab payload operations was transferred to the German Space Operations Center.**

twentieth launch of the Shuttle program. The commander and pilots were Joe Engle and Richard Covey and the astronauts included James van Hoften, Michael Lounge and William Fisher, whose wife, Anna Fisher, had flown aboard 51-A nine months before. During the eight-day mission, Fisher and van Hoften made two space walks to repair and redeploy the Leasat F3 satellite that had been launched during 51-D in April but had failed to activate. Joe Engle flew *Discovery* into position and over the period of two days, the two space-walking astronauts repaired the big Hughes-built spacecraft as Lounge held it in place with the Orbiter's remote manipulator arm.

Mission 51-J, launched on 3 October 1985 was the first flight of the Orbiter *Atlantis* (OV-104), the fourth and last of the space-rated Shuttle Orbiters. The mission was the second Defense Department all-military flight (51-C was the first), whose purpose was to launch a pair of Defense Satellite Communications System (DSCS) 'Discus-3' satellites. The crew included three Air Force officers, commander Karol Bobko, pilot Ronald Grabe and payload specialist Maj William Pailes as well as Army and Marine Corps mis-

Following the completion of a successful Spacelab D-1 mission the STS 61-A crew members emerge from *Challenger* at Edwards AFB on the morning of 6 November 1985. On the ground mission commander Henry Hartsfield, Jr shakes hands with George Abbey, director of flight crew operations at Johnson Space Center. Coming down the steps (*front to back*) are ESA payload specialists Reinhard Furrer, Ernst Messerschmid and Wubbo Ockels, and astronauts Bonnie Dunbar, Steven Nagel, James Buchli and Guion Bluford, Jr.

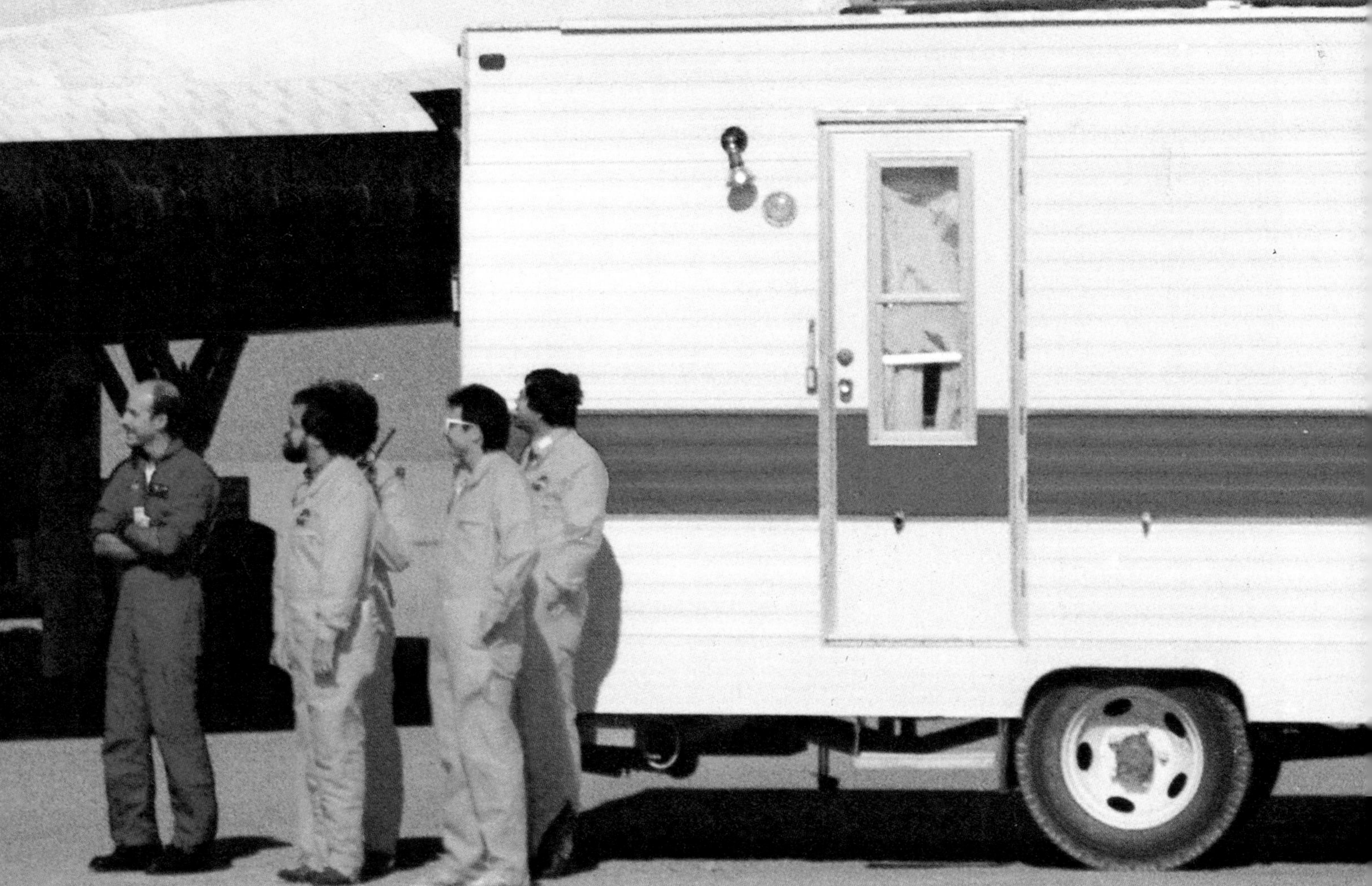
NASA
United States

MCDONNE

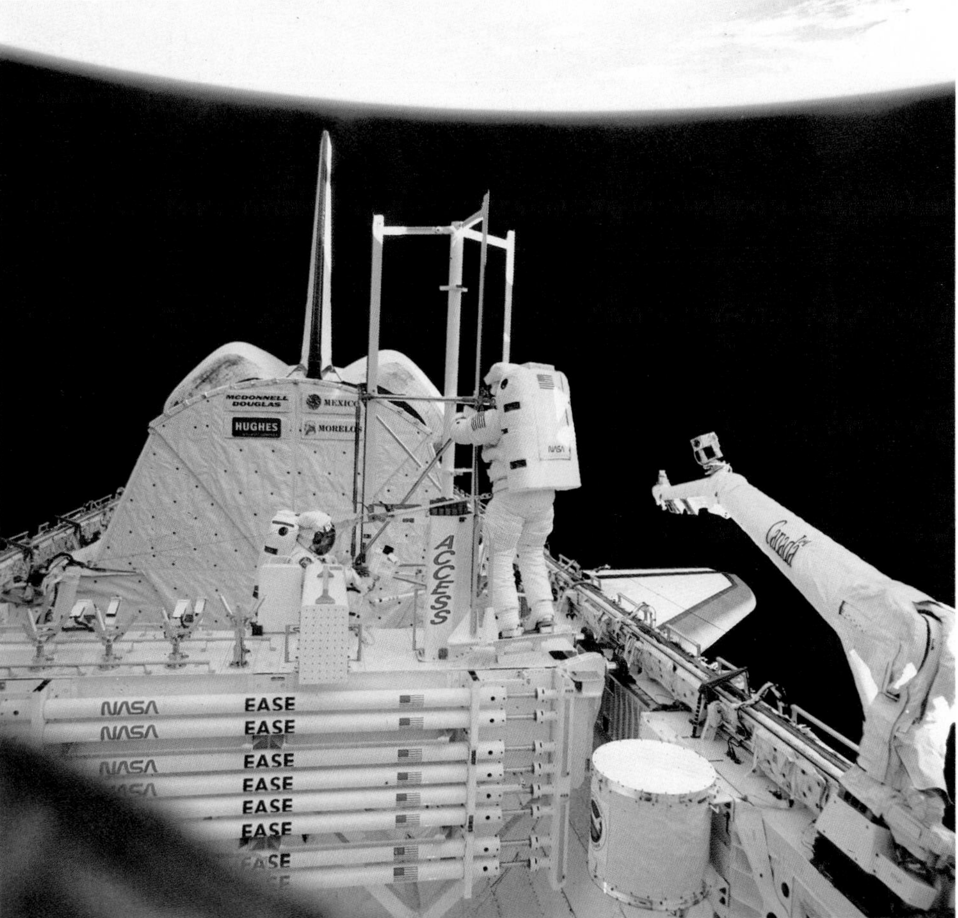

Above: **STS 61-B astronauts Jerry Ross (*left*) and Sherwood Spring in the early stages assembling the skeleton of a permanent manned space station. The RMS arm is in position to allow TV cameras to record the activity. *Left*: Sherwood Spring, photographed through *Atlantis's* cabin window, is shown connecting two more pieces of the space structure.**

sion specialist astronauts Robert Stewart and David Hilmers. During the four-day maiden voyage, *Atlantis* and its crew set a Space Shuttle program altitude record of 320 miles, which was about 50 percent of the theoretical maximum altitude of a Shuttle Orbiter. In September 1987, *Atlantis* was planned to fly to an altitude of 368 miles for observations with NASA's Hubble Space Telescope during a mission that would see the first major observatory to observe deep space from space.

Mission 61-A, launched on 30 October 1985, saw the ESA Spacelab flown for the fourth time, this time with the payload designation Spacelab D-1. Aboard *Challenger* for the seven-day mission was a record eight-member crew that included Henry Hartsfield, Jr as commander, Steven Nagel as pilot, and NASA astronauts Guion Bluford, James Buchli and Bonnie Dunbar. Also aboard were three ESA payload specialists, Ernst Messerschmid and Reinhard Furrer of West Germany as well as Wubbo Ockels of the Netherlands. As a precurser to expanded future European involvement, part of mission control for Spacelab D-1 payload operations was handed over from NASA in Houston to the German Space Operations Center in Oberpfaffenhofen, near Munich in West Germany. It was the first time that the mission control for any part of an American manned space flight had been transferred outside the United States.

On 26 November 1985, *Atlantis* thundered into the sky in the spectacular nighttime launch of mission 61-B. The mission commander was Brewster Shaw, Jr, with Bryan O'Conner as pilot. The other astronauts were Mary Cleave, Jerry Ross and Sherwood Spring, with McDonnell Douglas payload specialist Charles Walker accompanying the EOS equipment for the third time. Mexican payload specialist Rodolfo Neri also went along to observe the launch of the Morelos communications satellite and to monitor several Mexican experiments. Mission 61-B also saw the first assembly of the type of large structures that would form the skeleton of the permanent manned space station that was to become operational in the 1990s. As astronaut Mary Cleave operated the remote manipulator arm from inside *Atlantis,* astronauts Jerry Ross and Sherwood Spring went out into the open payload bay, where they began assembling a 45-foot truss tower composed of 93 tubu-

Sherwood Spring salutes from the end of the RMS arm after completing his extravehicular activity.

MEDICAL
CHECKLIST
STS
61-C
Columbia
STS 61-C

lar 6½ and 4½ foot beams. Ross and Spring also practiced assembling a large triangular component designed by MIT, scheduled for possible use in space station construction. They built and disassembled the tower twice and the MIT structure nine times during the 12 hours of EVA over a two-day period. The exercise proved that astronauts could build structures as high as a four-story building in space, even without the use of the self-contained Manned Maneuvering Units (MMU) that would allow the astronauts to fly around the object being built. The conclusion was that with the MMU structures the size of the planned permanent space station could be built in space with relative ease.

Nine American manned space flights took place in calendar year 1985, nearly double the number of 1965, 1966 and 1984, which were tied for second with five apiece. More Americans had flown into space aboard the Shuttle during 1985 than had flown in the entire Apollo program from 1968 through 1975. By the year end the four Orbiters had made 23 flights between them. *Challenger* (OV-99) had made nine, *Columbia* (OV-102) had made six, *Discovery* (OV-103) had made six and *Atlantis* (OV-104), which had first flown in October 1985, already had two space flights under its belt. During the year a number of non-NASA Americans went in orbit, either as technicians representing American aerospace firms or foreign governments, and the first US senator, Garn of Utah, made a flight into space.

On 12 January 1986, the Shuttle Orbiter *Columbia* was launched into space for the first time since November 1983. The first mission of the year, the seventh flight of *Columbia* had originally been scheduled for 18 December, but had to be postponed six times. Aboard *Columbia* for the six-day mission 61-C were Robert Gibson as commander, Charles Bolden, Jr as pilot and three NASA astronauts as mission specialists, George Nelson, Steven Hawley and Franklin Chang-Diaz. RCA payload specialist Robert Cenker was aboard to help launch an RCA Ku-band communications satellite. Flying as an observer was US Representative Bill Nelson (Democrat, Florida), chairman of the House Science and Technology subcommittee on space science and applications.

STS 61-C crew members use *Columbia*'s mid deck for the traditional in-flight portrait. Mission commander Robert Gibson (*lower right*) is surrounded by (*counterclockwise from upper right*) Charles Bolden, US Representative Bill Nelson of Florida, Robert Cenker, Steven Hawley, Franklin Chang-Diaz and George Nelson.

In calendar year 1986 NASA hoped to see its new Space Flight Participant Program begin, under which private citizens not associated with a governmental agency or aerospace firm would be selected to make space flights. As requested by President Ronald Reagan, the first participant in such a program was an American classroom teacher. By the February 1985 deadline, 11,146 teachers had submitted their 11-page applications to the space agency. From this group, NASA selected a group of finalists and eventually narrowed the list down to just two. The primary candidate was Sharon Christa McAuliffe, a 37-year-old high school social studies teacher from Concord, New Hampshire. The backup candidate, who was to undergo the same training, was Barbara Morgan, a 34-year-old second-grade teacher from McCall, Idaho.

Christa McAuliffe's long-awaited flight was the Shuttle program's mission 51-L. Scheduled for 26 January 1986, 51-L would be the program's twenty-fifth flight and the tenth for the Orbiter *Challenger.* The mission commander was Francis 'Dick' Scobee, who had first gone into space aboard *Challenger* in April 1984. *Challenger*'s pilot for the 51-L flight was Mike Smith, a former Navy fighter pilot. The three NASA payload specialists were rookie Ronald McNair and veterans Ellison Onizuka and Judy Resnik, the second American woman in space. The non-NASA personnel included McAuliffe and Greg Jarvis, a former Air Force pilot representing Hughes Aircraft. The crew of 51-L represented a true cross section of American life. Geographically, their home states spanned the nation from Hawaii to New Hampshire. There were two women, a black man and a Japanese-American. Both Scobee and Smith were former combat pilots and Resnik was a classical pianist.

The center of attention, however, was Christa McAuliffe. Other American private citizens had gone into space before, but they had been either politicians or (like Jarvis aboard this flight) aerospace engineers. There was something about a high-school teacher going into space that captured the imaginations of Americans of all ages. A special NASA video network was set up so that students in her own school back in Concord, New Hampshire, as well as thousands of others across the nation, could watch America's first space teacher go into space and teach her classes from earth orbit. It was to have been the first time that a 'regular person' would be speaking to the nation from space.

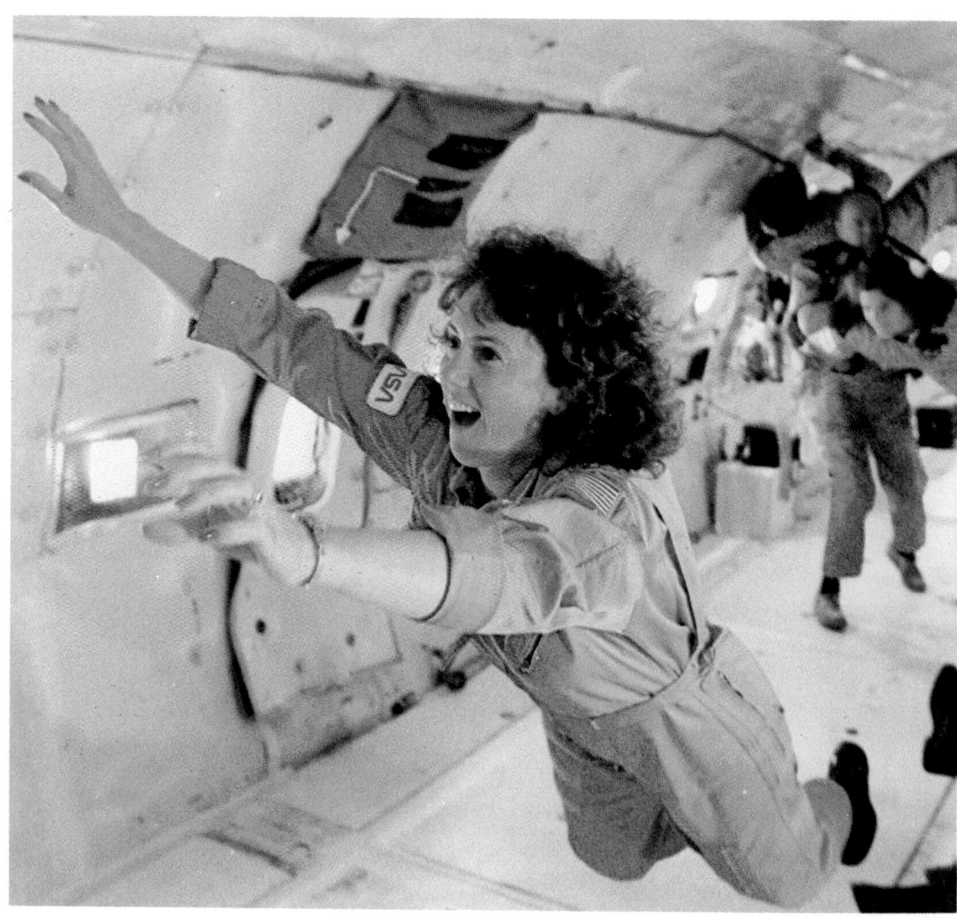

Above: **Sharon Christa McAuliffe, 51-L citizen observer/payload specialist representing the Teacher in Space Project, floats during moments of weightlessness aboard a KC-135.**

Below, from left: **Backup teacher-observer Barbara Morgan, 51-L pilot Mike Smith, a photographer, Christa McAuliffe and 51-L commander Dick Scobee during preflight training.**

Above: Five astronauts and two payload specialists made up the STS 51-L crew. In the front row (*left to right*) are Michael Smith, Dick Scobee and Ronald McNair. Behind are (*left to right*) Ellison Onizuka, Christa McAuliffe, Gregory Jarvis and Judy Resnik. Christa McAuliffe represented the Teacher in Space Project and Gregory Jarvis represented Hughes Co.

Below: Seated near the controls of the KC-135 aircraft Christa McAuliffe relaxes prior to participating in some zero-G rehearsals for her upcoming 51-L flight.

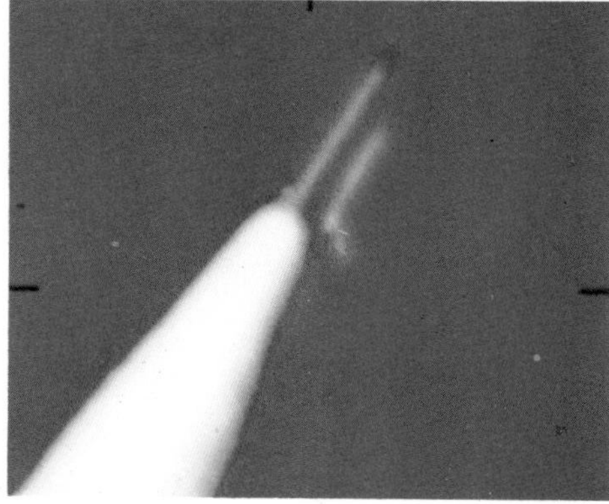

The fiery end of *Challenger* and 51-L: At 60.6 seconds, a small tongue of flame was visible at the base of the right solid rocket booster as an O-ring seal failed (*above left*). Two seconds later, the booster slammed the side of the external fuel tank, rupturing it and causing a leak of liquid hydrogen and liquid oxygen. Ten seconds later, the leak from the fuel tank was a torrent and at the 73.2-second mark (*above right*) it ignited and began to consume *Challenger* and her crew. At the 73.6-second mark, a huge explosion occurred, ripping the Orbiter into thousands of fragments while the two solid rocket boosters careened across the sky like blinded, panicked animals, only to be destroyed 37 seconds later by ground controllers when the boosters began to arc back toward populated areas.

The photograph at the right clearly shows the path of the Shuttle before the explosion, the explosion itself and the path of the two boosters afterward.

An icy cold front moved into Florida over the final weekend of the 51-L countdown, forcing the Sunday launch to be postponed to Tuesday, 28 January. Thus it came to be that students throughout the nation could watch the launch from their classrooms. Christa McAuliffe's own children, Scott, 9, and Caroline, 6, were on hand at Cape Canaveral with their father, Steve McAuliffe, and members of Scott's third-grade class, to watch *Challenger* go into space.

It was cold, just above freezing, as the seven members of the 51-L crew boarded the bus to take them out to the Orbiter on Pad 39B. As the crew entered *Challenger* they were smiling and appeared relaxed. A member of the ground crew handed teacher McAuliffe a shiny red apple as they climbed aboard. The textbook perfect launch came at 11:38 am. *Challenger* cleared the launch pad and climbed slowly into the sky. All the Shuttle's engines seemed to be running smoothly and Smith was in touch with ground control as he throttled down, right on cue. In Concord, New Hampshire, Christa McAuliffe's class cheered as they watched *Challenger* on television.

Challenger was at an altitude of 47,000 feet and traveling at a speed of 1800 feet per second when a small flame appeared at the base of the right solid rocket booster, and began to lick at the enormous fuel tank with its half-million gallons of liquid hydrogen and liquid oxygen. Fifteen seconds later and 73 seconds after launch, the Orbiter was enveloped in a fireball a hundred yards across as the fuel tank exploded. Both *Challenger* and the tank disintegrated in the explosion while the two solid rocket boosters twisted and turned across the sky like blinded, panicked animals. Across the nation, from Cape Canaveral where they watched the explosion in person to Concord where the scene was transmitted on live television, spectators stared dumbfounded, unsure of what had happened. Then, from mission control came the confirmation of what everyone feared but hoped wasn't true:

> Flight controllers are looking very carefully at the situation. Obviously a major malfunction. We have no downlink (communication with *Challenger*) . . . The vehicle has exploded.'

Nine years and one day after the Apollo 1 fire, seven people died in what would have been NASA's fifty-sixth manned space flight, but which became instead the worst disaster in a quarter century of manned space flight.

For nearly an hour debris drifted down from the cloud that had swallowed *Challenger*. Paramedics and rescue teams were on hand before the last fragments plunged into the Atlantic, but there was no hope of survivors. Over the days that followed, NASA began to sort out what had happened. The 14 Shuttle missions that were to have followed 51-L during 1986 were put on hold as investigators tried to piece together the cause of the fuel tank explosion.

Christa McAuliffe would never teach her classroom lesson from space, but her death and the death of her companions served to teach the lesson that the dangers and unknowns of space travel are more than equaled by the bravery of the men and women who seek to conquer mankind's final frontier.

THE SOVIET UNION

THE STAR CITY TWELVE

The Soviet space program, like that of the Americans, was born out of the ashes of World War II and built on the foundations laid by the Germans. The Soviets, like the Americans, imported German rocket scientists to help them develop a rocket program with an eye on a space program. Both programs moved at roughly the same pace, but it would be the Soviets who first reached beyond the final frontier and placed the first man-made object into outer space. Sputnik 1 was orbited on 4 October 1957 while the United States struggled with the hapless Vanguard. Sputnik 2 orbited on 3 November with the 'space dog' Laika aboard, but it was 31 January 1958 before the United States orbited Explorer 1.

Laika died a lonely, quiet death when her oxygen ran out a week into Sputnik 2's 103-day flight. By comparison the death of the American dream to be first in space was anything but quiet. American public opinion demanded that the United States catch up to the Soviet Union in the space race. The next arena that race could run would be manned space flight, and both nations set about evaluating their test pilots, looking for candidates from whom to choose their first men in space. The United States announced the selection of the seven Mercury astronauts in April 1959 and began their training amid a blizzard of publicity. The Soviets, meanwhile, went about their selection much more quietly. When they had funneled their list down to 20 pilots, there was no press release issued, nor did one appear when the roster was narrowed to 12.

On 14 March 1960 the final group of cosmonauts was selected. The men reported first to Zvyozdny Gorodok (Stellar Village) near Moscow for their initial training, then to Zvyezdograd (Star City) near the Baikonur Cosmodrome at Tyuratam in Khazakhstan east of the Aral Sea. While the first cosmonauts began their training, Soviet engineers were developing the spacecraft in which one of them would become the first Soviet man in space.

The men included in this 'Star City 12' were Pavel Belyayev, 28; Valeri Bykovsky, 26; Yuri Gagarin, 26; Viktor Gorbatko, 26; Yevgeny Khrunov, 27; Vladimir Komarov, 33; Alexei Leonov, 26; Andrian Nikolayev, 31; Pavel Popovich, 30; Georgi Shonin, 25; Gherman Titov, 25; and Boris Volynov, 26. All of the cosmonauts in the group were from the Soviet air force except Belyayev, who was chosen from the Soviet naval air arm.

VOSTOK

The first Soviet manned spacecraft program was called Vostok (East). Like the American Mercury capsule, Vostok was a one-man ballistic re-entry capsule. Unlike the bell-shaped Mercury, Vostok was spherical, more like a diving bell than a carillon bell. Vostok's diameter was half again greater than Mercury's and it weighed more than twice as much. For its launch, Vostok was enclosed within a cone-shaped aerodynamic shroud and attached to a barrel-shaped second-stage rocket motor, which made it look like the American Apollo CSM that was built much later.

Unlike the American space capsules from Mercury through Apollo, which were designed to be recovered at sea, Vostok was designed to parachute to a hard surface landing (like successor Soviet manned spacecraft). Also unlike the American capsules, Vostok was equipped with an aircraft-type ejection seat, used by the Soviet cosmonauts on all but the first Vostok flight.

By the spring of 1960, both the Americans and the Soviets were working feverishly toward the day when one of them would be the first to send a man into space. While the American Mercury program was surrounded by almost unprecedented publicity, the Soviets released little in the way of advance information, treating their space program like any other

Soviet cosmonauts (*left to right*) Boris Volynov, Yuri Gagarin and Andrian Nikolayev concentrate on their studies, in this case film-making, in January 1959. Nikolayev, the third cosmonaut to be named, later married Valentina Teveshkova, the first woman in space.

Cosmonaut number 1, Yuri Gagarin relaxes with his daughters in their Moscow apartment. The world's first man in space was killed in a military aircraft accident in March 1968 while training for Soyuz 3.

military flight-test program. The early Vostok capsule flight tests were even designated in the Sputnik series to conceal as much as possible. The first Vostok test, on 15 May 1960 and designated Sputnik 4 (Korabl Sputnik 1), failed when the capsule did not re-enter the earth's atmosphere. Two further tests were conducted in August and December. A pair of dogs carried aboard Sputnik 5 were ejected and recovered, and the dog aboard Sputnik 6 was killed when the recovery failed.

The Americans made two successful suborbital Mercury tests in December and January as the race to send the first man into space reached its final lap. The Americans successfully recovered space chimp Ham (the first primate in space) from their January test, while the Soviets successfully recovered the space dogs Chernushka and Zvezdochka from two Korabl Sputnik orbital test flights in March. The stage was set for man's first venture beyond the atmosphere.

On the morning of 12 April 1961, the waiting was over. Maj Yuri Gagarin, a former fighter pilot turned cosmonaut and just recently promoted from senior lieutenant, finished his coffee and marmalade and put on his blue pressure suit. Gagarin and backup pilot Gherman Titov were driven the short distance to the Baikonur Cosmodrome. Waiting at the launch pad at the Soviet equivalent of Cape Canaveral was the Vostok capsule that Gagarin had dubbed *Swallow.*

At 9:07 am Moscow time Vostok 1 left the launch pad in Kazakhstan. In the United States it was just after 4 am when reporters phoned NASA's Project Mercury public relations chief for a comment on the apparent Soviet success. His response, 'We're all still asleep down here,' was a prophetic summary of the way NASA felt.

Two hundred miles in space Yuri Gagarin was beyond the reach of earth's gravity, a place no man had ever been. 'When weightlessness appeared I felt excellent,' he later recalled. 'I did not sit as before, but was suspended in mid-air. The sunlit side of the earth is visible and one can easily distinguish the shores of the continents, islands and great rivers. Over Russia I saw distinctly the big squares of collective farm fields and it was possible to distinguish which was plowed and which was meadow. During the flight I saw for the first time with my own eyes, the earth's spherical shape. The horizon is dark blue, smoothly turning to black. The feelings that filled me I can express with one word: joy.'

Gagarin returned to earth near Smelovka on the Volga just 1 hour and 48 minutes after the launch, and after one complete orbit of the earth. Though the Americans put their first man into space three weeks later, no American would orbit the earth until the following year.

Two days after Vostok 1 slammed into the banks of the Volga, Yuri Gagarin's youthful face appeared on huge posters throughout Moscow and he was present to watch the huge parade through Red Square in his honor. As crowds chanted '*Slava* Yuri,' the young major received a huge bouquet from Premier Nikita Khrushchev. Like Kennedy, his counterpart half a world away, Khrushchev now saw manned space flight as more than just an isolated technological achievement. It was clear to the two leaders that manned space flight was the yardstick by which the two superpowers would be measured by the rest of the world and by each other.

Yuri Gagarin was a public relations man's dream come true. He was the ideal of the new Soviet hero and certainly a delight for Khrushchev. He charmed the press in Moscow and he traveled to the West, where he visited England and joined Queen Elizabeth for pleasant small talk over lunch. He was more than just a test pilot and he was more, even, than just the pioneer in a new chapter of mankind's exploration of the universe. The young cosmonaut with the engaging smile was a symbol of his nation's technological power.

Within a month of Gagarin's orbital flight, Alan Shepard made the first American suborbital flight and John Kennedy committed the United States to the goal of an American on the moon by the end of the 1960s. Prior to the flights of Gagarin and Shepard, neither nation had a firm outline of where to go with their manned space-flight programs, but thanks to Kennedy, the game plan was now in place and the goal was clear.

In the near term Khrushchev's strategy was to stay ahead of the Americans in the space race and to hopefully extend his lead—which is exactly what he did on 6 August 1961 with the flight of Vostok 2. This time the cosmonaut was Maj Gherman Stepanovich 'Herman' Titov, a 26-year-old Soviet air force pilot who had been Gagarin's backup for the April flight of Vostok 1. Titov's flight was the type of spectacle that must surely have pleased Premier Khrushchev. Whereas Gagarin had made one orbit of the globe, Titov made 17. While Gagarin had spent just under 2 hours in space, Titov spent 25 hours and 18 minutes. He was the first man to spend an entire day in outer space.

Although the flight had been marred by his severe space sickness, Titov returned to Moscow's Red Square a hero, and his picture joined Yuri's in the pantheon of new Soviet heroes high on the Kremlin wall. The era of manned space flight was less than four months old and both the US and USSR had sent two men into space. However, while the Americans had logged 31 minutes of space time, the Soviets had logged 1626.

The next Soviet flight did not take place for over a year, but when it did, it was another spectacle. The Americans seemed to plod along while the Soviets seemed determined to outdo themselves with each Vostok flight. The Americans had followed their two suborbital flights with two 3-orbit flights. Both John Glenn and Scott Carpenter had outdistanced Gagarin, but even their two flights together didn't approach Gherman Titov's full day in outer space.

The Soviets topped their own achievement not simply with a longer flight but with the flights of two manned spacecraft simultaneously. Vostok 3, nicknamed *Falcon* by its pilot Maj Andrian Nikolayev, was launched on 11 August 1962 and was followed the next day by Vostok 4, *Golden Eagle,* with Lt Col Pavel Popovich aboard. Nikolayev was in space for 94 hours and 27 minutes and Popovich for 70 hours and 29 minutes. At one point the two cosmonauts were within three miles of one another, but this was due to launch trajectory—the Vostok capsules didn't have the sophisticated manual maneuvering controls required for a rendezvous. The Americans didn't realize this and speculated that Nikolayev and Popovich may have been practicing for a rendezvous and docking maneuver, the next step in developing a more sophisticated generation of manned spacecraft. The Soviets were only too willing to let the Americans continue to speculate.

The two cosmonauts returned to the earth's atmosphere and ejected from their capsules just 6 minutes and 100 miles apart, two more Soviet heroes to warm the heart of showman Khrushchev.

Ten months later, when the Vostok program continued, it was with yet another dual launch and yet another new twist from a Soviet space program that seemed constantly choreographed to capture headlines. Lt Col Valeri Bykovsky was launched aboard Vostok 5, *Hawk,* on

14 June 1963. Although he established a new record space flight of 119 hours and 6 minutes, more than double the time logged by the *entire* American Mercury program, his feat was overshadowed by the flight of Vostok 6.

Bykovsky was two days into his epic flight when Vostok 6 thundered skyward from the Baikonur Cosmodrome. Aboard this spacecraft nicknamed *Sea Gull* was Jr Lt Valentina Tereshkova, the first woman to venture into space. Lt Tereshkova was also the lowest in rank of any of the Soviet cosmonauts and the first one to make a space flight who was not a member of the original group of 12. A 26-year-old former factory worker, she had been among a group of women selected for cosmonaut training in August 1962.

Valentina Tereshkova's historic space flight was a grueling ordeal. Though a veteran of 126 parachute jumps, she was not a jet pilot and as a result she wasn't as conditioned for the stress of the high-G re-entry as her male colleagues. When *Sea Gull* landed in the Southern Urals after her 70 hours and 50 minutes in space Valentina was described as being in 'pitiful condition,' but she recovered in time to be whisked to Moscow along with Bykovsky for a heroine's welcome.

The reaction to the first space flight by a woman was immediate but not prolonged. Premier Khrushchev proudly told the world that 'it is our girl who is *first* in space,' but the Soviet space program would send no *second* Soviet woman to follow her important first step until 1982. Congress and the press called for NASA to include women in its astronaut program, but the idea seemed to get lost in the cracks as the space agency concentrated on preparations for the upcoming Gemini program, for which the astronauts had already been selected. Nobody realized that it would be more than 19 years before the second woman would fly in space, and 20 years before an American woman would fly in space. When Valentina Tereshkova returned to earth on 19

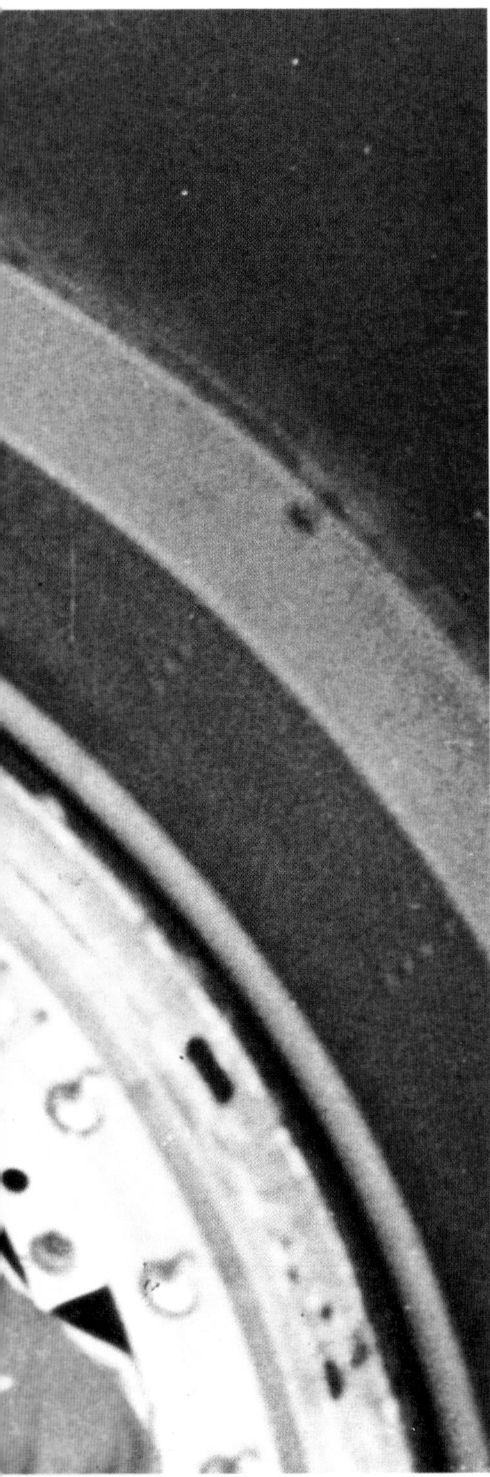

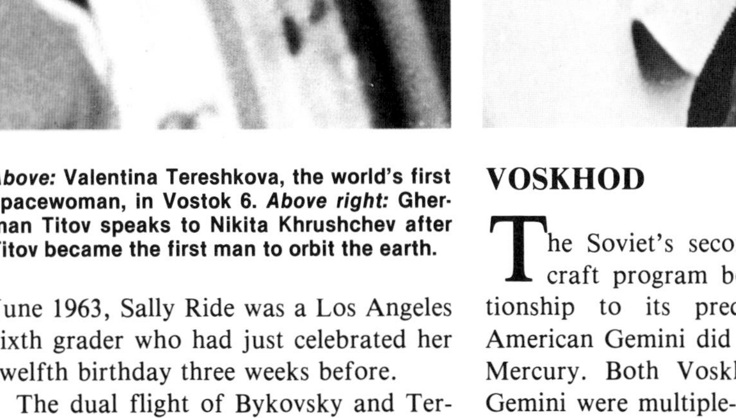

Above: **Valentina Tereshkova, the world's first spacewoman, in Vostok 6.** ***Above right:*** **Gherman Titov speaks to Nikita Khrushchev after Titov became the first man to orbit the earth.**

June 1963, Sally Ride was a Los Angeles sixth grader who had just celebrated her twelfth birthday three weeks before.

The dual flight of Bykovsky and Tereshkova aboard Vostok 5 and Vostok 6 marked the end of the Vostok program, just a bit more than a month after Gordon Cooper made the sixth and last flight of America's Mercury program. Each country had sent six people into space over the same two-year span of time, but the Vostok program had logged 382 hours in space to the Mercury's 54.

VOSKHOD

The Soviet's second manned spacecraft program bore the same relationship to its predecessor that the American Gemini did to its predecessor, Mercury. Both Voskhod (Sunrise) and Gemini were multiple-crew-member variations on the first-generation spacecraft and both were considered by their respective space agencies a means to obtain more detailed information about manned space flight that could be used in the development of future generation spacecraft. Both Mercury and Gemini were built by the McDonnell Aircraft Company and both were bell shaped, but Gemini was considerably larger. On the other hand Voskhod was virtually the same size as the Vostok and the spherical crew module was actually a greatly modified Vostok capsule. The major differences between the American and Soviet second-generation projects was that, while the Gemini program was designed to be a 10-flight series over a span of nearly two years, the Voskhod program planned two flights in five months, each designed around a specific unique mission.

Voskhod 1 was designed to be the first multiple-crew-member space flight. Nicknamed *Ruby,* it carried a three-man crew when it was launched on 12 October 1964. (The Americans had not yet made a single flight with their two-man Gemini capsule.) Aboard *Ruby* were the pilot, Col Vladimir Komarov, a familiar name from the original group of cosmonauts; Dr Boris Yegorov, a physician; and Konstantin Feoktistov, who had helped to design the spacecraft. In order to squeeze three couches into an area that originally held just one, the crew had to fly the mission without space suits. Spacecraft cabins were pressurized, but space suits were considered to be an extra measure of safety, especially during re-entry. The fact that the spacecraft's designer was aboard Voskhod 1 must have allowed the other two crew members a bit more confidence in the ship's ability to keep them safe during the long journey into space.

Without the bulky space suits, the crew was a good deal more comfortable and Dr Yegorov was able to move about and monitor the biologic effects on his two colleagues. In the midst of their 24 hour and 17 minute flight, the three cosmonauts chatted with Premier Nikita Khrushchev and other Kremlin leaders by radio. When Khrushchev closed with the offhand remark that Deputy Premier Anastas Mikoyan was 'pulling the receiver out of my hand,' few people realized that it would be the premier's last public statement. The day after Voskhod 1 landed, Khrushchev was stripped of his position, deposed by a Kremlin power struggle that brought Alexi Kosygin and Leonid Brezhnev to the upper rung of the Soviet hierarchy.

Voskhod 2, nicknamed *Diamond,* was launched on 18 March 1965 with a two-man crew, air force Col Alexei Leonov and Soviet navy Cdr Pavel Belyayev. The third couch had not been included aboard *Diamond* because the Voskhod 2 mission required the crew to wear space suits. *Diamond* had been designed with a special telescoping airlock that Leonov would use to leave the spacecraft and become the first man to venture in space. On the second orbit Leonov put on his space suit with its self-contained oxygen pack, squeezed through the hatch into the airlock and sealed himself in. He then opened the hatch at the other end and gently crawled out of the barrel-shaped airlock into the emptiness of space.

'I looked through the light filter and through the glass of the space suit,' he recalled.'The stars were bright and unblinking. I could distinguish clearly the Black Sea with its very black water, and the Caucasian outline. I saw the mountains with their snow tops looking through the cloud blanket covering the Caucasian Range. The Volga appeared

Left to right: **Commander of Voskhod 1 Colonel-Engineer Vladimir Komarov, physician Boris Yegorov and scientist Konstantin Feoktistov, photographed in 1964 before their flight. Komarov was selected as the pilot for the ill-fated first flight of the Soyuz 1 spacecraft three years later, and was the first man killed during a space flight when his parachute snarled on landing.**

and disappeared. The Urals floated under us. I saw the Ob and the Yenisey.'

The bedazzled Leonov spent 10 minutes outside the spacecraft while Belyayev filmed him for Soviet television. He floated freely as far as 15 feet from *Diamond,* attached to the ship only by a tether line and communications cable. It took him 8 minutes to squeeze back into the airlock and finally into the spacecraft. Once Leonov was back inside the capsule, the two cosmonauts jettisoned the airlock and excitedly discussed their adventure with ground control and the new Soviet leadership, basking in the glory of being the first Soviet manned space flight of the post-Khrushchev era.

Everything about Voskhod 2 had gone well until it came time to return to earth on the spacecraft's seventeenth orbit. The automatic re-entry sequence malfunctioned, and Soviet ground control reluctantly gave the go-ahead for Belyayev and Leonov to make the Soviet space program's first manual re-entry. It had to be delayed to the eighteenth orbit, which meant that Voskhod 2 would come down 1200 miles off target. At 11:02 am on 19 March 1965, after 26 hours and 2 minutes in space, *Diamond's* parachutes brought it down in a remote forest deep in the rugged snow-covered Urals. The scene that greeted the two men when they emerged from the capsule 5 minutes later was scarcely more hospitable than that which had received Leonov briefly in space.

The two were located by a helicopter 2½ hours later, but the terrain was too rugged for it to land and the men were forced to spend the night on the lonely hillside with the supplies dropped by the helicopter. The following day a rescue party was landed by helicopter at the nearest level spot about 12 miles away, but the rescuers did not reach the stranded cosmonauts until midday. The group requested another supply drop in order to spend a second night near *Diamond* and use the entire next day to hike to where helicopters could land. Leonov and Belyayev finally reached civilization on 21 March, having spent twice as long in the wilderness of the Urals as they had in the wilderness of space.

As intended, that final flight of the short Voskhod series had demonstrated man's ability to function outside a spacecraft in space, but it had accidentally proven to the Soviet controllers a lesson that NASA had already learned—that in a manned spacecraft, the men aboard can be counted on to reliably 'fly' the vehicle if automated systems should fail. One of the features that distinguished Voskhod from Gemini was that the former used manual control only as a backup system for extreme emergencies; the Gemini spacecraft were designed to be flown by the crew. It was their reluctance to use their cosmonauts as pilots to a higher degree that would cost the Soviets their impressive lead in the space race.

THE MIDDLE YEARS

Two days after Alexei Leonov and Pavel Belyayev trudged out of the Urals, the Americans launched their first Gemini mission. It was not until after the conclusion of the 10-flight Gemini series that the Soviet Union resumed manned space flight. During those two years of absence the Soviets developed a new all-purpose spacecraft called Soyuz (Union) as well as new spacecraft procedures, and they trained new cosmonauts.

When Voskhod ended the Soviet Union was clearly ahead in the space race. The Soviets had flown 11 men in space to the American 6. They had flown the only two multiple-crew space flights and Leonov had been the only man to walk in space. The Soviets had accumulated 504 man hours in space and the Americans still had just 54.

Of the 12 men in the first cosmonaut group, eight had made space flights during Vostok and Voskhod. Five remained among the corps of cosmonauts who would fly during Soyuz. Pavel Belyayev, pilot of Voskhod 2, died in January 1970 of internal troubles without making a

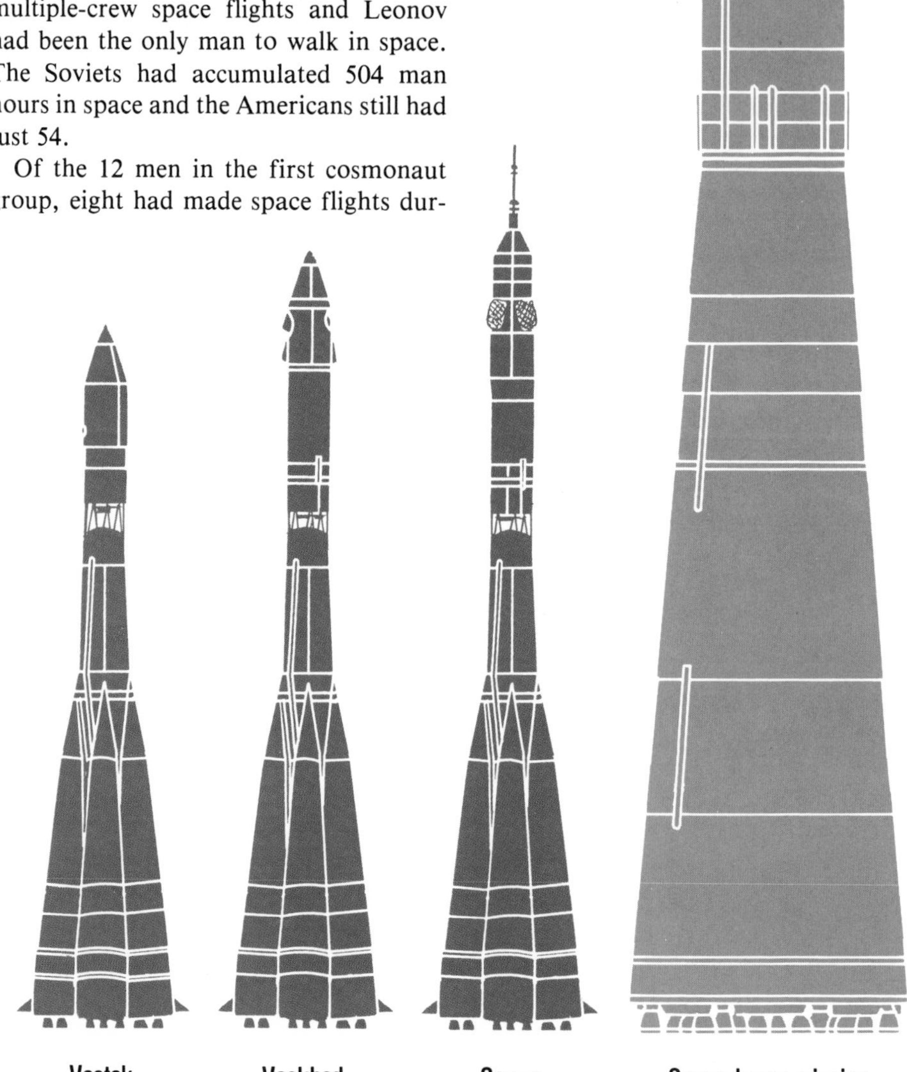

Vostok (D Class rocket) 1961-1963

Voskhod (D Class rocket) 1964-1965

Soyuz (D Class rocket) 1967-present

Soyuz lunar mission (G Class rocket) scheduled for 1969 but never flown second flight. Valeri Bykovsky flew in Vostok 5 and made his second flight 13 years later aboard Soyuz 22. Yuri Gagarin, the first man in space, stayed with the cosmonaut program and almost certainly would have flown again during the Soyuz program had he not been killed in the crash of a MiG-15 trainer during a routine flight near Star City on 27 March 1968. In the years after his space flight Gagarin had become almost an ambassador for the Soviet space program. It is interesting to speculate that Gagarin, aged 41, might have been a likely choice for the Soyuz crew during the 1975 Apollo-Soyuz rendezvous. Gagarin's ashes are buried in the Kremlin wall and the Soviet Cosmonaut Training Center and a lunar crater bear his name.

Vladimir Komarov, commander of Voskhod 1, was the first man killed in space when he piloted the ill-fated Soyuz 1 mission in 1967. Alexei Leonov, the first man to walk in space during Voskhod 2, commanded Soyuz 19, which docked with the American Apollo in the 1975 Apollo-Soyuz Test Project. Andrian Nikolayev flew in Vostok 3 and later married Soyuz 6 cosmonaut Valentina Tereshkova. He remained in the cosmonaut program to command Soyuz 9 in 1970. Pavel Popovich, the first cosmonaut chosen and the fourth to fly, remained with the cosmonaut program to command Soyuz 14 in 1974. Gherman Titov, the second cosmonaut in space, developed inner ear problems that may have been attributable to his flight in Soyuz 2, and he never flew in space a second time.

Of the 4 other men chosen in the first 12 who didn't fly during Vostok or Voskhod, all saw service aboard a Soyuz spacecraft. Viktor Gorbatko flew in Soyuz 7 in 1979 and commanded Soyuz 24 eight years later. Yevgeni Khrunov flew in Soyuz 5 in 1979 and commanded Soyuz 18. Georgi Shonin commanded Soyuz 6 in 1969. Boris Volynov commanded both the flight of Soyuz 5 in 1969 and Soyuz 21 in 1976.

Among the personnel who flew in either Vostok or Voskhod, three were not part of the original cosmonaut group and none of them was ever to make another space flight. Konstantin Feoktistov, the spacecraft designer, and Dr Boris Yegorov, the physician who had flown aboard Voskhod 1 with little cosmonaut training, were dropped from the roster as the Soviet Union realized that space flights were better made with trained cosmonauts. Valentina Tereshkova, the sixth cosmonaut and the first woman in space, married Andrian Nikolayev with whom she'd carried on a romance prior to her space flight. The couple were married in November 1963, five months after her flight, in a wedding that found Nikita Khrushchev serving as toastmaster. She gave birth to a daughter, Yelena, in June 1964. Soviet scientists monitored Yelena's early development, keen to measure any possible effects that might manifest themselves in the child of two people who'd flown in space. While Nikolayev remained on flight status as a cosmonaut, Valentina completed her technical training and retired to a desk job at the Soviet Cosmonaut Training Center, later renamed for Yuri Gagarin. In 1967 she was elected a member of the Supreme Soviet from Yaroslavl and in 1974 she became a member of the Presidium of the Supreme Soviet.

SOYUZ

The Soyuz (Union) was the Soviet Union's third manned type of spacecraft, and like its predecessors it was designed by engineer Sergei Korolev. It is larger than Vostok or Voskhod but not significantly, and at 33 feet, it is slightly shorter than the Apollo CSM. It has a diameter of between 7 and 8 feet, or about two thirds that of the American Apollo CSM. Soyuz is composed of three modules: a barrel-shaped Instrument Module (IM) that corresponds in placement and function to the Apollo SM; a dome-shaped Descent, or re-entry, Module (DM), a ballistic re-entry capsule like the Apollo CM and a spherical Orbital Module (OM) that is used as the 'work room' while the cosmonauts are in space and which is discarded before re-entry. The OM had no equivalent in the American Apollo, but because the overall Soyuz diameter is less than that of Apollo, the OM/DM combination serve to give the cosmonauts roughly the same internal volume as the Apollo CM.

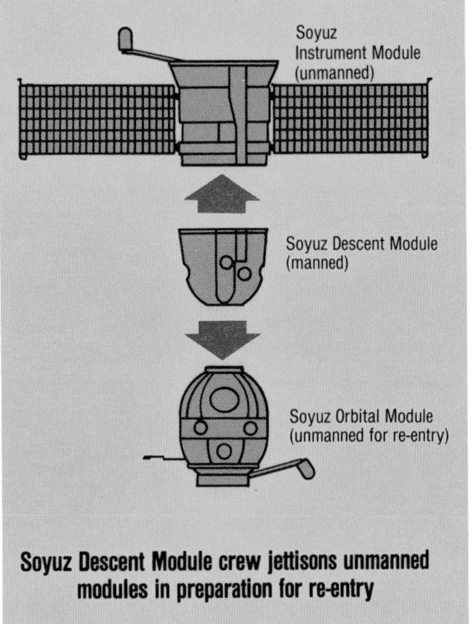

Soyuz Descent Module crew jettisons unmanned modules in preparation for re-entry

Soyuz and Apollo were the first spacecraft to give their respective countries a real operational capability in space that went beyond the idea of merely putting people into space. Both spacecraft had more maneuverability and were capable of longer flights than their predecessors, and both were designed to be able to rendezvous and dock with another spacecraft. While Apollo was designed specifically for a lunar mission, Soyuz was designed to be a workhorse spacecraft that could perform a variety of missions over a long period of time. A specified number of Apollo spacecraft were built and they made all their flights within a period of seven years. On the other hand, the Soyuz assembly line remained open for two years and the original Soyuz series was not completely phased out in favor of the Soyuz T-series until 1981.

Soyuz was also designed in conjunction with a series of space stations. Called Salyut (Salute), these earth-orbit space stations are about half the size of the American Skylab and are about 60 feet long, roughly the same size as the Space Shuttle payload bay. Salyut is similar in size and function to the European Space Agency's Spacelab. Spacelab is carried entirely within the Space Shuttle payload bay, however, and Salyut is launched independently as an unmanned spacecraft like the American Skylab. Soyuz spacecraft are used to fly the Salyut crews to and from their space stations.

While Soyuz has come to be associated strictly with operations in earth orbit, particularly in conjunction with Salyut, it should be recalled that in the beginning Soyuz was the centerpiece of the Soviet manned lunar landing program. That project was reluctantly abandoned in 1969 when it became clear that the Americans would get to the moon first.

On 23 April 1967 Vladimir Komarov was the test pilot for Soyuz 1. The former Voskhod 1 commander was the first experienced cosmonaut to return to space and the first cosmonaut to go into space in 25 months. The Soyuz DM had been designed to carry a three-man crew, but as the Soyuz 1 mission was a test flight, only the pilot was required. Things went well for Komarov up to his fifteenth orbit, when malfunctions began to occur in the retro-rocket systems used to maneuver the spacecraft. He tried to align the spacecraft for a re-entry on the seventeenth orbit, but failed. He succeeded on the

Cosmonaut Alexei Yeliseyev took part in the Soyuz 4/Soyuz 5 double launch spectacular that offset the gloom associated with the Soyuz 1 disaster.

eighteenth, but because of the problems with the retro-rockets, he couldn't stop the DM from spinning after re-entry. The huge parachute designed to slow the capsule's fall to earth deployed properly, but as the spacecraft continued to spin, the parachute cords became twisted and the parachute deflated. With nothing to brake its fall, the Soyuz 1 DM hit the ground at more than 200 mph and burst into flames. Komarov was the first man to be killed during a space flight.

The Soyuz 1 disaster came just three months after America lost three astronauts during preflight tests of the Apollo 1 spacecraft. In both countries there was a sober reassessment of the breakneck speed with which the respective space programs were pursuing the space race. Though several flights had been scheduled by both countries, Soyuz 1 was the only manned space flight of 1967 and the only such space flight for almost two years. Neither country launched another man into space until the last quarter of 1968.

The lost time struck a serious blow to Soviet hopes to obtain the kind of rendezvous and docking experience that the United States had gained in 1966 during Gemini. Although the United States had already flown missions in which the astronauts controlled the spacecraft manually, the Soviets decided to try it first by remote control using unmanned Soyuz spacecraft. In October 1967 two such Soyuz capsules were launched under the designations Cosmos 186 and Cosmos 188 (the Cosmos name is a catch-all designation used by the Soviet Union for unmanned spacecraft of many unrelated types). The rendezvous and docking between Cosmos 186 and Cosmos 188 was successful and the spacecraft were recovered intact. The mission could have been done with cosmonauts aboard, but the Soviets decided to try it once again by remote control. In April 1968 two more unmanned Soyuz spacecraft were launched (Cosmos 212 and Cosmos 213) and once again the rendezvous and docking were successful. This was the green light for the first rendezvous and docking attempt by a manned Soviet spacecraft. Soyuz 2 was launched on 25 October 1968 as an unmanned docking target and Soyuz 3 followed the next day with Georgi Beregovoi at the controls. A member of the cosmonaut corps since 1964, the 47-year-old Beregovoi was the oldest man yet to fly in space. He was able to maneuver his spacecraft to within 500 feet of the target but he was unable to dock with it. Though the official reports denied that docking had been part of the plan, there was great disappointment.

In the meantime, Soviet engineers were busily putting what they hoped would be the final touches on the other hardware needed to send the first cosmonauts to the moon. This involved developing a G-Class launch vehicle that would have more than 10 times the thrust of the A-Class rockets used for all the earlier Soviet manned space flights and 5 times the thrust of the D-Class rockets used for unmanned planetary probes. The G-Class rocket would be the equivalent of the Saturn 5 that the Americans planned to use for their Apollo lunar missions. However, while Saturn 5 development was proceeding on schedule, the G-Class rocket was falling behind. By early 1968, it was clear that the Americans would reach the moon with the Saturn 5 before the G-Class would be operational.

While the G-Class rocket would be needed to support a lunar *landing* attempt, Soviet engineers reasoned that they might be able to put a manned Soyuz spacecraft into lunar *orbit* using a D-Class launch vehicle. Using such a launch vehicle, a Soyuz spacecraft was successfully placed into deep space in March 1968 under the designation Zond 4. Another unmanned Soyuz was launched under the designation Zond 5 on 15 September 1968. This time the spacecraft reached the moon

and looped around it at an altitude of 1100 miles. On 22 September the Zond 5 splashed down in the Indian Ocean and was successfully recovered by the Soviet navy. The experiment was successfully repeated between 10 and 17 November, and Zond 6 was successfully recovered on land within the Soviet Union. The Americans had launched their first manned Apollo spacecraft into earth orbit in October, but the Soviet Union had sent to the moon two spacecraft that were capable of carrying a human being. It seemed for a brief moment in the autumn of 1968 as though the first man to orbit the moon, like the first man to orbit the earth, would be a cosmonaut.

On Christmas Eve 1968, however, the race to put a man in orbit around the moon ended when America's Apollo 8 astronauts watched the earth dip below the lunar horizon. The Soviet manned space program lacked the capability to land on the lunar surface, and having lost the race to lunar orbit, it changed gears. The moon race abandoned, the USSR refocused its emphasis on manned space activities in earth orbit.

On 16 January 1969, the long-awaited first docking between two manned Soyuz spacecraft finally took place. Soyuz 4, piloted by Vladimir Shatalov, had been launched on 14 January and followed the next day by Soyuz 5. The latter was the first Soyuz to carry a full three-man crew. It included Boris Volynov as commander, Alexei Yeliseyev as flight engineer and Yevgeni Khrunov as research engineer. For the docking Shatalov took manual control of Soyuz 4 at a distance of about 300 feet. Once the two spacecraft were linked, Khrunov and Yeliseyev donned space suits and made their way to Soyuz 4's OM. After 4 hours, the two spacecraft were detached and Soyuz 4 returned to earth, leaving Volynov alone in Soyuz 5. The exercise demonstrated the capability of one spacecraft to rescue personnel from another. Volynov returned to earth on 18 January after 72 hours and 46 minutes in space, an hour and 32 minutes longer than Soyuz 4.

The next Soyuz launch did not take place until October 1969, and was designed to be a 'space spectacular' in the style of the Soviet space program of the early 1960s. For the first time in history three manned spacecraft would be in orbit simultaneously. Soyuz 6 was launched on 11 October with Georgi Shonin and Valeri Kubasov; Soyuz 7 followed on the 12th with Anatoli Filipchenko, Viktor Gorbatko and Vladislav Volkov. The next day Soyuz 8 was launched with Alexei Yeliseyev and overall mission commander Vladimir Shatalov, both veterans of the Soyuz 4/Soyuz 5 rendezvous in January. Though the spacecraft were maneuvered manually while in orbit, no docking maneuvers took place. Aboard Soyuz 6 Shonin and Kubasov sealed off their OM and conducted some remote control experiments in zero-gravity welding.

With choreographed precision, the three spacecraft landed one day apart with almost identical mission durations. Soyuz 6 was in space for 118 hours and 42 minutes. The other two had identical flight times, just one minute shorter than Soyuz 6.

Mission duration was the raison d'être for Soyuz 9, launched on 1 June 1970 with Vitali Sevastyanov and Andrian Nikolayev. Commanded by Vostok 3 veteran Nikolayev, Soyuz 9 set a duration record of 424 hours, beating the 1965 record of 330 hours set by Gemini 7. While in space Nikolayev spoke by radio to his daughter Yelena on the occasion of her sixth birthday, as well as to his wife, Valentina Tereshkova, the first woman in space.

On 20 April 1971, the first of the Salyut space stations was launched atop a D-Class rocket, and three days later Soyuz 10 was launched with a three-man crew to rendezvous with it. Commanded by Vladimir Shatalov, who was commanding an unprecedented third space mission, Soyuz 10 also included first-time cosmonaut Nikolai Rukavishnikov and Alexei Yeliseyev, a veteran of Soyuz 5 and Soyuz 8. Using manual controls, Shatalov was able to dock with the space station on the twelfth orbit of Soyuz 10. They remained attached to the space station for over 5 hours, but did not enter the space station. After detaching themselves from Salyut they remained in space for 16 hours while Rukavishnikov recovered from his space sickness, which had been extremely severe during the early part of the flight and may have played a role in the decision not to enter Salyut for a long-duration visit. They returned to earth after 48 hours and 45 minutes in space. The flight of Soyuz 10 was the last for Vladimir Shatalov. Promoted to the rank of major general, he was made director of cosmonaut training and became a major figure in charting the future course of the Soviet manned space program.

Less than two months later, the crew of Soyuz 11 was knocking at the door of Salyut 1. Launched on 6 June, the second crew to rendezvous with the space station included Georgi Dobrovolsky, Vladislav Volkov and Viktor Patsayev. Of the group, only flight engineer Volkov had been in space before. They docked with Salyut on the second day and set up housekeeping in the space station for what would be a 23-day stay. After completing their assigned projects and having set a new record for duration in space, the crew locked up the space station and returned to Soyuz. The automated re-entry seemed to go like clockwork. The parachute set the spacecraft down gently after 570 hours in space, but inside something had gone dreadfully wrong. One of the valves designed to open after the spacecraft re-entered the earth's atmosphere to equalize air pressure inside and out had accidently opened while Soyuz 11 was still in space. The entire atmosphere of the spacecraft had been sucked into the void

The crew of Soyuz 11 — commander Georgi Dobrovolsky (*lying down*), test engineer Viktor Patsayev and flight engineer Vladislav Volkov — were killed in 1971 when a valve in their spacecraft malfunctioned.

of space in a single screeching instant before the crew had a chance to react. They had been dead before the automated re-entry sequence even began.

Once again, as with Soyuz 1, fate had dealt a cruel blow to the Soviet space program just as Salyut 1 had become operational. A second mission to the space station was canceled because the valve system on future Soyuz spacecraft could not be modified before Salyut 1's orbit decayed and it burned up in re-entry on 11 October 1971. It was nearly two years later, on the eve of the American Skylab launch, that another Salyut was launched. There were actually two Salyuts launched in the six weeks before the United States launched its space station, but neither of them reached a stable orbit. Salyut 2 was launched on 3 April 1973, but was lost on 28 May. The Salyut 2 backup, designated Cosmos 557, was launched on 11 May but lost on 22 May.

In the meantime, Soviet manned space flights were suspended for over two years because of the Soyuz 11 disaster. By the time the flight of Soyuz 12 took place on 27 September 1973, a number of important changes had been made. The pressure equalization valves had been replaced, of course, but the most obvious modification was that Soyuz was no longer a three-man spacecraft. The configuration had been altered for a two-man crew because a two-man crew would have the room within the Soyuz DM to wear space suits during re-entry. The two crewmen were Oleg Makarov and Dr Vasili Lazarev, the second physician to fly as a cosmonaut. The purpose of the flight was to evaluate performance of the modified Soyuz, so it lasted a relatively short 47 hours and 16 minutes.

The 189-hour flight of Soyuz 13 was launched on 18 December 1973 while the American Skylab space station was manned. However, Pyotr Klimuk and Valentin Lebedev aboard the Soyuz did not sight Skylab and didn't communicate with the Americans because their respective radios were not tuned to the same frequency.

The launch of Soyuz 14 on 3 July 1974 followed the successful launch of the Salyut 3 space station by eight days. Yuri Artyukhin and Vostok 4 veteran Pavel Popovich reached the station 26 hours after launch and docked successfully. The two men spent 377 hours and 30 minutes in space conducting scientific observa-

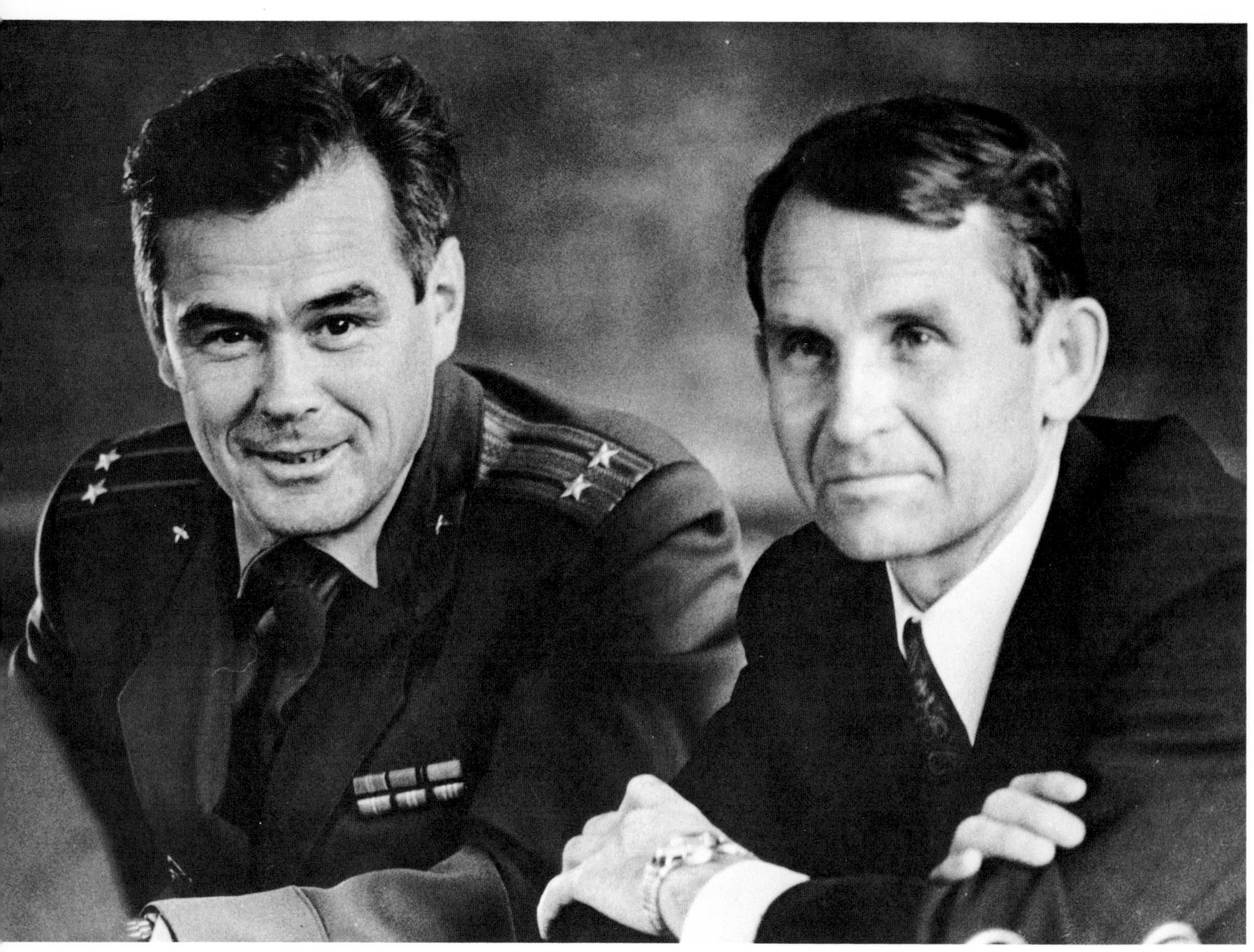

tions of the earth and working on a project to evaluate Salyut as a military reconnaissance platform. They ended their flight six days short of the duration record set by the last crew to occupy a Salyut, thankful that their flight ended less eventfully.

A month later, on 26 August, Soyuz 15 was launched for the dual purpose of a month-long operational stay aboard Salyut 3 and a test of an automatic docking system that would allow future cosmonauts to resupply Salyut space stations using unmanned cargo tugs. Gennadi Sarafanov and Lev Demin (the first grandfather in space) reached Salyut on the sixteenth orbit, but a failure of the automatic docking system sent Soyuz 15 reeling out of control and forced an emergency termination of the flight after a disappointing 48 hours and 12 minutes.

Soyuz 16, launched on 2 December 1974, was a rehearsal for the upcoming Soyuz 19 mission, and cosmonauts Anatoli Filipchenko and Nikolai Rukavishnikov made no attempt to reach Salyut 3 during the 147 hour and 24 minute flight.

Soyuz 17 was launched just after midnight on 11 January 1975 to rendezvous with Salyut 4, which had been launched 16 days before. Alexei Gubarev and Georgi Grechko reached the new space station and took up their positions for a 29-day mission. It was a new record for a Soviet Salyut crew, but still short of the 84-day record set by the American Skylab 4 astronauts.

On 5 April 1975 Dr Vasily Lazarev and Oleg Makarov, both veterans of Soyuz 12 two years before, were launched on what was to have been Soyuz 18, a 60-day stay aboard Salyut 4. Moments after the launch, however, the third stage of the launch vehicle failed and the automatic abort system brought the crew down safely near Gorno-Altaisk in Siberia. Despite fears that they might land in China and the fact that it took rescuers a day to find them, the two cosmonauts survived and were reported to be 'feeling well.'

A new Soyuz 18 mission was successfully launched six weeks later on 24 May 1975, this time with Pyotr Klimuk and Vitali Sevastyanov. Klinuk was a veteran

Above: **Design engineer Oleg Makarov accompanied commander Lt-Col Vasili Lazarev (*left*) on Soyuz 12 in 1973. Their next flight, aboard Soyuz 18 in 1975, was aborted after launch and the two men ended up in Siberia.**

Right: **Soyuz 16 commander Anatoli Filipchenko (*left*) and flight engineer Nikolai Rukavishnikov outside the OM of the Soyuz simulator.**

of Soyuz 13 and Sevastyanov, who had flown on Soyuz 9, had become a popular television commentator on the program 'Man, Earth and Universe' in the five years since his earlier space flight. The Soyuz 18 was to provide a new platform for his commentaries. The two cosmonauts set a Soviet duration record of 63 days, of which 61 were spent aboard Salyut. It was while they were in orbit that the historic rendezvous between Soyuz 19 and the last American Apollo mission took place.

Soyuz 19 was the most widely publicized of any Soyuz flight. It had been in the planning stages since 24 May 1972, when Soviet Premier Alexei Kosygin and American President Richard Nixon signed

СОЮЗ

СОЮЗ
APOLLO
VII-1975

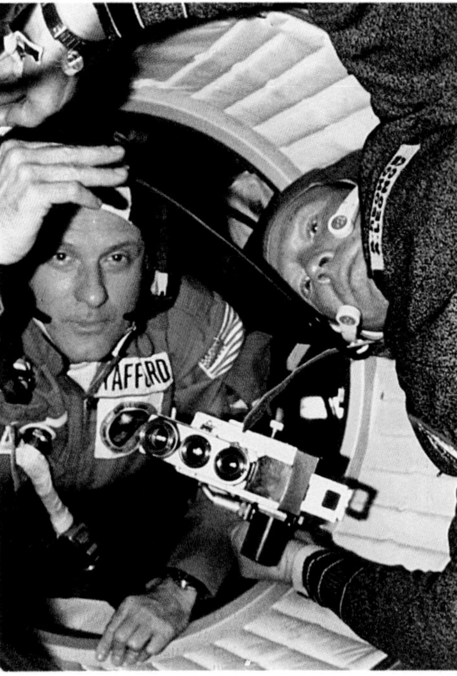

Soyuz 19 docked with Apollo in the July 1975 earth-orbit mission during the joint Apollo-Soyuz Test Project. Soyuz 19 commander Alexei Leonov greets US commander general Thomas Stafford (*above*) in the docking module. *Left:* Engineer Valeri Kubasov at work in the Soyuz Orbiter module.

a letter of understanding that called for a joint US-Soviet space mission. One of the ideas discussed was for an Apollo to visit a Salyut space station or to have a Soyuz visit Skylab, but eventually the plan evolved for Apollo and Soyuz spacecraft to rendezvous and dock with one another in earth orbit. Technicians from both countries went to work on the logistics of integrating communications and developing the hardware needed to dock the two dissimilar spacecraft. In the meantime, the two nations named the crews for their respective spacecraft.

The Apollo was manned by Gen Tom Stafford, a veteran of two Gemini and one previous Apollo mission, and Vance Brand and Deke Slayton, both of whom were making their first flight. Slayton had been one of the original seven American astronauts but had not flown earlier because of a heart condition. The Soviet crew for Soyuz 19, or the Apollo-Soyuz Test Project (ASTP) as the Americans called it, was Alexei Leonov, commander of Voskhod 2 and Valeri Kubasov, the flight engineer aboard Soyuz 6. The back-up cosmonauts were Anatoli Filipchenko and Nikolai Rukavishnikov, who had flown on Soyuz 7 and Soyuz 10, respectively. They had flown together on Soyuz 16, the December 1974 Soviet rehearsal for the Apollo-Soyuz rendezvous mission.

Both spacecraft were launched on 15 July 1975, half a world apart, with Soyuz 19 preceding Apollo by 7 hours and 30

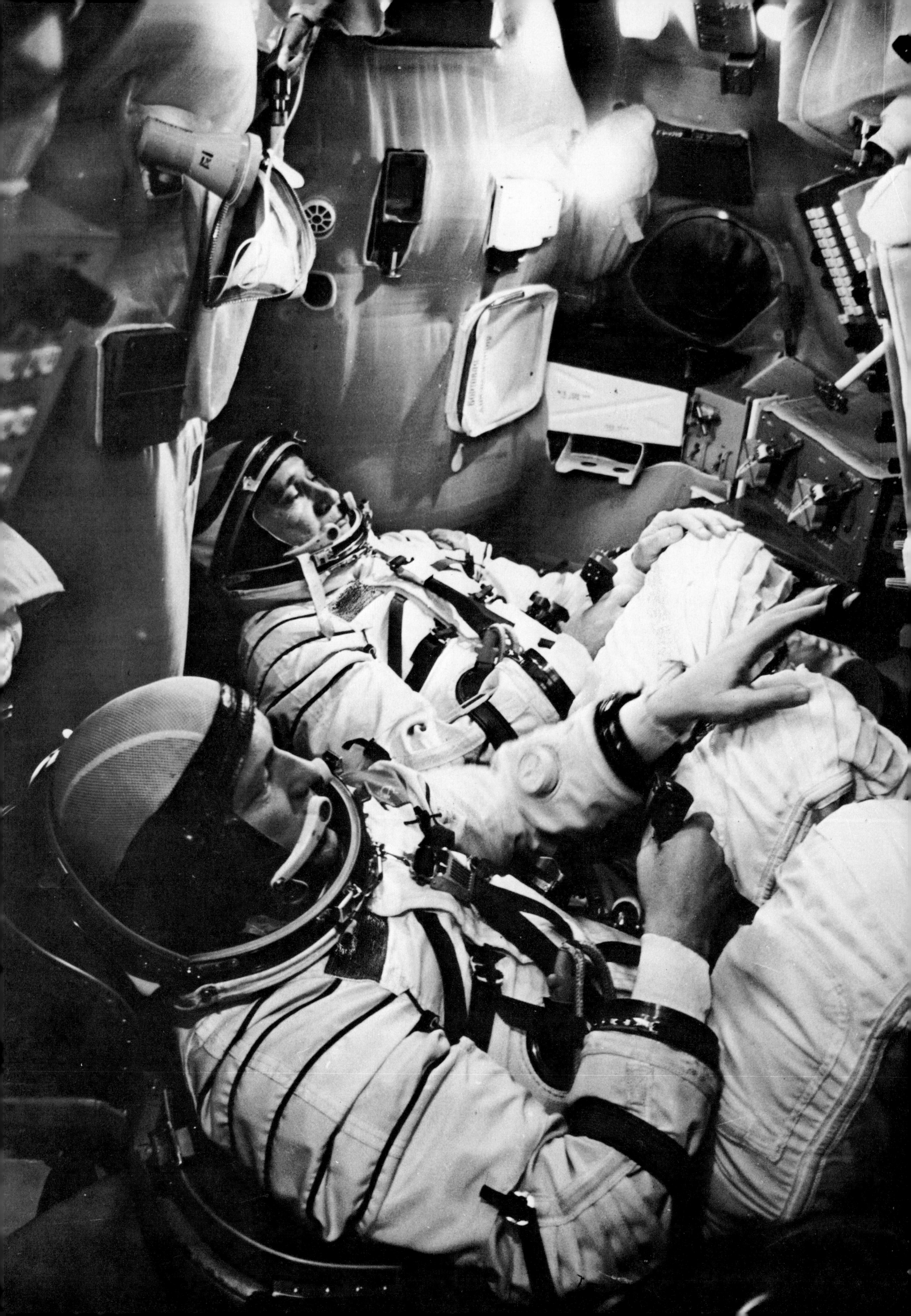

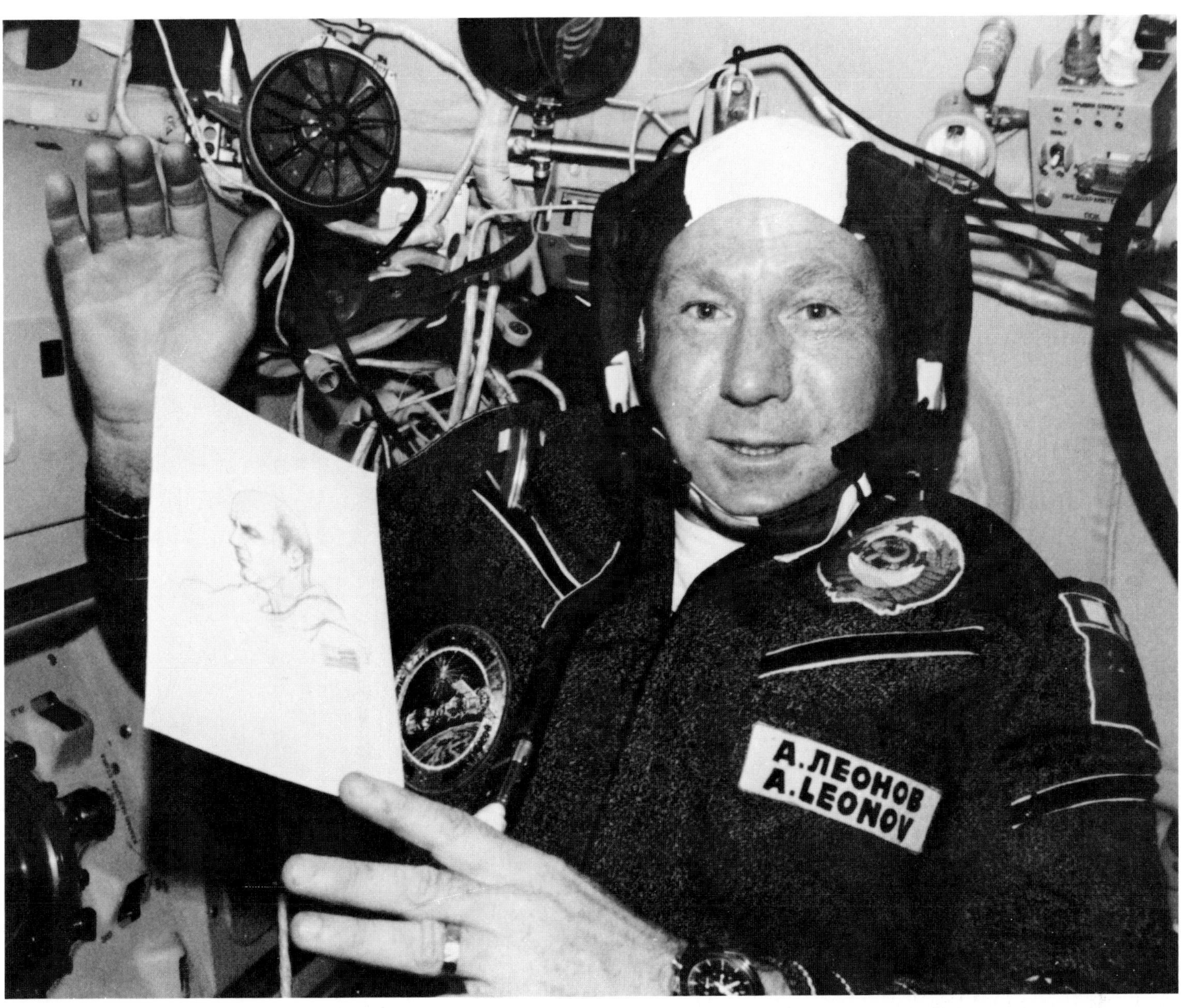

Above: **Soyuz 19 commander Alexei Leonov, an accomplished draftsman, with a portrait he drew of Thomas Stafford, who visited the spacecraft while it was docked with Apollo.**

Left: **Soyuz 16 crewmen Anatoli Filipchenko (*rear*) and Nikolai Rukavishnikov in the Soyuz DM training module. The DM was originally designed for a crew of three without space suits.**

minutes. The two spacecraft made their historic rendezvous 51 hours after the Soyuz launch, on 17 July. At 51 hours and 55 minutes, the two spacecraft docked. Stafford and Slayton entered the DM that Apollo had carried, and equalized the pressure from that common to Apollo to one that would be common to Soyuz. Two hours and 55 minutes after docking, the hatch between the DM and the Soyuz OM was opened and American astronauts shook hands with Soviet cosmonauts in space for the first time. During 18 July the two crews exchanged visits to one another's spacecraft and carried out joint activities. The two spacecraft were detached on 19 July after nearly 44 hours.

Soyuz 19 returned to earth on 21 July after 142 hours and 31 minutes in space, landing in Kazakhstan. Apollo landed near Hawaii on 24 July after 217 hours and 23 minutes. Soyuz 18, which had been docked with Salyut 4 during the entire flight of Soyuz 19, returned to earth on 26 July, five days after Soyuz 19. These three landings in late July of 1975 brought the space programs of the two nations to yet another turning point. That month saw the last American manned space flight for six years and the last Soviet manned flight for over a year.

It was not the last Soyuz flight for that year, however. On 17 November 1975 Soyuz 20 was launched without a crew and guided to Salyut 4, where it successfully docked with the space station. This was the first successful test of the Soyuz as an unmanned cargo tug using the automatic docking system that had caused so much trouble for Sarafanov and Demin when they tried unsuccessfully to use it to dock with Salyut 3 during the Soyuz 15 flight a year before. Without a crew present aboard the space station when Soyuz 20 arrived, it could not retrieve supplies from the Salyut. Soyuz 20, the first unmanned Soyuz spacecraft to actually carry a Soyuz designation, was undocked and returned to earth on 16 February 1976.

After four years of disappointing results, it finally appeared that Salyut operations were becoming routine. In the beginning it had been hoped that during its six-month lifespan, each Salyut could be used to support two or perhaps even three crews. However, out of the first four Salyut space stations launched into space (including the Salyut 2 backup), only two had been used by crews, and once each in both cases. Salyut 4 had supported two crews for a total of 29 days, and had also served in the unmanned supply tug experiment. Excluding the Apollo-Soyuz docking, manned Soviet spacecraft

had conducted docking maneuvers only six times, and two of those efforts involved Salyut 4. The Salyut 4 space station also managed to remain in orbit until February 1977, more than two years after it was launched and over a year after it was last used, demonstrating a durability not apparent in its predecessors.

Salyut 5 was launched on 22 June 1976, while Salyut 4 was still in orbit. Soyuz 21, with Boris Volynov and Vitali Zholobov aboard, were launched on 6 July 1976 and reached the space station the following day for a 49-day sojourn in outer space. The flights of Soyuz 22 and Soyuz 23 were much shorter flights and did not visit Salyut. Valeri Bykovsky, on his first flight since Vostok 3, joined Vladimir Aksyonov on the eight-day military reconnaissance flight of Soyuz 22 launched on 15 September. During this flight a multispectral camera developed by Zeiss in East Germany was used to observe NATO exercises in Western Europe as well as to study geologic features in East Germany and the Soviet Union. Soyuz 22 was the last Soyuz flight whose mission plan did not involve a rendezvous with a space station.

Salyut 23, launched on 14 October 1976 with Vyacheslav Zudov and Valeri Rozhdestvensky, was intended to dock with Salyut 5 and to perhaps go for the duration record still held by the American Skylab 4 crew. Even before the two first-time cosmonauts reached the space station they began to suffer guidance problems, so the mission was aborted and Soyuz 23 returned to earth after 48 hours. The spacecraft came down in Lake Tengiz near Tselinograd in the middle of a blinding snowstorm, and was the first water landing of a Soviet manned spacecraft.

Above: **Soyuz 21 commander Boris Volynov at the Gagarin training center, photographed in 1976 after a session in the centrifuge as he was greeted with a bouquet of flowers by one of the center's nurses.** ***Right:*** **Vladimir Aksyonov works with the multizone MKF-6 camera in the 'photo department' of the orbital module of Soyuz 22.**

Soyuz 24, launched on 7 February 1977, carried the Soyuz 23 flight plan and the two men who had been the backup crew for Soyuz 23, Viktor Gorbatko and Yuri Glazkov. They were able to dock successfully with Salyut 5 the following day for a 17-day visit and to continue the research projects begun by the Soyuz 21 cosmonauts in July 1976. By this time Salyut 5 had been occupied twice on three attempts for a total of 65 days, compared to 92 days in two visits for Salyut 4, 14 days on one visit for Salyut 3 and 18 days on the single visit for Salyut 1.

A NEW ERA IN SPACE

On 1 October 1977 Lt Gen Vladimir Shatalov, the former cosmonaut and current head of the cosmonaut program, announced that 'future (space) stations much larger than the present Salyuts with crews of 12 to 20 people' would eventually be deployed by the Soviet Union to help develop and produce 'superpure metals, monocrystals, vaccines and other useful products.'

Even as the general spoke a new space station, launched on 29 September, had already taken up its position. Designated Salyut 6, the space station was a new generation long-duration space station and a far cry from the likes of Salyut 1 and Salyut 3. For the first time in history a space station was equipped with two docking ports to allow more than one spacecraft to service it or be served by it. With Salyut 6 a crew could dock at one of the ports and leave the second one free for a supply tug or for a second spacecraft. This opened the way for the possibility of a continuously manned space station, a permanent presence in space.

The immediate plan called for a 'host' crew to spend durations of about three months in Salyut 6, with two or three 'guest' crews visiting them for one-week periods during that time. In between the visits from the guest crews, unmanned Progress supply tugs would be sent up carrying food, fuel and other supplies to support the crews. The engines of the Progress tugs would also be used to boost the orbit of Salyut, thus extending its service life.

On 9 October Soyuz 25's first attempt to dock with the new space station failed, and Valeri Ryumin and Vladimir Kovalyonok reluctantly set a course for home after 49 hours in space. On 10 December, however, Soyuz 26 was launched for a successful docking with the space station. Noting that Soyuz 25 had trouble with Salyut's forward docking port, Yuri Romanenko and Georgi Grechko used the aft port and found it operable. On 20 December they ventured outside into space for an 88-minute EVA to check and clear the problem with the forward docking port.

On 11 January 1978, Vladimir Dzhanibekov and Oleg Makarov arrived at Salyut 6 aboard Soyuz 27, and for the first time there were two crews aboard a Salyut space station. The Soyuz 27 cosmonauts remained aboard the space station for six days before returning to earth in the Soyuz 26 spacecraft. On 22 January, Progress 1, an unmanned supply tug and successor to the Soyuz 20 experiment, arrived at Salyut with 2205 pounds of propellant and 2866 pounds of food, water, compressed air and other supplies. By 7 February Progress 1 had been filled with two months' worth of garbage and was sent back to earth for a fiery re-entry over the Pacific.

On 3 March Romanenko and Grechko received their second group of visitors

These diagrams show typical examples of a Soyuz spacecraft docking with an unmanned (*below*) and with a manned (*bottom*) Salyut space station. *Right:* In June 1978 Vladimir Kovalyonok and Alexander Ivanchenkov docked their Soyuz 29 spacecraft with Salyut 6 and set a record as the first flight to exceed 100 days in space.

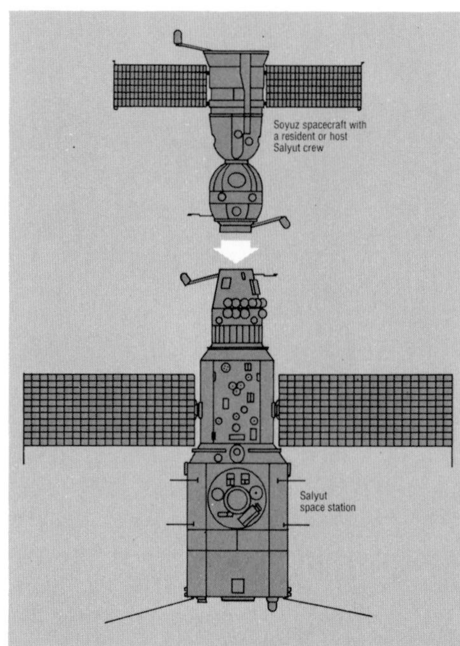

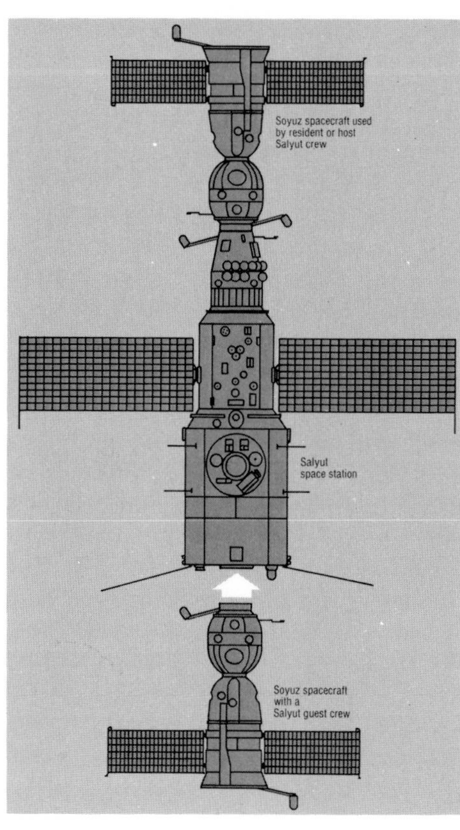

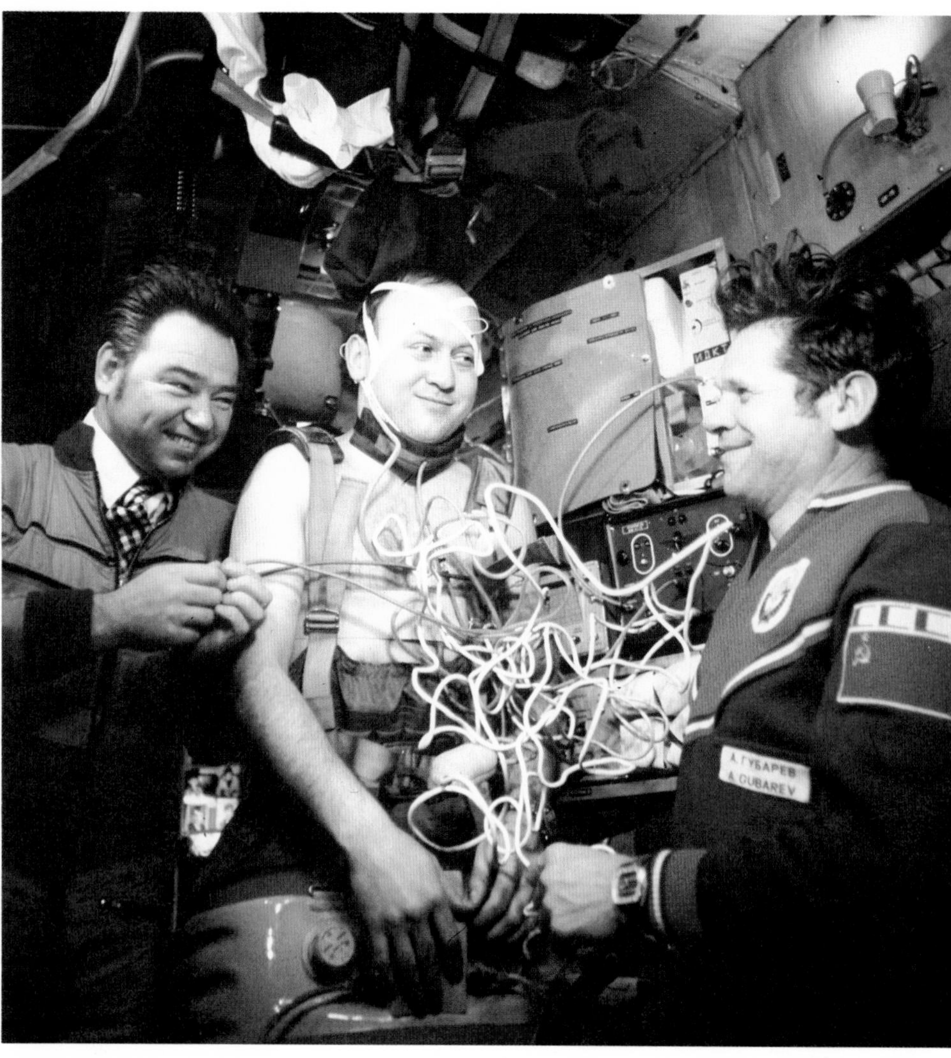

Above: **Georgi Gretchko (*left*) and Alexei Gubarov help Vladimir Remek (*center*) during a medical experiment aboard Salyut 6. A Soyuz spacecraft undocking from a Salyut space station (*below left*) and an unmanned progress supply tug docking with a manned Salyut space station (*below right*). *Right:* Soyuz 29 commander Vladimir Kovalyonok relaxes.**

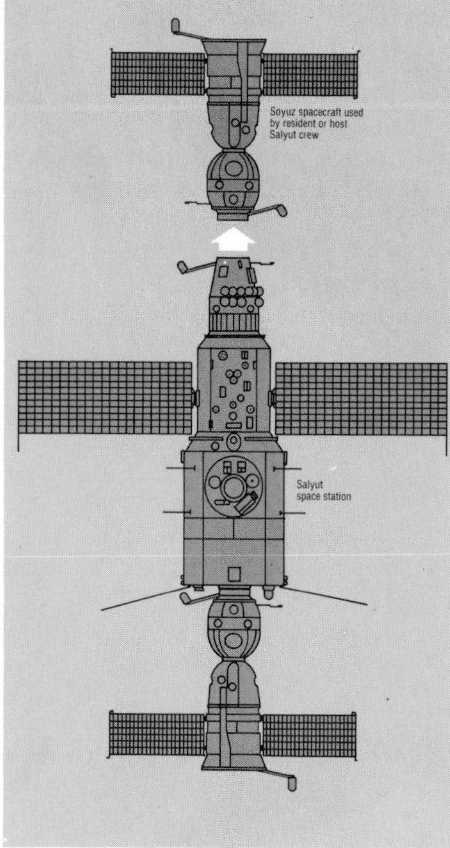

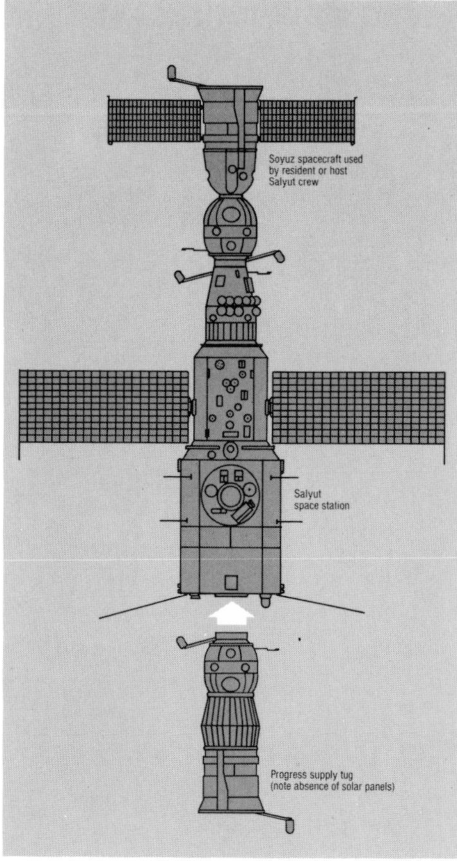

when Soyuz 28 docked with Salyut 6. Aboard were Alexei Gubarev and Vladimir Remek, a captain in the Czechoslovakian air force and the first man in space who was neither Russian nor American. Gubarov and Remek remained in space for eight days before returning to earth on 10 March. Grechko and Romanko returned to earth six days later, having established a new space-flight duration record of 96 days and 10 hours, 12 days longer than the American Skylab 4 crew three years before. Over the next five years cosmonauts from nine communist countries visited the Salyut 6 space station as part of the Soviet Intercosmos Program.

Salyut 6 remained empty until the arrival of Vladimir Kovalyonok and Alexander Ivanchenkov aboard Soyuz 29 on 16 June 1978. On 27 June Soyuz 30 docked with the space station carrying Pyotr Klimuk and the second Intercosmos cosmonaut, Polish air force Maj Miroslaw Hermaszewski. The Soyuz 30 crew remained until 5 July conducting earth resources photography and biomedical experiments devised by Polish scientists. Three days after Klimuk and Hermaszewski ended their eight-day visit, the unmanned Progress 2 cargo tug made its first supply delivery to the Soyuz 29 crew. A month later Progress 3 arrived with another load of supplies when Kovalyonok and Ivanchenkov extended their tour aboard Salyut 6 for a new record.

Progress 3 was jettisoned on 23 August and three days later the sixth Soyuz mission to reach Salyut 6 arrived. Aboard Soyuz 31 were Valeri Bykovsky, veteran of Vostok 5 and Soyuz 22, and his guest, East German cosmonaut Sigmund Jähn. Their visit lasted eight days, a duration that was by then routine for crews visiting manned space stations. Bykovsky and Jähn used Soyuz 29 for their return to earth, leaving the newer Soyuz 31 for the Soyuz 29 crew. Kovalyonok and Ivanchenkov took another delivery from Progress 4 on 5 October, and on 2 November they returned to the Soviet Union in Soyuz 31 with a new long-term duration record of 139 days and 14 hours.

The next host crew arrived at Salyut 6 on 26 February 1979 aboard Soyuz 32. Vladimir Lyakhov was making his first flight and Valeri Ryumin was making his second after the first unsuccessful attempt to reach Salyut 6 in 1977. Though no one realized it in February 1979, over the next five years, these two men became the first to each exceed a duration of 300 days in outer space.

The first visitor to Salyut 6's third host crew was the Progress 5 cargo tug, which

Not the Tblisi trolley! The large Soyuz 31 launch vehicle is towed by rail from its hangar to the Baikonur launch pad in preparation for the 20 August 1978 launch.

Right: On 3 September 1978 the international crew of Valeri Bykovsky of the USSR and cosmonaut-researcher of Eastern Germany Sigmund Jähn returned to earth after successfully concluding the program of joint work aboard the Salyut 6/Soyuz 29/Soyuz 31 research complex.

arrived on 13 March bringing supplies in advance of a planned visit by Soyuz 33 in April. Soyuz 33 was launched as planned on 10 April with Nikolai Rukavishnikov and Bulgarian cosmonaut Georgi Ivanov aboard, but they failed to dock with Salyut because of a systems failure in the engines used to maneuver the spacecraft. The Soyuz 33 crew returned to earth, touching down after dark on 12 April.

It was the first docking failure in two years of routine Salyut 6 operations, and it left Soviet controllers with a dilemma. Rukavishnikov and Ivanov were supposed to have flown back to earth in Soyuz 32, leaving the newer Soyuz 33 for Lyakhov and Ryumin. The choice was either to recall the two men in the space station before Soyuz 32 exceeded a safe usable duration or to send up another spacecraft. They chose the latter route, and on 6 June 1979 they launched Soyuz 34 without a crew, the first unmanned Soyuz-designated launch since the Soyuz 20 remote docking experiment in 1975. Supplied with the fresh Soyuz 34 ship, Lyakhov and Ryumin jettisoned Soyuz 32. The two men remained in space until 19 August, setting yet another space-duration record of 175 days.

While Lyakhov and Ryumin were setting their duration record, Soviet engineers were putting the finishing touches on a new-generation manned spacecraft. The new ship was based on the standard Soyuz but it had a large enough internal volume to carry a *troika,* or trio, of cosmonauts in space suits. The first flight of what was designated the Soyuz T-series was launched on 16 December 1979 after two preliminary test flights under the Cosmos 1001 and Cosmos 1074 designations. The unmanned Soyuz T-1 docked with the unmanned Salyut on 17 December for what was to be a 101-day stay. On 29 March, four days after Soyuz T-1 was detached by remote control, the unmanned Progress 8 tug visited Salyut.

On 9 April 1980, Soyuz 35, a conventional Soyuz spacecraft, docked with Salyut 6, bringing the space station's fourth long-duration host crew. This new crew

Left: **Valeri Ryumin and Leonid Popov piloted Salyut 6 in 1980 (note the cassettes taped to the wall). Both cosmonauts established endurance records, and Ryumin was in space for 361 days over a 20-month period.** ***Above:*** **Alexei Leonov, member of the Voskhod 2 crew that came down in the Urals in March 1965, consults with Nikolai Rukavishnikov and Georgi Ivanov (in tent) during landing training for Soyuz 33.**

consisted of Leonid Popov, making his first flight, and Valeri Ryumin, who had returned from nearly six months in space less than a year before, and was a last-minute replacement for Valentin Lebedev who had suffered a knee injury a couple of weeks earlier.

Popov and Ryumin unloaded and jettisoned Progress 8 on 26 April and received Progress 9 three days later, which they left attached until 20 May. On 27 May Soyuz 36 arrived with the first guest crew to reach the space station in nearly two years. Aboard were Valeri Kubasov and the fifth member of the Intercosmos group, Hungarian cosmonaut Bertalan Farkas. After eight days aboard, they departed in Soyuz 35 as Popov and Ryumin made ready for the first arrival at Salyut 6 of a manned Soyuz T-series spacecraft. Three days later on 6 June Yuri Malyshev and Vladimir Aksyonov docked Soyuz T-2 on the space station's aft docking port for a three-day visit.

Over the course of the next four months Ryumin and Popov took delivery of another load of supplies and entertained two more eight-day visits from Intercosmos space travelers. Vietnamese cosmonaut Pham Tuan arrived on 24 July with Viktor Gorbatko aboard Soyuz 37 and left aboard the Soyuz 36 spacecraft used by Kubasov and Farkas in June. Yuri Romanenko and Cuban cosmonaut Arnaldo Mendez made a round trip in Soyuz 38 between 18 and 26 September, leaving Soyuz 37 for Ryumin and Popov, who returned on 11 October after yet another duration record of 184 days and 19 hours. By the time Soyuz 37 floated down to earth near Dzhezkazgan, Ryumin had spent nearly 12 out of the past 20 months in space. In three space flights he logged 361 days in space.

On 27 November 1980 Leonid Kizim, Oleg Makarov and Gennadi Strekalov were launched on the first test flight of a

Left: **Leonid Popov of the USSR with the cocky Dumitru Prunariu (*left*), Romania's first cosmonaut, in a Salyut simulator prior to the flight of Soyuz 40, the last original-series Soyuz flight. Popov and Prunariu were the last guest crew to visit Salyut 6. *Above:* Popov with Valeri Ryumin after their return from Soyuz 37's record-breaking flight in 1980.**

Soyuz T-series spacecraft with a full three-man crew aboard. On 28 November they docked with Salyut 6 for a 12-day maintenance visit in which they installed a new temperature control pump and a new fuel system converter.

On 13 March 1981 Soyuz T-4 arrived at Salyut 6 carrying Vladimir Kovalyonok and Viktor Savinykh, the space station's fifth and last resident crew. On 23 March they were joined for an eight-day visit by Vladimir Dzhanibekov and Mongolian cosmonaut Jugderdemidiyn Gurragcha aboard Soyuz 39. On 15 May Leonid Popov returned to Salyut 6 on Soyuz 40 along with Romanian cosmonaut Dumitru Prunariu. Their eight-day space flight marked the ninth and last space flight in the Intercosmos series, which saw first space flights for the cosmonauts of nine nations. Soyuz 40 was the last flight by one of the original Soyuz-series spacecraft.

On 22 May 1981, Popov and Prunariu departed Salyut 6 in Soyuz 40, and four days later Kovalyonok and Savinykh followed them in Soyuz T-4. After their 75 days in space, they were the last men to see Salyut 6, the most successful Soviet space station to date. In four years, Salyut 6 had entertained visits by the crews of no fewer than 17 manned Soyuz spacecraft and supported them during an unprecedented 676 days of manned occupancy. Within its walls men set three successive space-duration records and it had received the cosmonauts of 9 of the 11 countries to have sent men into space.

On 19 April 1982, nearly a year after Salyut 6 was abandoned for the last time, its successor was launched from the Baikonur Cosmodrome atop a D-Class launch vehicle. A month later, on 14 May, Anatoli Berezovoi and Valentin Lebedev arrived in Soyuz T-5 to inaugurate manned occupancy of Salyut 7.

On 25 June Berezovoi and Lebedev were joined by Soyuz T-6 carrying Vladimir Dzhanibekov to his third space station visit and Alexander Ivanchenkov to his second. With them for the eight-day mission was Jean-Loup Chrétien, the first Frenchman in space and the first non-Soviet cosmonaut who was also not part of the Intercosmos program.

Soyuz T-7, launched for an eight-day mission on 19 August, six weeks after Soyuz T-6, carried Leonid Popov, Alexander Serebrov and Svetlana Savitskaya, the second woman to fly in space. Savitskaya, a 33-year-old aerobatic pilot, was apparently moved to the head of the list of those scheduled for a space flight when NASA announced that Sally Ride was about to be the first American woman in space. It was the first time in the 19 years since Valentina Tereshkova's flight in 1963 that a woman had flown aboard a spacecraft. Popov, Serebrov and Savitskaya returned to earth aboard Soyuz T-5

Left: **Svetlana Savitskaya, the second woman in space, with Leonid Popov and Alexander Serebrov during training for their Soyuz T-7 flight on 19 August 1982, almost a year before Sally Ride became the first US woman in space.**

Below: **A film crew scampers into position in the preset landing area near Dzhezkazgan to film a Soviet ground crew as they prepare to open the Soyuz T-12 Descent Module contain-**

ing Vladimir Dzhanibekov, Igor Volk and Svetlana Savitskaya on 29 July 1984. She was the first Soviet woman to fly in space twice.

Right: **Vladimir Dzhanibekov and Svetlana Savitskaya share a chuckle at the Gagarin training center as they check out the space suits that they would use on their Soyuz T-12 mission. During this flight Savitskaya became the first woman to walk in space.**

The Soyuz T-8 crew: commander Vladimir Titov, cosmonaut-researcher Alexander Serebrov and flight engineer Gennadi Strekalov.

on 27 August, leaving Berezovoi and Lebedev for what would be another four and a half months in space. When they did return in January 1983, they had set a new single-flight duration record of 211 days and 8 hours, eclipsing the 184 day and 19 hour record set by Ryumin and Popov two years before.

On 20 April 1983 Soyuz T-8 was launched on what was destined to be the first unsuccessful attempt to dock with Salyut 7. Vladimir Titov (no relation to Vostok 2 cosmonaut Gherman Titov), Gennadi Strekalov and Alexander Serebrov returned to earth after just two days in space. Soyuz T-9, with Vladimir Lyakhov and Alexander Alexandrov, was launched two months later on 27 June and successfully docked with the space station. During two lengthy space walks, the two cosmonauts added two solar panels to Salyut 7, the first of many planned improvements to the station. On 27 September the first guest crew scheduled to visit them climbed aboard Soyuz 10 at Baikonur Cosmodrome. The two-man crew consisted of Titov and Strekalov, two members of the Soyuz 8 crew who had attempted to reach Salyut 7 in April. They were in the midst of the launch sequence when sensors in the booster rocket detected a serious malfunction. This activated the escape sequence that fired the spacecraft's escape tower, pulling Soyuz 10 several hundred feet into the air as the launch vehicle exploded in a huge fireball. The Soyuz IM separated and parachutes were deployed, safely returning the DM and the two cosmonauts to earth.

Meanwhile Alexandrov and Lyakov were having serious problems of their own as they entered their sixteenth week in space. On 9 September Salyut's main oxidizer line ruptured, spilling two thirds of the station's nitric oxide propellant into space. The accident damaged two of Salyut's three propellant tanks, rendering them unusable. The two men put on their space suits and began to prepare for an emergency return to earth. Soviet ground control, monitoring the problem from the ground, determined that no hazard existed and decided to let the two men remain aboard Salyut 7. The loss of the propellant, however, seriously limited their ability to fire the rockets aboard the space station that would allow it to be placed into a higher orbit when its present orbit decayed under gravitational pressure from earth. On 22 October, Progress 18 arrived at Salyut 7 with a new load of propellant to top off the one remaining usable fuel tank. Progress could be left attached to Salyut for as long as necessary, its supply tanks serving as auxiliary fuel tanks for the space station. A month later, on 23 November, Lyakov and Alexandrov left the troubled space station, returning to earth aboard Soyuz T-9 after 149 days and 10 hours in space. Theirs had been a troubled stay, and they were the first resident crew aboard one of the new class of space stations to not entertain another crew.

On 8 February 1984 a new Soyuz spacecraft was launched to Salyut 7 under the designation Soyuz T-10B (the original Soyuz T-10 launch aborted in September was referred to as Soyuz T-10A). Aboard for the mission were Leonid Kizim, Vladimir Solovyev and Oleg Atkov, the first three-man crew to reach Salyut 7 in more than a year. On 3 April, after being resupplied by Progress 19, they received their first guest crew. Aboard Soyuz T-11 for the eight-day visit were Yuri Malyshev, Gennadi Strekalov and India's first cosmonaut, Rakesh Sharma. After the guest crew departed in the Soyuz T-10B spacecraft, Kizim and Solovyev conducted a series of lengthy space walks to repair the damage that had occurred to the space station's fuel tanks and propulsion system. During four EVAs, which took place between 23 April and 4 May, the two cosmonauts logged a total of 35 hours of EVA time, more than had been logged in the 25-year history of the Soviet space program. Between 1965 and 1983, Soviet cosmonauts had walked in space for a total of 28 hours during 12 EVAs, and 25½ of those hours were associated with either Salyut 6 or Salyut 7.

On 18 July Soyuz T-12 docked with Salyut 7 carrying Vladimir Dzhanibekov, Igor Volk and Svetlana Savitskaya, the first soviet woman to fly in space twice and the first woman to walk in space on 25 July. Her 3 hour and 35 minute EVA involved routine testing of cutting and soldering tools. Savitskaya and her two Soyuz T-12 companions returned to the Soviet Union on 29 July after 12 days in space, a longer-than-typical duration for a visiting crew. The original team of Oleg Atkov, Leonid Kizim and Vladimir Solovyev returned to earth on 2 October 1984 after 237 days in space, breaking the previous record of 211 days that had been set by the Salyut 7 crew. The fact that the Soyuz T-11 vehicle in which they returned had been in space for 180 days demonstrated that the new T-series Soyuz ships could remain in space much longer than had been tried with the earlier series Soyuz spacecraft.

With the completion of this record flight, the Soviet Union logged a total of more than 87,600 cosmonaut hours in space, compared to 30,012 astronaut hours for the United States after Shuttle mission 41-D in August 1984. The Soviet total exceeded the equivalent of 10 years in space.

Salyut 7 remained unoccupied for half a year until Vladimir Dzhanibekov and Viktor Savinykh arrived on 6 June 1985 aboard Soyuz T-13. On 23 June Progress 24 arrived and docked with the space station to unload supplies for the crew, whose mission involved routine repairs to Salyut 7 and agricultural photography of areas within the Soviet Union in connection with the Kursk-85 project. On 15 July the crew jettisoned Progress 24 and six days later Cosmos 1669 arrived. Similar in configuration to Progress (and to Soyuz, too), Cosmos 1669 was a laboratory module that could function under its own electical system.

Cosmos 1669 was jettisoned on 30 August in anticipation of the arrival on 18 September of the Soyuz T-14 crew Vladimir Vasyutin, Georgi Grechko and Alexander Volkov. On 26 September, Soyuz T-13 commander Dzhanibekov, along with Georgi Grechko, returned to earth aboard Soyuz T-13, leaving Savinykh and the Soyuz T-14 crew aboard Salyut 7, thus effecting a partial exchange of resident crews. This was the first time in Salyut operations that two resident crews had been aboard a space station simultaneously. Previous resident crews had re-

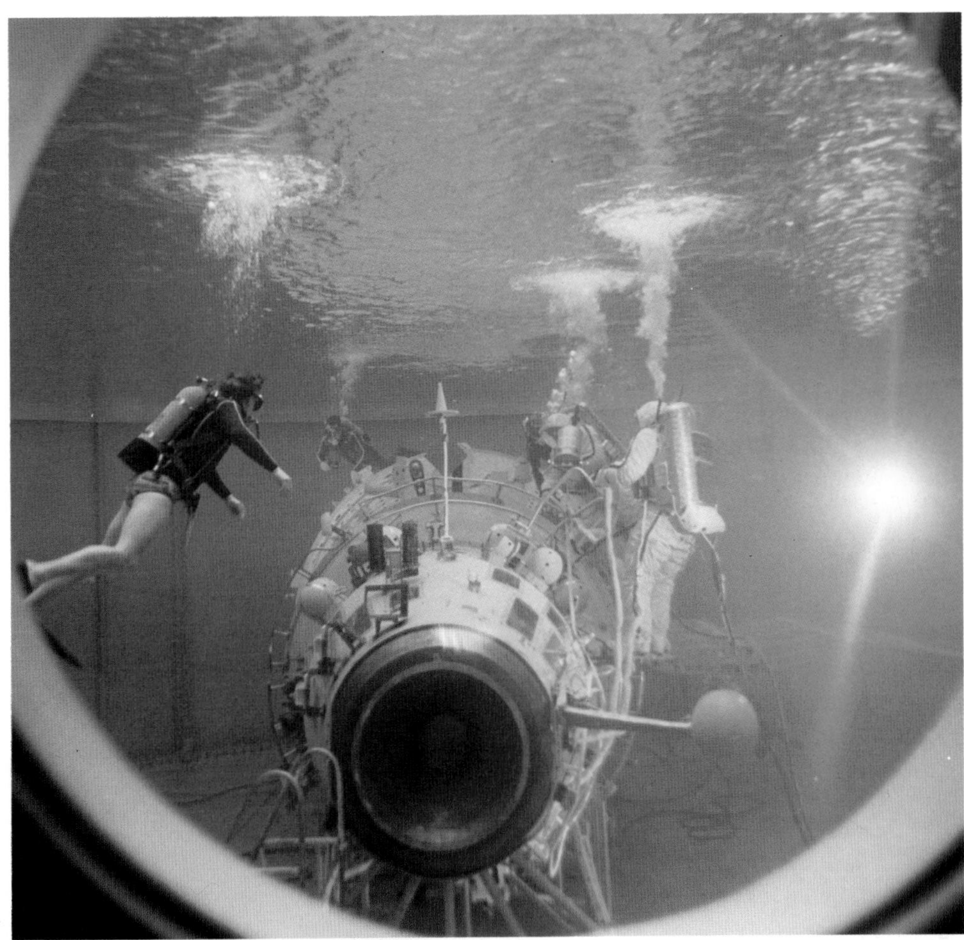

Right: **Soyuz T-5 cosmonauts Anatoli Berezovoi and Valentin Lebedev train in an underwater environment that approximates the weightlessness of space. This view from a Salyut mockup shows the cosmonauts and two divers working with a full-scale mockup of a Soyuz spacecraft, one of whose solar 'wings' is visible on the right.** ***Below:*** **The Soyuz T-10 crew — Leonid Kizim, Vladimir Solovyev and Oleg Atkov — rest after landing.**

ceived guests during their respective watches, but Salyuts had always been vacant for several months between resident crews.

On 27 September 1985 the Soviets launched Cosmos 1686, a new habitable module that could function as a true Salyut 'annex.' Docked at one of Salyut 7's forward docking bays, it served to nearly double the space station's length and increase the station's habitable volume by roughly 50 percent.

With two manned space flights in excess of 200 days during 1982 and 1984, the Soviet Union had demonstrated the ability of both its cosmonauts and its T-series spacecraft to function normally for half a year in space. The incorporation of Cosmos 1686 into the Salyut 7 complex demonstrated that large space stations could be constructed in space from self-contained modules. The routine resupply of Soviet space stations with the Progress tugs had been demonstrated over several years, and the Soyuz T-13/Soyuz T-14 crew exchange had gone so smoothly that it hardly seemed out of the ordinary. All of these factors combined to show that a permanent Soviet presence in space was an easily attainable goal.

Right: **Salyut cosmonauts Viktor Savinykh, Vladimire Vasyutin and Alexander Volkov. Savinykh arrived at Salyut 7 in Soyuz T-13; Vasyutin and Volkov arrived in Soyuz T-14.** ***Below:*** **The Cosmos 1686 module (Salyut annex) docking with a manned Salyut space station.**

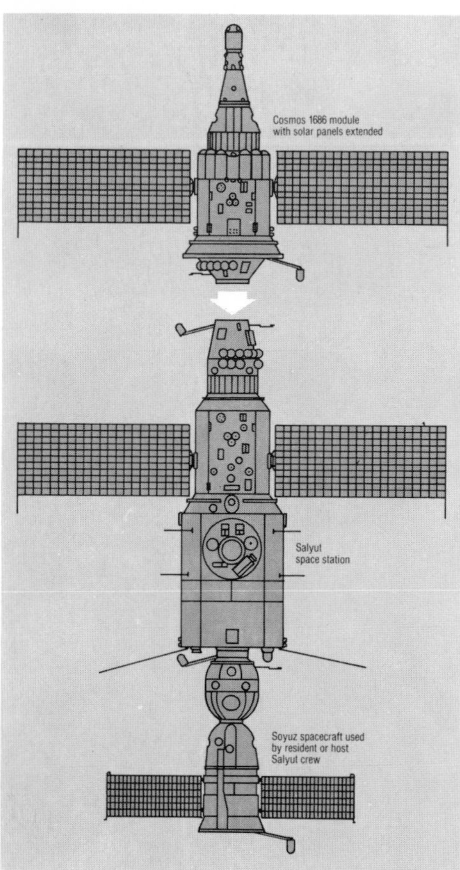

OTHER MANNED SPACE FLIGHT PROGRAMS

CANADA

With the launch of the Alouette 1 research satellite in 1962, Canada became the third country to have a satellite in orbit, but it was 20 years before Canada developed a manned space program. The Canadian Astronaut Program (or Programme Astronauts Canadians) is under the direction of the National Research Council Canada in cooperation with NASA in the United States, and the first group of six astronauts were selected on 5 December 1983. Because Canada has no manned spacecraft program of its own, all of the Canadian astronauts will fly as payload specialists aboard the American Space Shuttle.

The first member of the Canadian team to go into space was Marc Garneau, who flew on the eight-day 41-G mission aboard the Shuttle Orbiter *Challenger* in 1984. Born in February 1949 in Quebec City, Quebec, Garneau has a bachelor of engineering physics degree from the Royal Military College of Kingston and a doctorate in electrical engineering from the Imperial College of Science and Technology in London, England. A pilot and scuba diver, Garneau has also twice been a member of the crew of a 59-foot yawl on transatlantic voyages.

Garneau's first voyage into space was on board *Challenger* on 5 October 1984. During his flight he observed at close range the operation of the Canadian-built remote manipulator arm that is standard equipment on all American Shuttle Orbiters. He also monitored a number of Canadian scientific experiments including those involving the Atmospheric Environment Service Sunphotometer and the Department of Communications Advanced Composite Materials Exposure experiment. He was also responsible for three National Research Council projects, the Space Vision experiment, the Shuttle Glow and Atmospheric Emission experiment and the Space Adaptation Syndrome experiments, which were cosponsored by McGill University, the Medical Research Council and the Department of National Defense.

The other Canadian astronauts include Bob Thirsk of New Westminster, British Columbia, who trained as Garneau's backup for the first flight in 1984; Roberta Bondar of Sault Sainte Marie, Ontario; Steve MacLean of Ottawa, Ontario; Ken Money of Toronto, Ontario and Bjarni Tryggvason, a native of Reykjavik, Iceland who has lived in Canada since attending primary school in Nova Scotia and British Columbia. Like Garneau, all of Canada's astronauts hold doctorate degrees: Thirsk and Bondar in medicine, MacLean in astrophysics, Money in physiology and Tryggvason in engineering (with a specialization in applied mathematics and aerodynamics).

Left: **Marc Garneau flew aboard *Challenger* in 1984, and was Canada's first man in space, representing the National Research Council.** ***Below:*** **The Canadian astronaut corps: Bjarni Tryggvason, Robert Thirsk, Roberta Bondar, Steve MacLean, Ken Money and Marc Garneau.**

EUROPEAN SPACE AGENCY (ESA)

In December 1977 the European Space Agency (or Agence Spatiale Européenne) selected its first group of astronauts, who would train to fly under the payload specialist designation aboard the American Space Shuttle when it carried ESA's Spacelab experiment module. The four original ESA astronauts were Franco Malerba (Italy), Ulf Merbold (West Germany), Claude Nicollier (Switzerland) and Wubbo Ockels (Netherlands). Malerba later left the program and Lodewijk van den Berg of the Netherlands was added. Even though the ESA is headquartered in Paris, there are no Frenchmen included among its astronauts because France maintains its own astronaut program through its national space agency, CNES.

The first Spacelab flight was scheduled as early as 1980 put postponed until Space Shuttle mission 41-A launched on 28 November 1983. Aboard the Orbiter *Challenger* for the flight was ESA's first astronaut in space, Ulf Merbold, a pilot and research physicist born in Greiz, Germany in 1941. Merbold, who was the first non-American astronaut to go into space in a US spacecraft, operated the Spacelab experiments in conjunction with three American payload specialists during the 10-day flight. During the flight, on 5 December, Merbold and members of the American crew spoke with President Reagan and German Chancellor Helmut Kohl on live television.

The second ESA astronaut to go into space was Holland's Lodewijk van den Berg, who joined the crew of the Orbiter *Challenger* for Shuttle mission 51-B. Launched on 29 April 1985, the seven-day mission 51-B carried the Spacelab 3 experiments. Spacelab 2, originally scheduled ahead of Spacelab 3 was postponed until June 1985 and was accompanied only by NASA astronauts. The Spacelab 3 module included geophysical flow experiments and atmospheric chemistry experiments. Van den Berg also grew a series of bright red mercuric oxide crystals. An experiment involving a large number of research animals became a nuisance when crumbs and rat droppings got out of some of the cages and began floating around in the weightless Spacelab.

The third ESA astronaut to fly in space was Wubbo Ockels, Merbold's backup on Spacelab 1 in 1973. Ockels was a 39-year-old Dutch physicist with a doctorate from the Nuclear Physics Accelerator Institute in Groningen. The fourth flight of Spacelab was largely a German effort and hence flew under the designation Spacelab D-1. It was launched on 30 October 1985 and, like the earlier Spacelab flights, it was carried aboard the Orbiter *Challenger*. In addition to Ockels and five Americans, the Spacelab D-1 flight carried two German payload specialists representing the German Aerospace Research Agency (DFVLR), Reinhard Furrer and Ernst Messerschmid. During part of the seven-day flight, operational control of Spacelab was handed over to the German Space Operations Center at Oberpfaffenhofen near Munich in West Germany, the first time that any portion of the operational control of an American space flight had been transferred outside of the United States. In the German Space Operations Center, the crew interface coordinator for the mission was ESA's first man in space, Ulf Merbold.

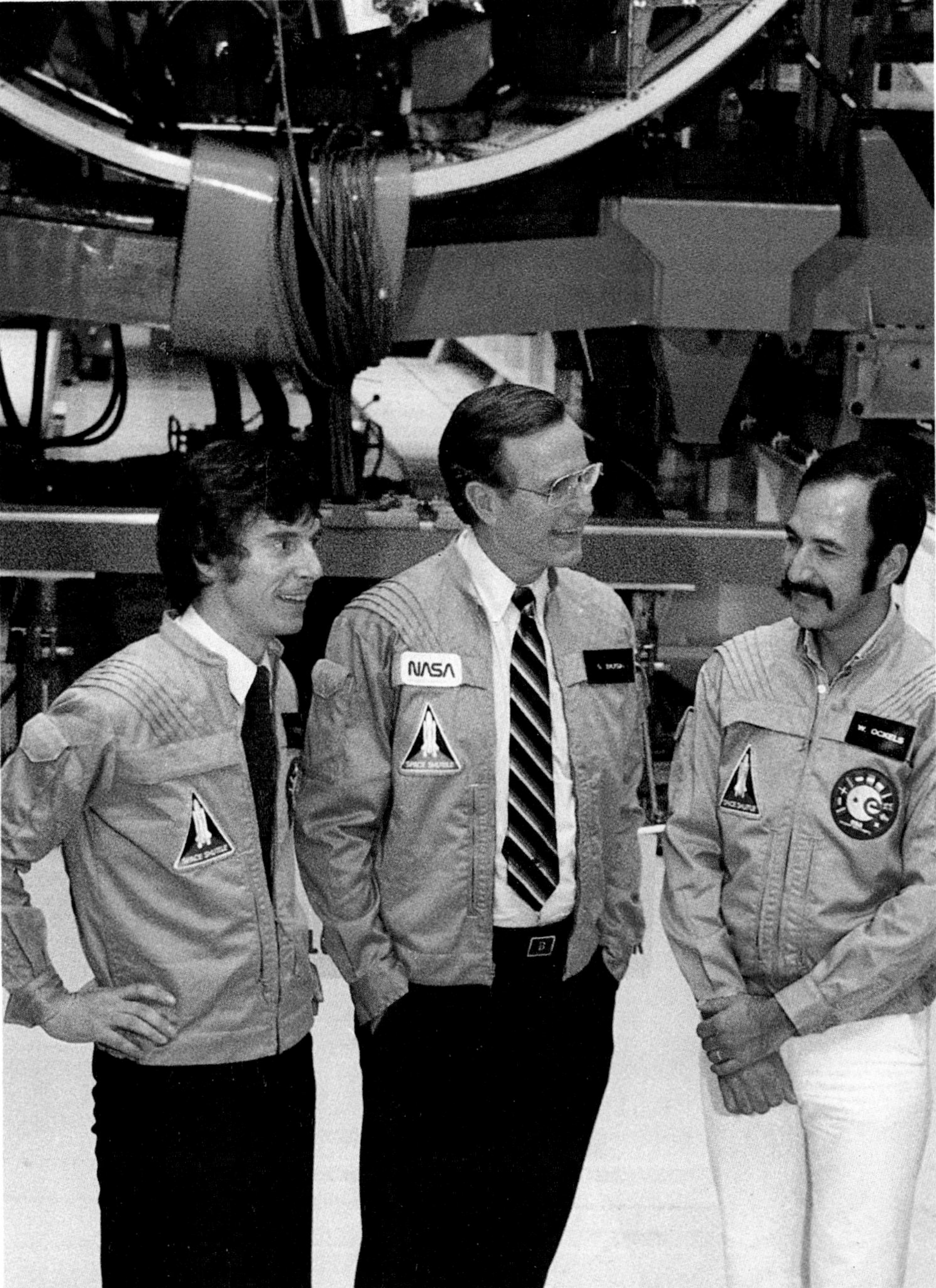

ESA's men in space. ***Above:*** **Vice President George Bush confers with Ulf Merbold (*left*) from West Germany and Wubbo Ockels (*right*) from The Netherlands.** ***Below:*** **Lodewijk van den Berg was a payload specialists for Spacelab 3.**

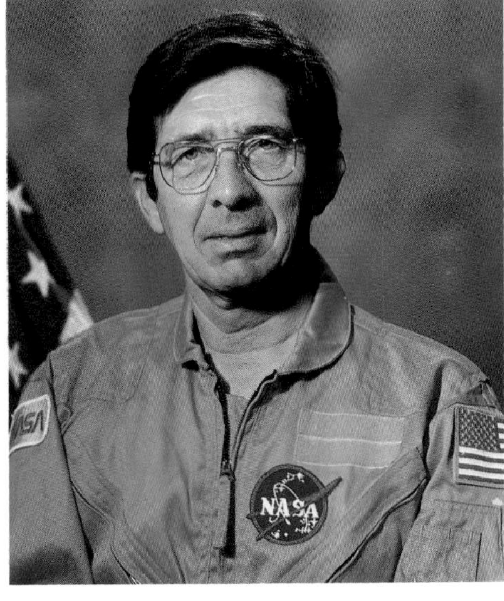

FRANCE

Paris is a unique city in many ways, and among them is that the City of Lights is the headquarters of two of the world's manned space programs, the European Space Agency on Rue Mario-Nikis and the French National Space Agency on Place Maurice Quentin.

The French National Space Agency (Centre National d' Etudes Spatiales) was founded in 1962, and in 1965 France became the third country to independently build, launch and maintain spacecraft. France was also the third nation to undertake the development of its own manned spacecraft. In its manned spacecraft program, France decided to forgo using ballistic return capsules (such as were used by the United States from 1961 to 1975 and by the Soviet Union since 1961) and move directly to the reusable space plane concept that the United States has used operationally since 1981. Called Hermes, the spacecraft will first fly in the mid 1990s and will be developed by the nation's two leading aerospace firms, Dassault-Breguet and Aerospatiale.

In the meantime, the CNES manned space program has had two of its men fly in space since France has been the only country to boast both an astronaut *and* a cosmonaut. In 1980, CNES picked the two men from 400 applicants.

The first to fly was Jean-Loup Chrétien, born in La Rochelle in August 1938. A colonel in the French air force, Chrétien

Below: Patrick Baudry and Jean-Loup Chrétien as cosmonauts in Moscow in 1982, and Baudry (_right_) in space as an astronaut aboard _Discovery_ in June 1985, using shades to shield his eyes from the strong sun.

France's Patrick Baudry and Jean-Loup Chrétien (*above*) in hybrid CNES/NASA flight suits prior to Baudry's flight on *Discovery* on 17 June 1985. Chrétien served as Baudry's backup for the flight. India's Rakesh Sharma (*below*) flew on Soyuz T-11.

also has a masters degree in aeronautical engineering and acquired 6000 hours of flying time first as a fighter pilot (1962–1970) and later as an air force test pilot (1970–1977). After his selection, he underwent two years of training in France and at Star City, USSR. On 25 June 1982 he was a member of the Soyuz T-6 crew that was launched into orbit for a rendezvous the following day with the Soviet Salyut 7 spacecraft. During his 189-hour space flight, cosmonaut Chrétien implemented nine scientific experiments in the fields of medicine, biology, astronomy and materials processing in space. During re-entry he functioned as Soyuz copilot.

France's second man in space was Patrick Baudry, who trained along with Chrétien and who was his backup on the Soyuz T-6 flight. Born in West Africa in March 1946 when it was still a French colony, Baudry is a lieutenant colonel in the French air force and a fighter pilot with 4000 hours of flying time in a variety of aircraft. Baudry's first space flight was on 17 June 1985 aboard the Space Shuttle Orbiter *Discovery* on mission 51-G. Baudry conducted a series of cardiovascular and sensorimotor tests and an echocandiograph experiment during the seven-day mission. He repeated some of the experiments that had been conducted aboard Salyut three years before so that the results could be compared. In 1982 Chrétien had been unable to make his initial measurements for 48 hours because of the time required for Soyuz T-6 to reach Salyut 7. In Baudry's case, *Discovery* was in position within 3 hours.

At the end of mission 51-G, in which Chretien served as Baudry's backup, the two men returned to France to participate in CNES preparations for the first flight of Hermes.

INDIA

India did not launch its first unmanned spacecraft until 1980, and over the years most of its satellites have been launched on a contract basis by the United States, the Soviet Union or France. The manned space program of the Indian Space Research Organization has depended entirely on the Soviet Union, and the first Indian cosmonaut spent the better part of an eight-day trip into space aboard Salyut 7 in 1984. Launched along with two Soviet cosmonauts aboard Soyuz T-11 on 2 April was Sqn Ldr Rakesh Sharma, a 35-year-old Indian air force pilot. During the flight Sharma conducted multispectral photography of northern India in anticipation of the construction of hydroelectric power stations in the Himalayas. Sharma and his backup, Wing Cdr Ravish Malhotra, also prepared an elaborate series of zero-gravity Yoga exercises that Sharma practiced aboard Salyut 7.

INTERCOSMOS

The Intercosmos series consisted of nine space flights involving cosmonauts from nine communist countries undertaken by the Soviet Union between 1978 and 1981. These flights included medical and other scientific experiments designed by the guest nations as well as multispectral earth resources photography of the guest nations. They were all launched aboard original-series two-man Soyuz spacecraft and all were planned for an eight-day duration, including six days aboard Salyut 6. All of the flights were successfully launched and recovered, but one mission failed to dock with Salyut because of a malfunction of the Soyuz maneuvering engines.

The first nation to participate in the manned Intercosmos program was Czechoslovakia, which had produced technical hardware for a number of the Intercosmos unmanned satellites, but did not see its first domestically developed satel-

Czech cosmonaut Vladimir Remek (*above*) was the first man not from the US or USSR to go into space, aboard Soyuz 28 in March 1978. *Below:* Miroslaw Hermaszewski of Poland confers with Soviet cosmonaut Pyotr Klimuk prior to Soyuz 30.

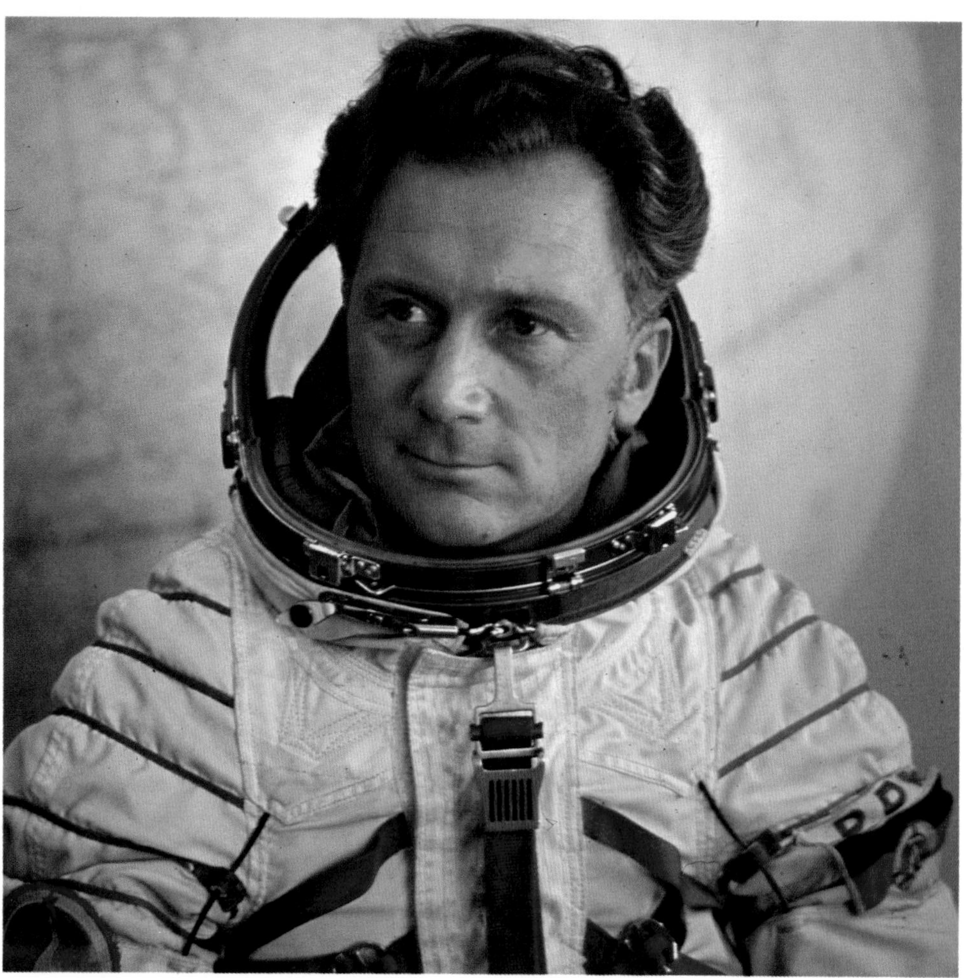

East Germany's Sigmund Jähn (*above*), the third Intercosmos cosmonaut, flew aboard Soyuz 31 in 1978, and Bulgaria's Georgi Ivanov (*below*) went into space aboard Soyuz 33 the following year. Jähn spent a week in the Salyut 6 space station.

lite (Magion) launched until after its first cosmonaut had been into space. The first Czech cosmonaut and the first man other than a Russian or an American to fly in space, was army Capt Vladimir Remek. Born in September 1948, Remek flew with Soviet cosmonaut Alexei Gubarev aboard Soyuz 28 launched on 2 March 1978 for a duration of seven days and 22 hours.

The second manned Intercosmos flight featured Polish air force Sqn Ldr Miroslaw Hermaszewski, who went into space with Soviet cosmonaut Pyotr Klimok aboard Soyuz 30 on 15 June 1978. Born in September 1941, Hermaszewski was selected for cosmonaut training in 1976 and spent seven days and 22 hours in space.

The third and oldest of the Intercosmos cosmonauts was Lt Col Sigmund Jähn of the East German air force, who was born in February 1937. He went into space with veteran Soviet cosmonaut Valeri Bykovsky aboard Soyuz 31 on 26 August 1978 and returned to earth aboard Soyuz 29 after spending seven days and 21 hours in space.

The fourth manned Intercosmos flight involved the youngest member of the program, Bulgarian air force Maj Georgi Ivanov, who was born in July 1940. Ivanov went into space with Soviet cosmonaut Nikolai Rukavishnikov aboard Soyuz 33 on 4 October 1979 and returned after 47 hours when the spacecraft was unable to dock with Salyut 6. Ivanov's mission was the only docking failure in the Intercosmos program.

The fifth Intercosmos launch took place on 25 June 1980 and involved Hungarian air force Lt Col Bertalan Farkas, born in August 1949. Farkas went into space along with Soviet cosmonaut Valeri Kubasov aboard Soyuz 36, and returned with him aboard Soyuz 35 after seven days and 21 hours in space.

The sixth Intercosmos flight featured the first space flight by a person from outside Europe or North America. Lt Col Pham Tuan of the Vietnamese air force, born in February 1947, went into space with Soviet cosmonaut Viktor Gorbatko on 23 July 1980 aboard Soyuz 37 and returned with him aboard Soyuz 36 after seven days and 22 hours in space.

The seventh Intercosmos flight saw the first space flight by a person from a Western Hemisphere country outside the United States. Cuban air force pilot Arnaldo Tamayo Mendez, born in 1942, went into space aboard Soyuz 38 with Soviet cosmonaut Yuri Romanenko on 18 September 1980 and returned after seven days and 21 hours in space.

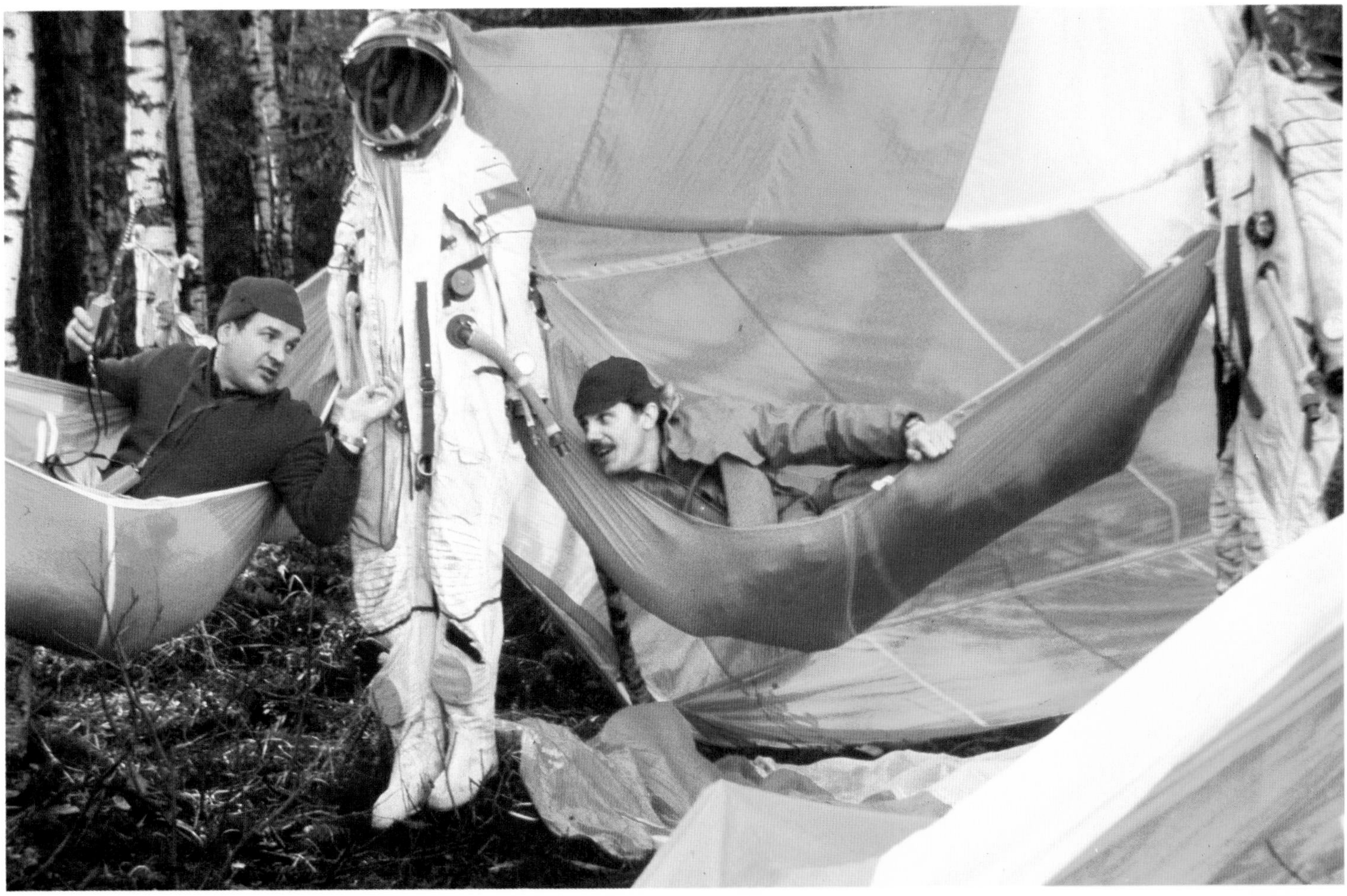

Intercosmos training exercises in 1980 were not entirely hard work. *Above:* Hungary's Bertalan Farkas and Soviet cosmonaut Valeri Kubasov (in blue) used parachutes to construct an elaborate tent during survival training in the birch woods near Moscow. Cuba's Arnoldo Mendez (*below left*) was obviously having a better time practicing for a Soyuz 38 water landing with his Soviet cosmonaut counterpart, Yuri Romanenko.

The eighth Intercosmos flight featured Capt Jugderdemidiyn Gurragcha, a Mongolian aircraft engineer born in December 1947. Selected as a cosmonaut in 1978, Gurragcha went into space with Soviet cosmonaut Vladimir Dzhanibekov aboard Soyuz 39 on 22 March 1981, and returned after seven days and 21 hours in space.

The ninth and final manned Intercosmos flight featured the youngest cosmonaut in the program, Sr Lt Dumitru Prunariu, an engineer in the Romanian air force who was born in September 1952. Prunariu went into space along with Soviet cosmonaut Leonid Popov in Soyuz 40 on 14 May 1981 and returned to earth after seven days and 20½ hours in space.

MEXICO

On 26 November 1985 Mexico became the fourth Western Hemisphere country to have a man fly in space. The first flight by a Mexican payload specialist followed first flights by the United States in 1961, Cuba in 1980 and Canada in 1984. Astronaut Rudolfo Neri went into space aboard the Orbiter *Atlantis* on Space Shuttle mission 61-B to observe the launch of the Mexican Morelos B communications satellite. The American-built Morelos, a Hughes HS-376, was launched by the *Atlantis* crew at 1:47 am CST on 27 November after a nighttime liftoff at 7:29 pm. The satellite was designed to play a key role in communications within Mexico following the devastating series of earthquakes that had struck the country in September 1985.

Payload specialist Neri, an electromagnetic engineer, had played a key role in the development of Mexican communications, but participated in the Morelos launch only as an observer. For the remainder of the eight-day flight, Neri conducted medical experiments and took photographs of his homeland that would later be used in land-use planning or mineral and petroleum exploration.

SAUDI ARABIA

On 17 June 1985 Sultan Salman Abdel-aziz Al-Saud, son of His Royal Highness Prince Salman bin Abdul Aziz, became the first Saudi Arabian and the first member of a royal family to fly in space. Born in Riyadh, Saudi Arabia in June 1956, the sultan has a bachelor's degree in mass communications from the University of Denver, Colorado. He is an

Left: Mongolian Judgerdemindiyn Gurragcha, selected in 1978 as the eighth intercosmos cosmonaut, was cosmonaut-researcher of Soyuz 39 in March 1981.

Above: **Payload specialist Rodolfo Neri, on the STS 61-B mission aboard *Atlantis,* begins one of the experiments for Mexico, testing plants and bacteria. *Right:* Payload specialist Sultan Salman Al-Saud participates in the French Postural Experiment on the mid deck of *Discovery* during mission 51-G.**

experienced pilot with 1000 hours in jet aircraft and helicopters, and he served as deputy director in the Saudi Olympic Information Committee during the 1984 Summer Olympics.

Sultan Al-Saud went into space aboard the Orbiter *Discovery* on Space Shuttle mission 51-G to observe the launch of Arabsat-2, the second telecommunications satellite of the Arab Satellite Communications Organization, a group whose member nations span the breadth of the Arab world, and whose headquarters is in Riyadh. The spacecraft, an American-built Hughes HS-376, was launched on the third day of the seven-day mission. The Saudi payload specialist also participated in French biomedical experiments conducted by French payload specialist Patrick Baudry.

INDEX

Picture Credits

Author's collection 6
Boeing Aerospace Co 90-91
Centre National d'Etudes Spatiales 182, 184 top
Senator Jake Garn's Office 122
Senator John Glenn's Office 12, 83
Grumman Aerospace 52 top
Ian Hogg 6
McDonnell Douglas 1, 14, 16 both, 18, 28-29 both, 30-31, 33
NASA 2-3, 4-5, 6-7, 8-9, 11 both, 13, 17, 19 both, 20, 20-21, 22-23, 23, 24-25, 26-27 all 4, 31, 32 both, 34-35 both, 36-37, 38 left, 40 both, 41 both, 42-43 all 3, 44, 45, 46-47, 48, 49, 50, 51, 52 bottom, 53, 54, 55 all 3, 56, 57, 58-59 all 3, 60-61, 62-63, 63, 64 both, 65 both, 66-67 both, 68-69 all 3, 72-73 both, 75, 76, 77, 78, 79, 80 both, 81, 82, 84, 85 both, 86-87, 88-89, 92 both, 93, 94 both, 95 both, 96 both, 97, 98, 99 all 3, 100-01, 102-03 both, 104-05 all 3, 106-07 both, 108, 109 both, 110-11 all 3, 112, 113 (both), 114, 115 both, 116-17, 118, 119 both, 120-21, 123 both, 124-25 both, 126-27, 128, 129, 130-31, 132-33 both, 134-35, 136-37, 138-39 all 4, 140 both, 158-59, 159, 180 both, 181 both, 182-83, 189 both, 192
NASA via Harrison Schmitt 10, 70-71 both
TASS from Sovfoto 142-43, 144, 146-47, 148-49, 152-53, 154-55, 156, 157, 162, 163, 164-65, 166 top, 167, 168-69, 169, 170-71, 172, 173, 174-75 all 3, 176, 177 both, 178-79, 184 bottom, 185 both, 186 both, 187 both, 188
Wide World Photos 140-41
© **Bill Yenne** 38-39, 39, 74, 150, 151, 164 both, 166 bottom both, 178

Edited by Susan Garratt
Designed by Bill Yenne

Overleaf: **Group Eight astronaut Norman Thagard with his son Daniel just prior to his STS-7 flight aboard *Challenger* in 1983.**

GLOSSARY

AFB	Air Force Base	FY	Fiscal year
ALSEP	Apollo Lunar Surface Experiments Package	IM	Instrument Module (Soyuz)
AOK	All OK	LEM	Lunar Excursion Module (later LM)
ASTP	Apollo-Soyuz Text Project	LM	Landing Module/Lunar Module (Apollo)
ATDA	Augmented Target Docking Adapter (Gemini)	LRV	Lunar Roving Vehicle
CDT	Central Daylight Time	MMU	Manned Maneuvering Unit
CM	Command Module (Apollo)	MOL	Manned Orbital Laboratory
CSM	Command plus Service Module unit (Apollo)	NASA	National Aeronautics and Space Administration
CST	Central Standard Time	OM	Orbital Module (Soyuz)
DSCS	Defense Satellite Communications System	OMS	Orbital Maneuvering System
EDT	Eastern Daylight Time	OV	Orbiting Vehicle (Space Shuttle)
DM	Descent Module (Soyuz)	OWS	Orbital Workshop (Skylab space station)
ESA	European Space Agency	PAM	Payload Assist Module
EST	Eastern Standard Time	SM	Service Module (Apollo)
EVA	Extravehicular activity ('space walk')	STS	Space Transportation System (Space Shuttle)